'As Time Goes By'

Written by
JOSHUA HALE FIALKOV

Art by
MATTHEW DOW SMITH

Colors by
CHARLIE KIRCHOFF

Lettering by
SHAWN LEE

Series Edits by **DENTON J. TIPTON**

Cover by **MARK BUCKINGHAM**

Cover Colors by **CHARLIE KIRCHOFF**

Collection Edits by **JUSTIN EISINGER AND ALONZO SIMON**

Collection Design by **BEN D. BROWN**

Special thanks to Kate Bush, Georgie Britton, Caroline Skinner, Denise Paul, and Ed Casey at BBC Worldwide for their invaluable assistance.

IDW founded by Ted Adams, Alex Garner, Kris Oprisko, and Robbie Robbins | International Rights Representative, Christine Meyer: christine@gfloystudio.com

ISBN: 978-1-61377-216-4

15 14 13 12 1 2 3 4

IDW

Ted Adams, CEO & Publisher
Greg Goldstein, President & COO
Robbie Robbins, EVP/Sr. Graphic Artist
Chris Ryall, Chief Creative Officer/Editor-in-Chief
Matthew Ruzicka, CPA, Chief Financial Officer
Alan Payne, VP of Sales

Become our fan on Facebook facebook.com/idwpublishing
Follow us on Twitter @idwpublishing
Check us out on YouTube youtube.com/idwpublishing
www.IDWPUBLISHING.com

Originally published as DOCTOR WHO II Issues #13–16.

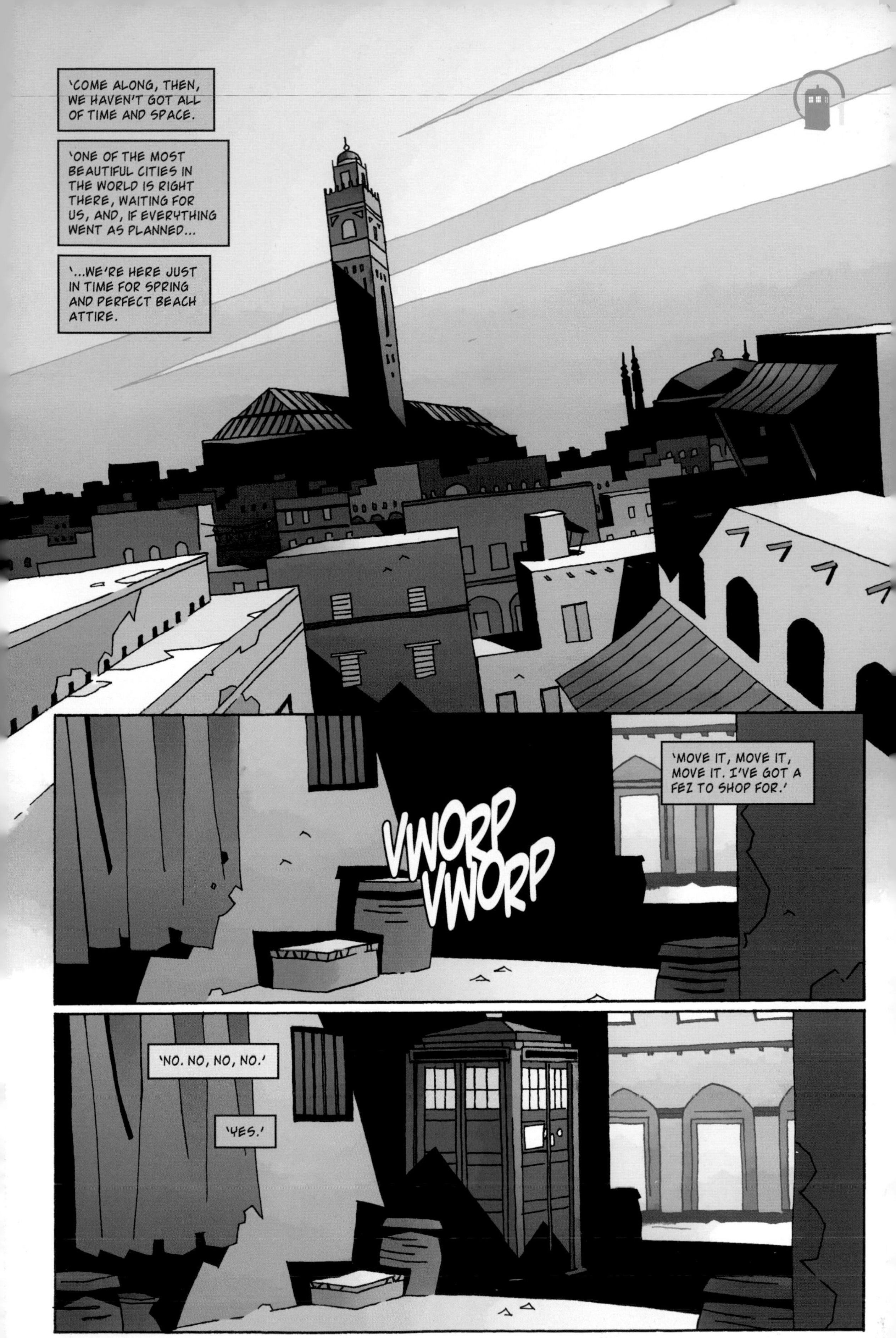
'COME ALONG, THEN, WE HAVEN'T GOT ALL OF TIME AND SPACE.
'ONE OF THE MOST BEAUTIFUL CITIES IN THE WORLD IS RIGHT THERE, WAITING FOR US, AND, IF EVERYTHING WENT AS PLANNED...
'...WE'RE HERE JUST IN TIME FOR SPRING AND PERFECT BEACH ATTIRE.
VWORP VWORP
'MOVE IT, MOVE IT, MOVE IT. I'VE GOT A FEZ TO SHOP FOR.'
'NO. NO, NO, NO.'
'YES.'

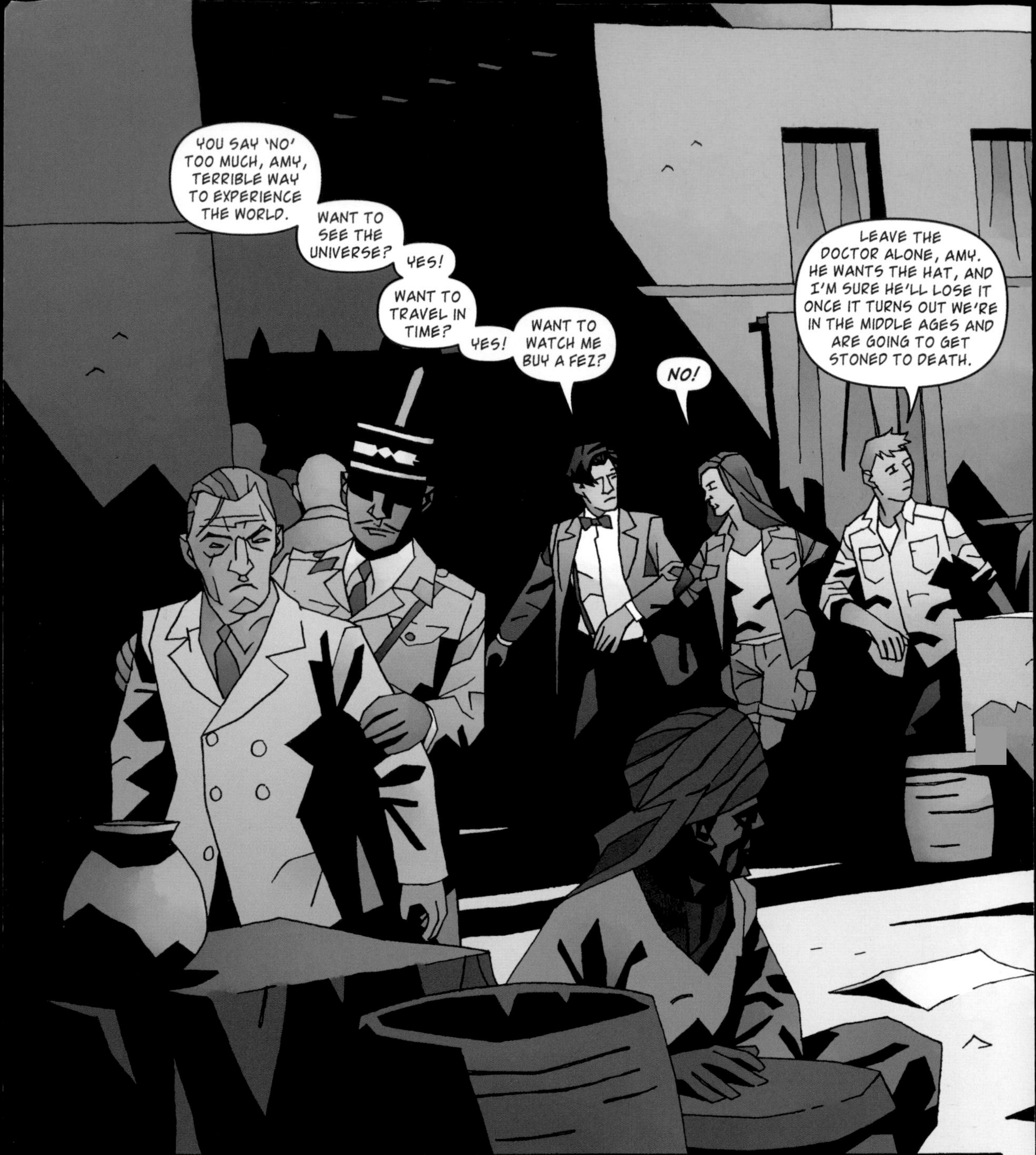
YOU SAY 'NO' TOO MUCH, AMY, TERRIBLE WAY TO EXPERIENCE THE WORLD.
WANT TO SEE THE UNIVERSE?
YES!
WANT TO TRAVEL IN TIME?
YES!
WANT TO WATCH ME BUY A FEZ?
NO!
LEAVE THE DOCTOR ALONE, AMY. HE WANTS THE HAT, AND I'M SURE HE'LL LOSE IT ONCE IT TURNS OUT WE'RE IN THE MIDDLE AGES AND ARE GOING TO GET STONED TO DEATH.

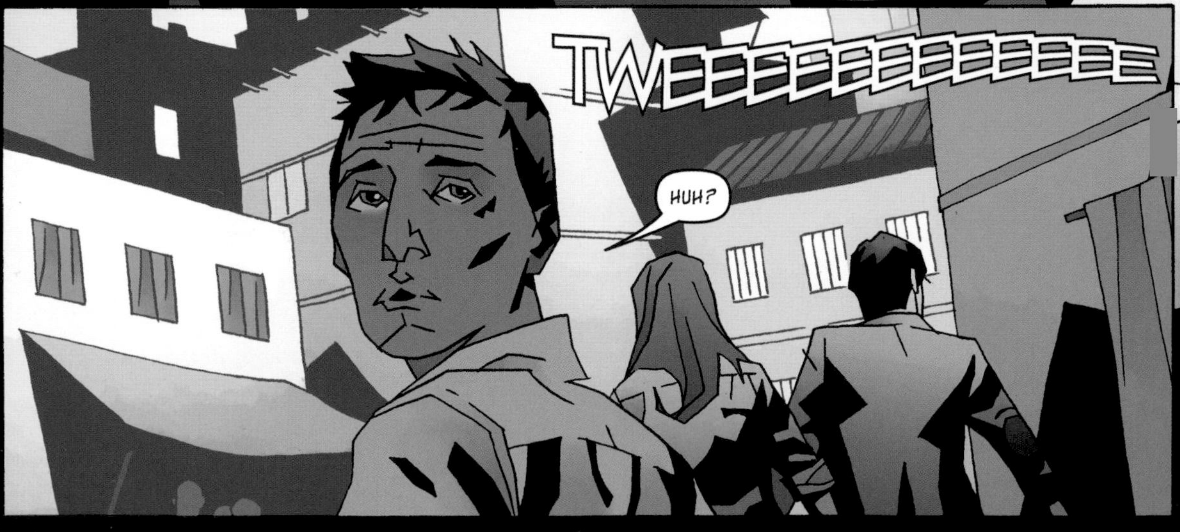
TWEEEEEEEEEEEEEE
HUH?

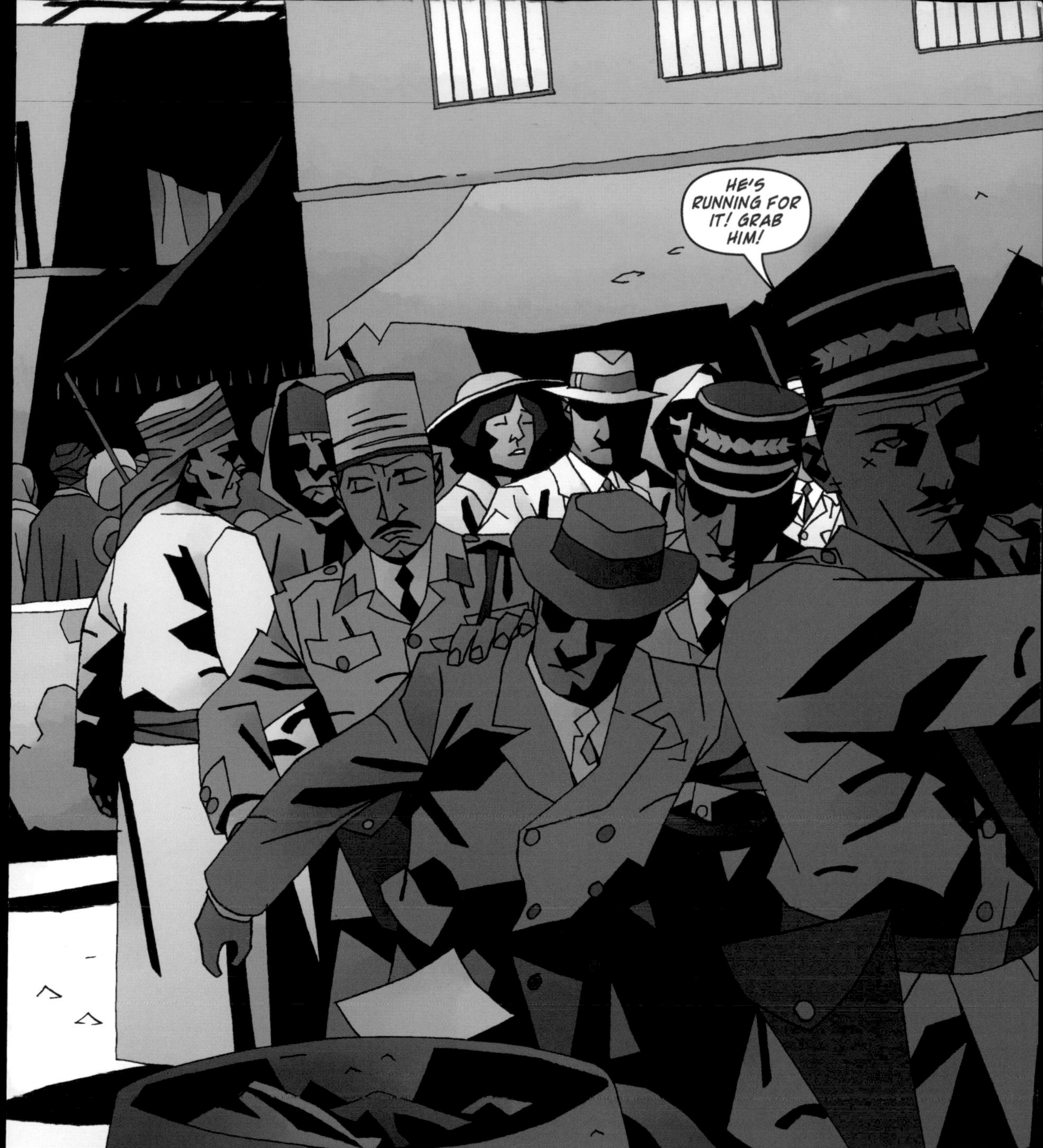
HE'S RUNNING FOR IT! GRAB HIM!

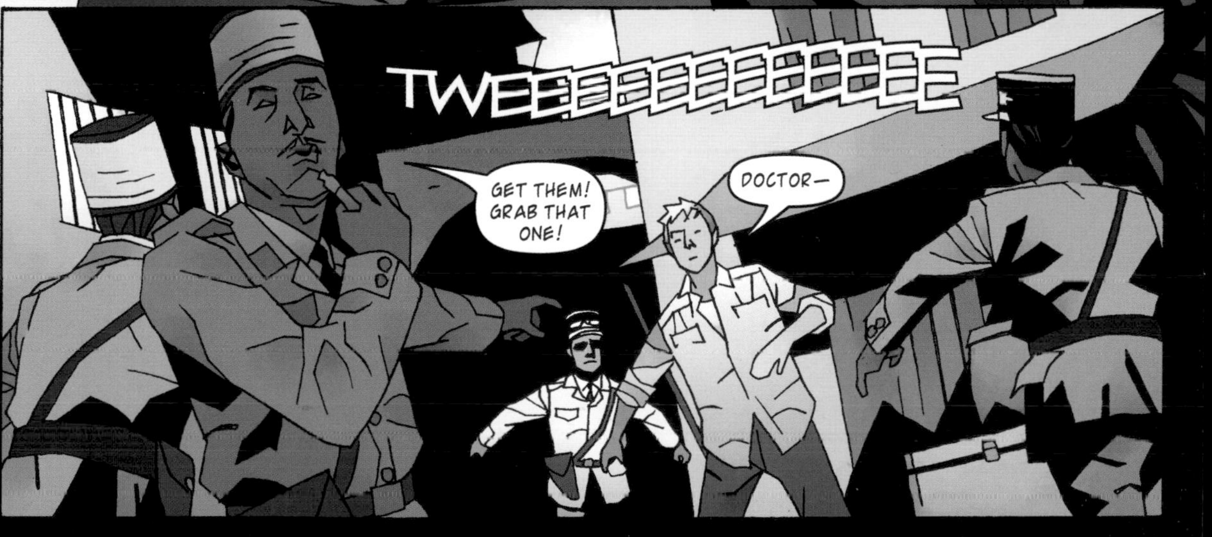
TWEEEEEEEEEEEEEE
GET THEM! GRAB THAT ONE!
DOCTOR—

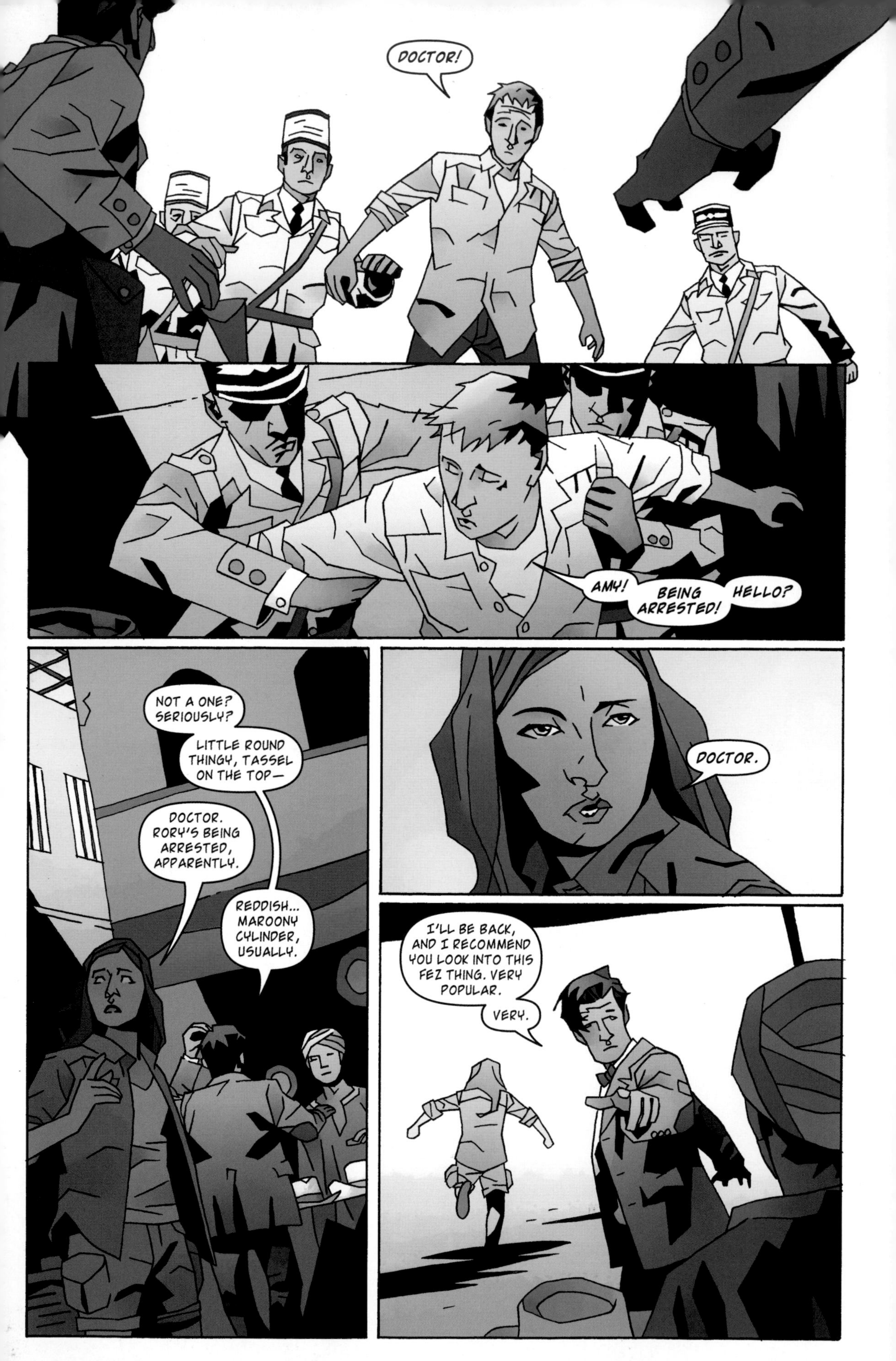
DOCTOR!
AMY!
BEING ARRESTED!
HELLO?
NOT A ONE? SERIOUSLY?
LITTLE ROUND THINGY, TASSEL ON THE TOP—
DOCTOR. RORY'S BEING ARRESTED, APPARENTLY.
REDDISH... MAROONY CYLINDER, USUALLY.
DOCTOR.
I'LL BE BACK, AND I RECOMMEND YOU LOOK INTO THIS FEZ THING. VERY POPULAR.
VERY.

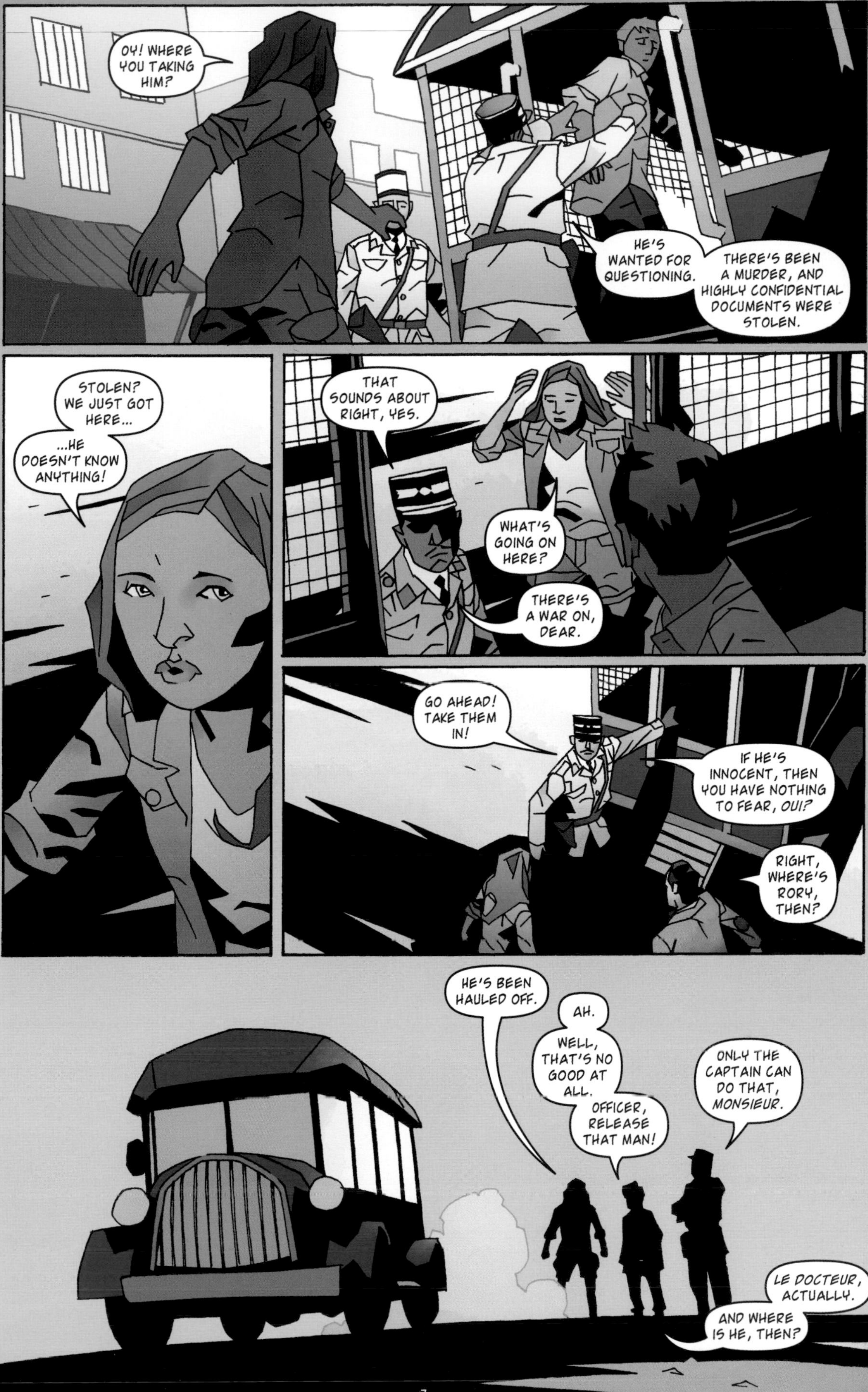
OY! WHERE YOU TAKING HIM?
HE'S WANTED FOR QUESTIONING.
THERE'S BEEN A MURDER, AND HIGHLY CONFIDENTIAL DOCUMENTS WERE STOLEN.
STOLEN? WE JUST GOT HERE...
...HE DOESN'T KNOW ANYTHING!
THAT SOUNDS ABOUT RIGHT, YES.
WHAT'S GOING ON HERE?
THERE'S A WAR ON, DEAR.
GO AHEAD! TAKE THEM IN!
IF HE'S INNOCENT, THEN YOU HAVE NOTHING TO FEAR, OUI?
RIGHT, WHERE'S RORY, THEN?
HE'S BEEN HAULED OFF.
AH.
WELL, THAT'S NO GOOD AT ALL.
OFFICER, RELEASE THAT MAN!
ONLY THE CAPTAIN CAN DO THAT, MONSIEUR.
LE DOCTEUR, ACTUALLY.
AND WHERE IS HE, THEN?

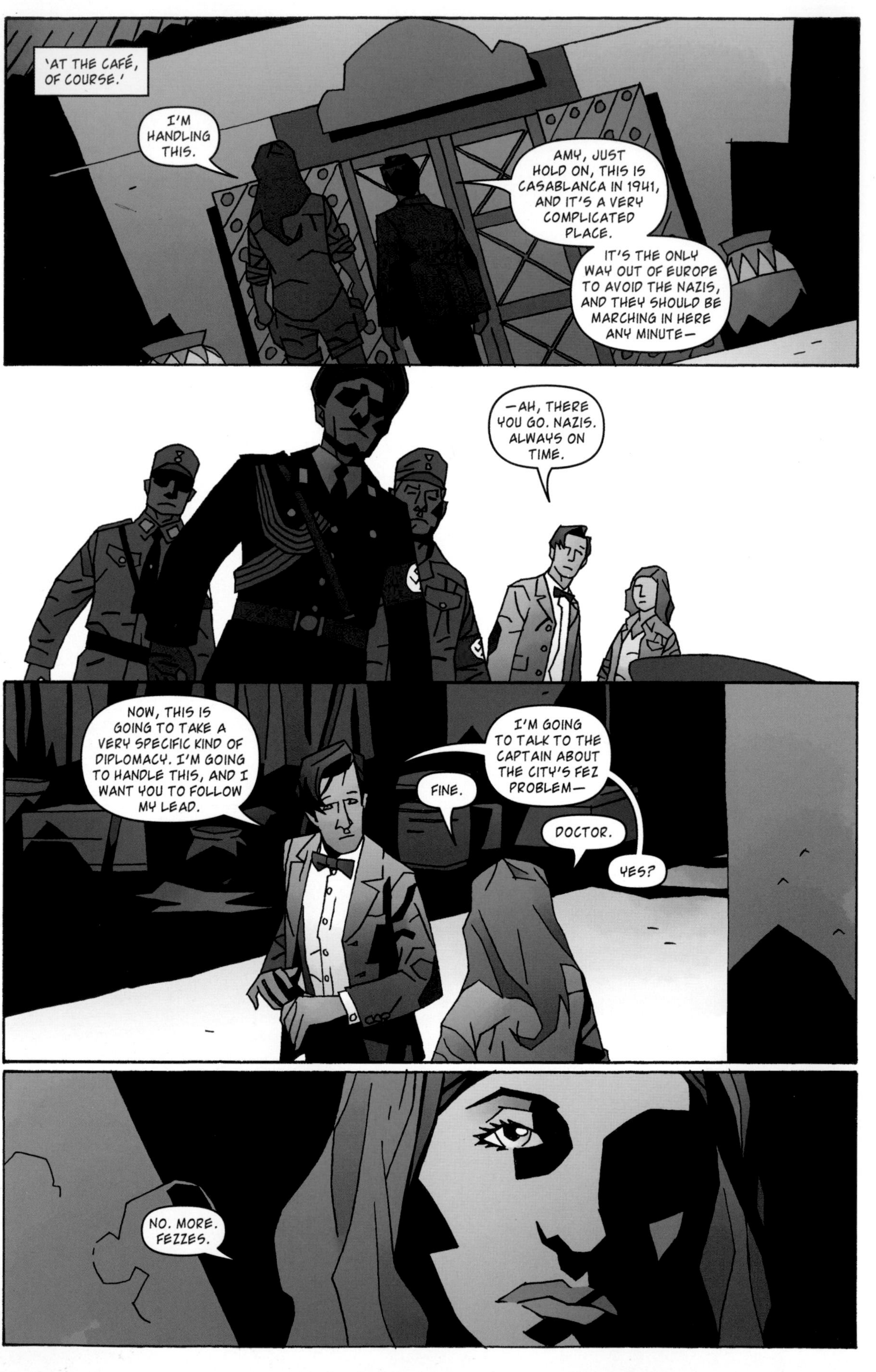

'AT THE CAFÉ, OF COURSE.'
I'M HANDLING THIS.
AMY, JUST HOLD ON, THIS IS CASABLANCA IN 1941, AND IT'S A VERY COMPLICATED PLACE.
IT'S THE ONLY WAY OUT OF EUROPE TO AVOID THE NAZIS, AND THEY SHOULD BE MARCHING IN HERE ANY MINUTE—
—AH, THERE YOU GO. NAZIS. ALWAYS ON TIME.
NOW, THIS IS GOING TO TAKE A VERY SPECIFIC KIND OF DIPLOMACY. I'M GOING TO HANDLE THIS, AND I WANT YOU TO FOLLOW MY LEAD.
FINE.
I'M GOING TO TALK TO THE CAPTAIN ABOUT THE CITY'S FEZ PROBLEM—
DOCTOR.
YES?
NO. MORE. FEZZES.

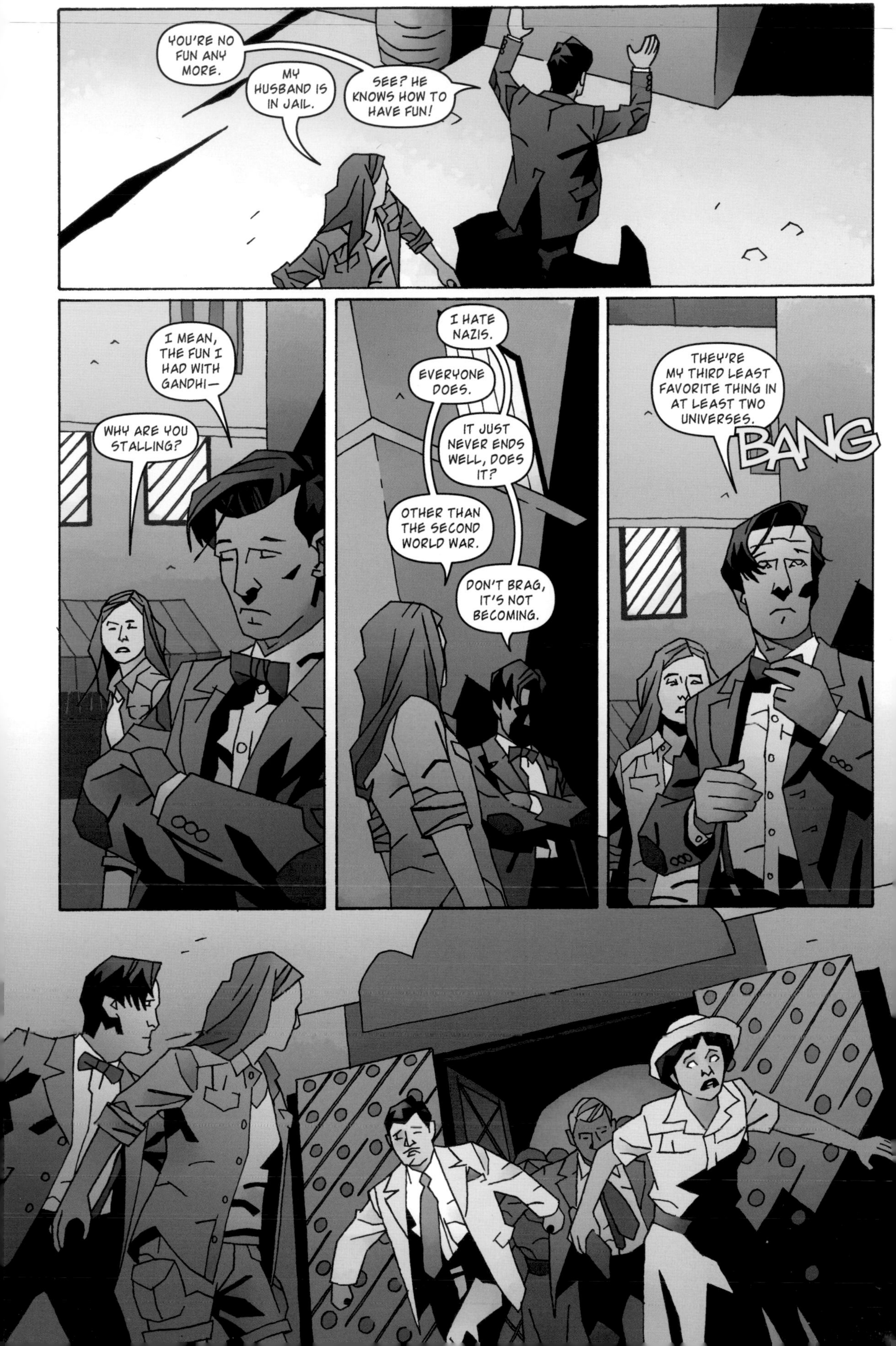
YOU'RE NO FUN ANY MORE.
MY HUSBAND IS IN JAIL.
SEE? HE KNOWS HOW TO HAVE FUN!
I MEAN, THE FUN I HAD WITH GANDHI—
WHY ARE YOU STALLING?
I HATE NAZIS.
EVERYONE DOES.
IT JUST NEVER ENDS WELL, DOES IT?
OTHER THAN THE SECOND WORLD WAR.
DON'T BRAG, IT'S NOT BECOMING.
THEY'RE MY THIRD LEAST FAVORITE THING IN AT LEAST TWO UNIVERSES.
BANG

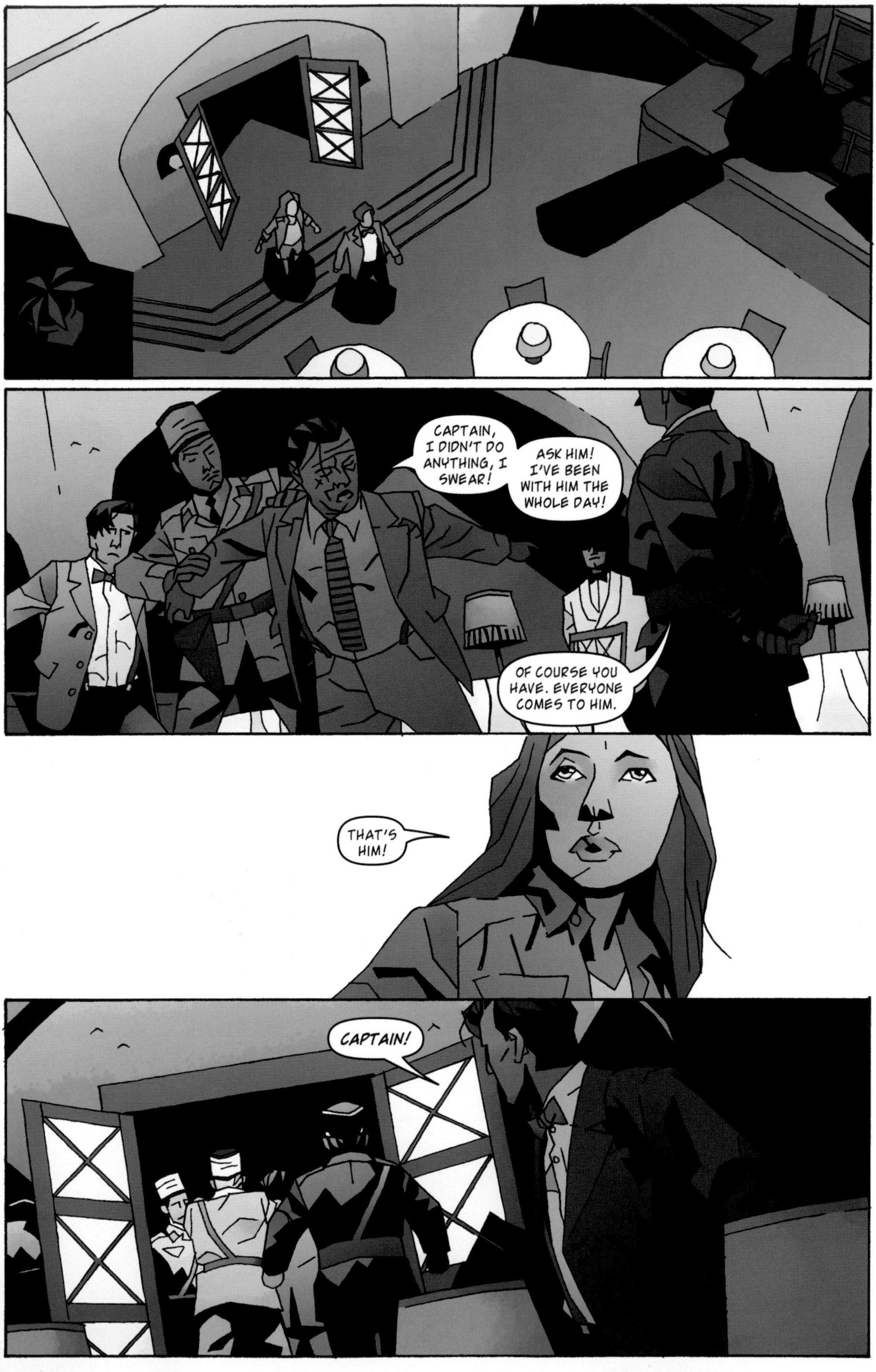
CAPTAIN, I DIDN'T DO ANYTHING, I SWEAR!
ASK HIM! I'VE BEEN WITH HIM THE WHOLE DAY!
OF COURSE YOU HAVE. EVERYONE COMES TO HIM.
THAT'S HIM!
CAPTAIN!

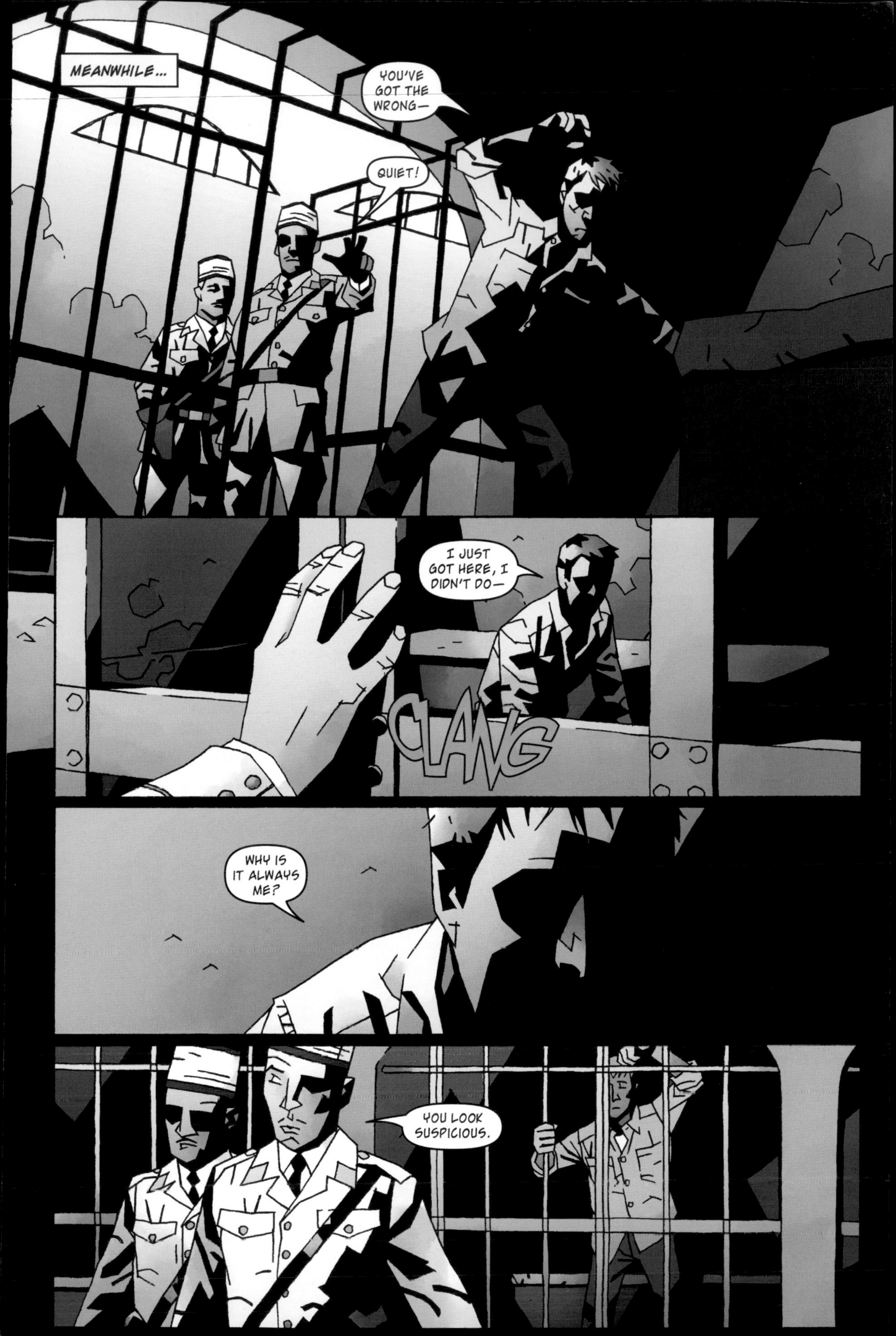
MEANWHILE...
YOU'VE GOT THE WRONG—
QUIET!
I JUST GOT HERE, I DIDN'T DO—
CLANG
WHY IS IT ALWAYS ME?
YOU LOOK SUSPICIOUS.

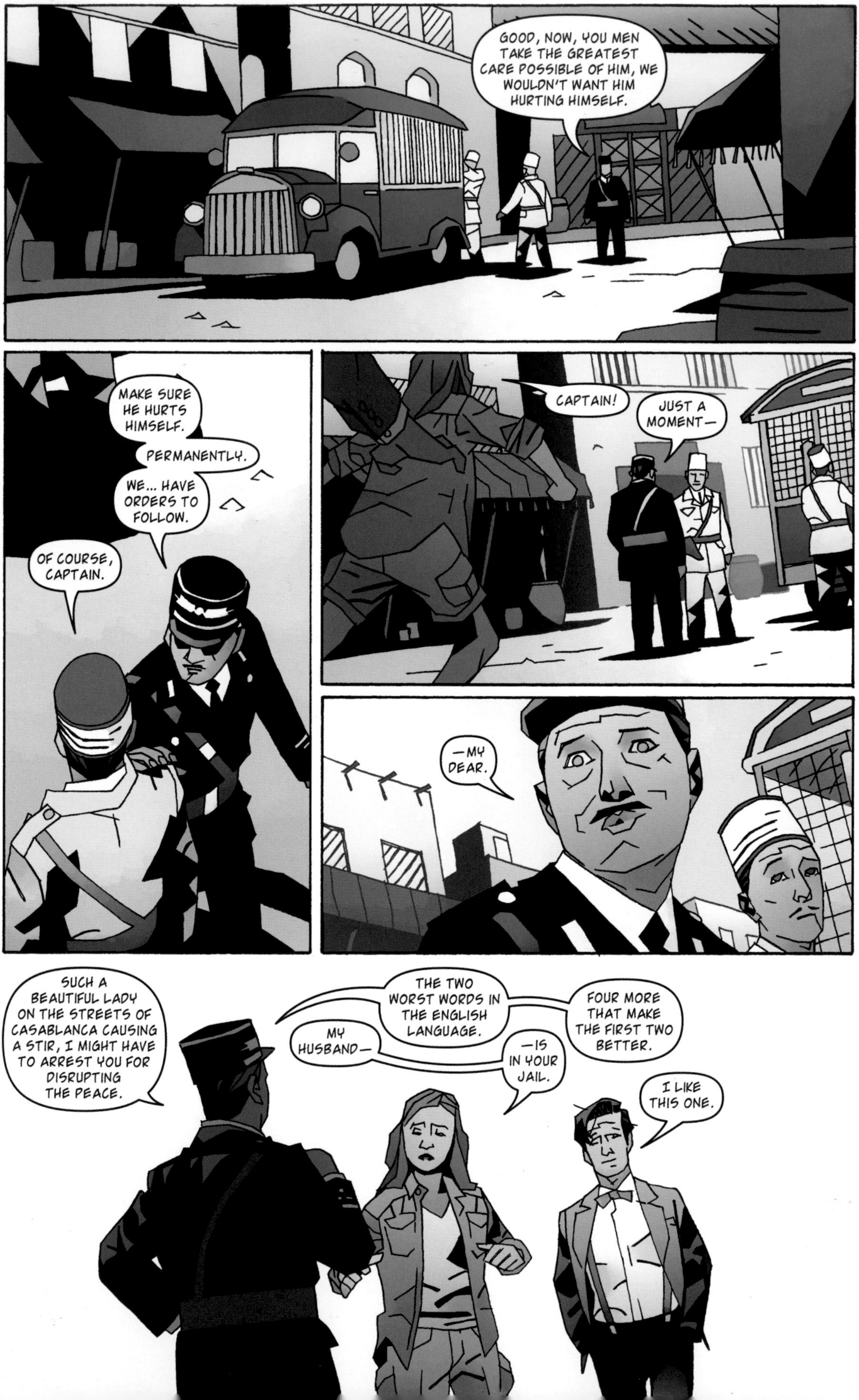
GOOD, NOW, YOU MEN TAKE THE GREATEST CARE POSSIBLE OF HIM, WE WOULDN'T WANT HIM HURTING HIMSELF.
MAKE SURE HE HURTS HIMSELF.
PERMANENTLY.
WE... HAVE ORDERS TO FOLLOW.
OF COURSE, CAPTAIN.
CAPTAIN!
JUST A MOMENT—
—MY DEAR.
SUCH A BEAUTIFUL LADY ON THE STREETS OF CASABLANCA CAUSING A STIR, I MIGHT HAVE TO ARREST YOU FOR DISRUPTING THE PEACE.
MY HUSBAND—
—IS IN YOUR JAIL.
THE TWO WORST WORDS IN THE ENGLISH LANGUAGE.
FOUR MORE THAT MAKE THE FIRST TWO BETTER.
I LIKE THIS ONE.

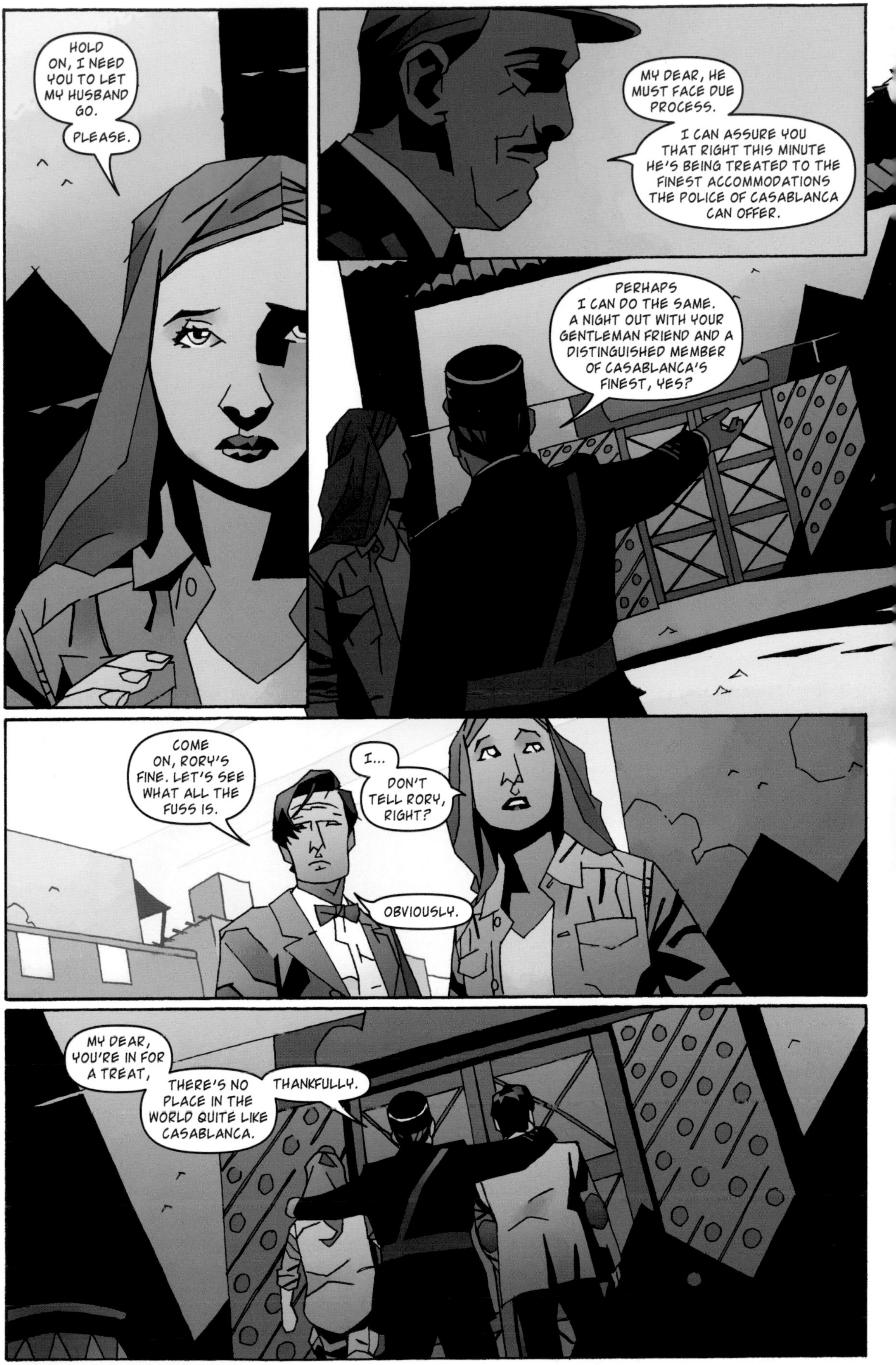
HOLD ON, I NEED YOU TO LET MY HUSBAND GO.
PLEASE.
MY DEAR, HE MUST FACE DUE PROCESS.
I CAN ASSURE YOU THAT RIGHT THIS MINUTE HE'S BEING TREATED TO THE FINEST ACCOMMODATIONS THE POLICE OF CASABLANCA CAN OFFER.
PERHAPS I CAN DO THE SAME. A NIGHT OUT WITH YOUR GENTLEMAN FRIEND AND A DISTINGUISHED MEMBER OF CASABLANCA'S FINEST, YES?
COME ON, RORY'S FINE. LET'S SEE WHAT ALL THE FUSS IS.
I...
DON'T TELL RORY, RIGHT?
OBVIOUSLY.
MY DEAR, YOU'RE IN FOR A TREAT,
THERE'S NO PLACE IN THE WORLD QUITE LIKE CASABLANCA.
THANKFULLY.

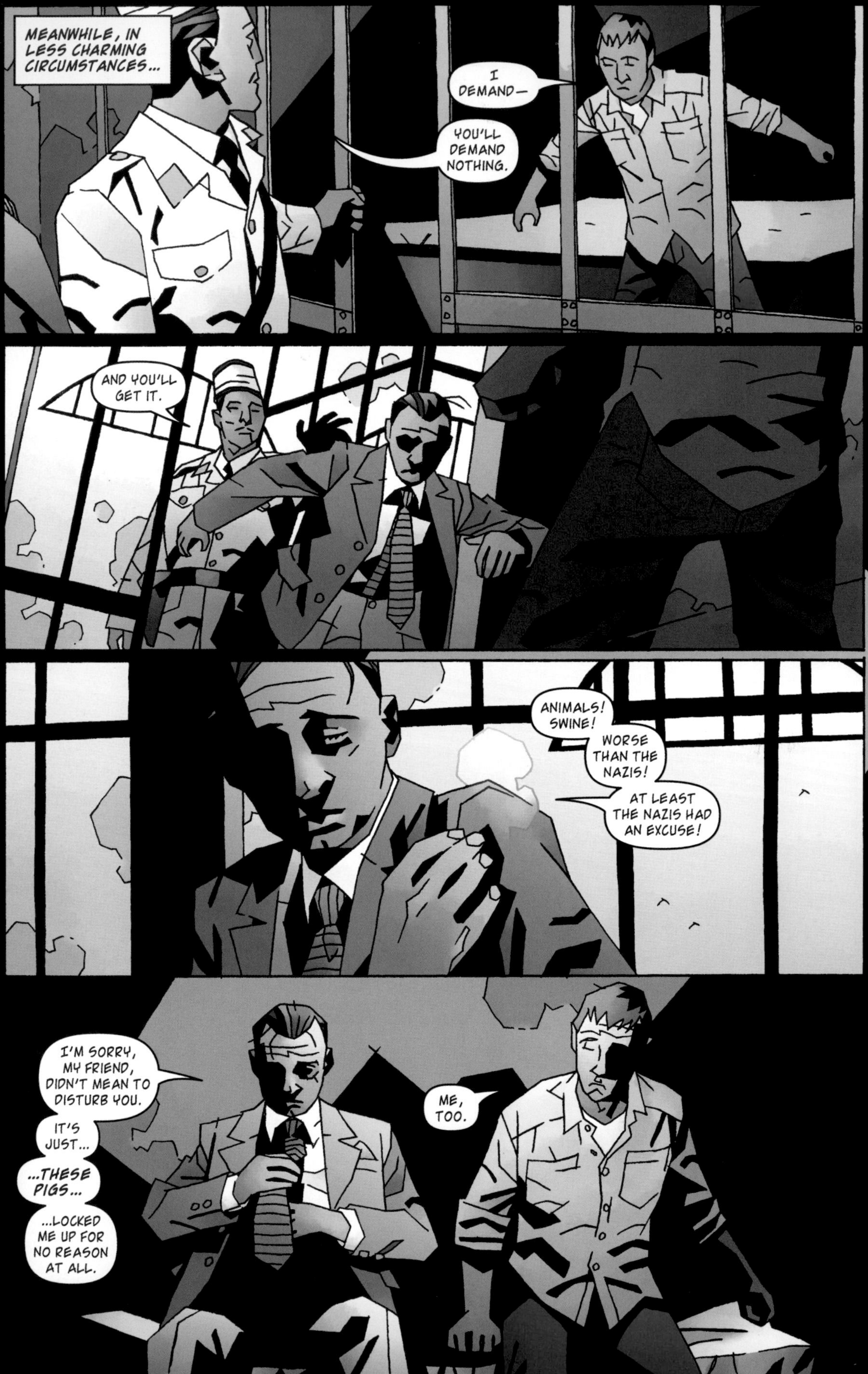
MEANWHILE, IN LESS CHARMING CIRCUMSTANCES...
I DEMAND—
YOU'LL DEMAND NOTHING.
AND YOU'LL GET IT.
ANIMALS! SWINE!
WORSE THAN THE NAZIS!
AT LEAST THE NAZIS HAD AN EXCUSE!
I'M SORRY, MY FRIEND, DIDN'T MEAN TO DISTURB YOU.
IT'S JUST...
...THESE PIGS...
...LOCKED ME UP FOR NO REASON AT ALL.
ME, TOO.

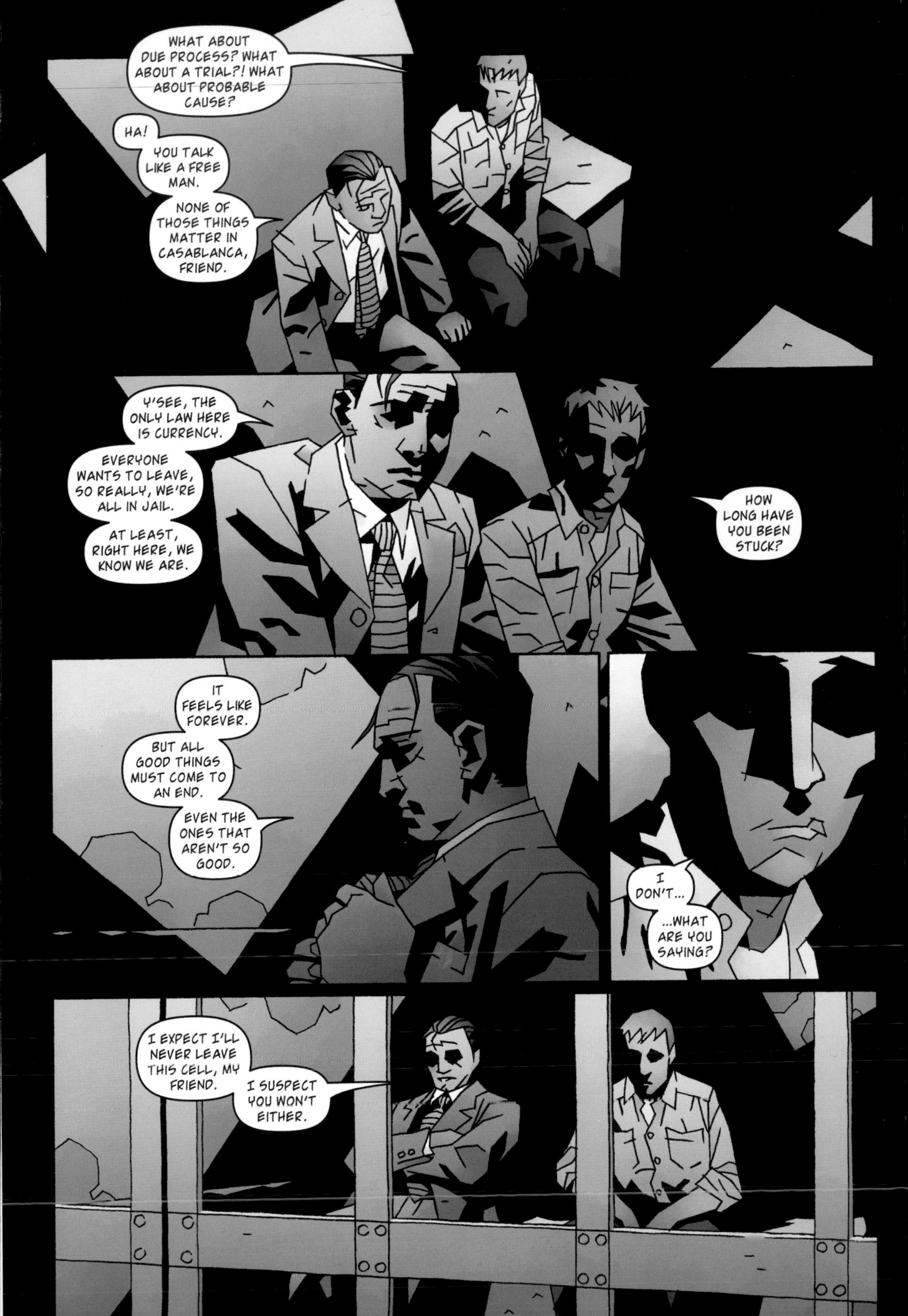
WHAT ABOUT DUE PROCESS? WHAT ABOUT A TRIAL?! WHAT ABOUT PROBABLE CAUSE?
HA!
YOU TALK LIKE A FREE MAN.
NONE OF THOSE THINGS MATTER IN CASABLANCA, FRIEND.
Y'SEE, THE ONLY LAW HERE IS CURRENCY.
EVERYONE WANTS TO LEAVE, SO REALLY, WE'RE ALL IN JAIL.
AT LEAST, RIGHT HERE, WE KNOW WE ARE.
HOW LONG HAVE YOU BEEN STUCK?
IT FEELS LIKE FOREVER.
BUT ALL GOOD THINGS MUST COME TO AN END.
EVEN THE ONES THAT AREN'T SO GOOD.
I DON'T...
...WHAT ARE YOU SAYING?
I EXPECT I'LL NEVER LEAVE THIS CELL, MY FRIEND.
I SUSPECT YOU WON'T EITHER.

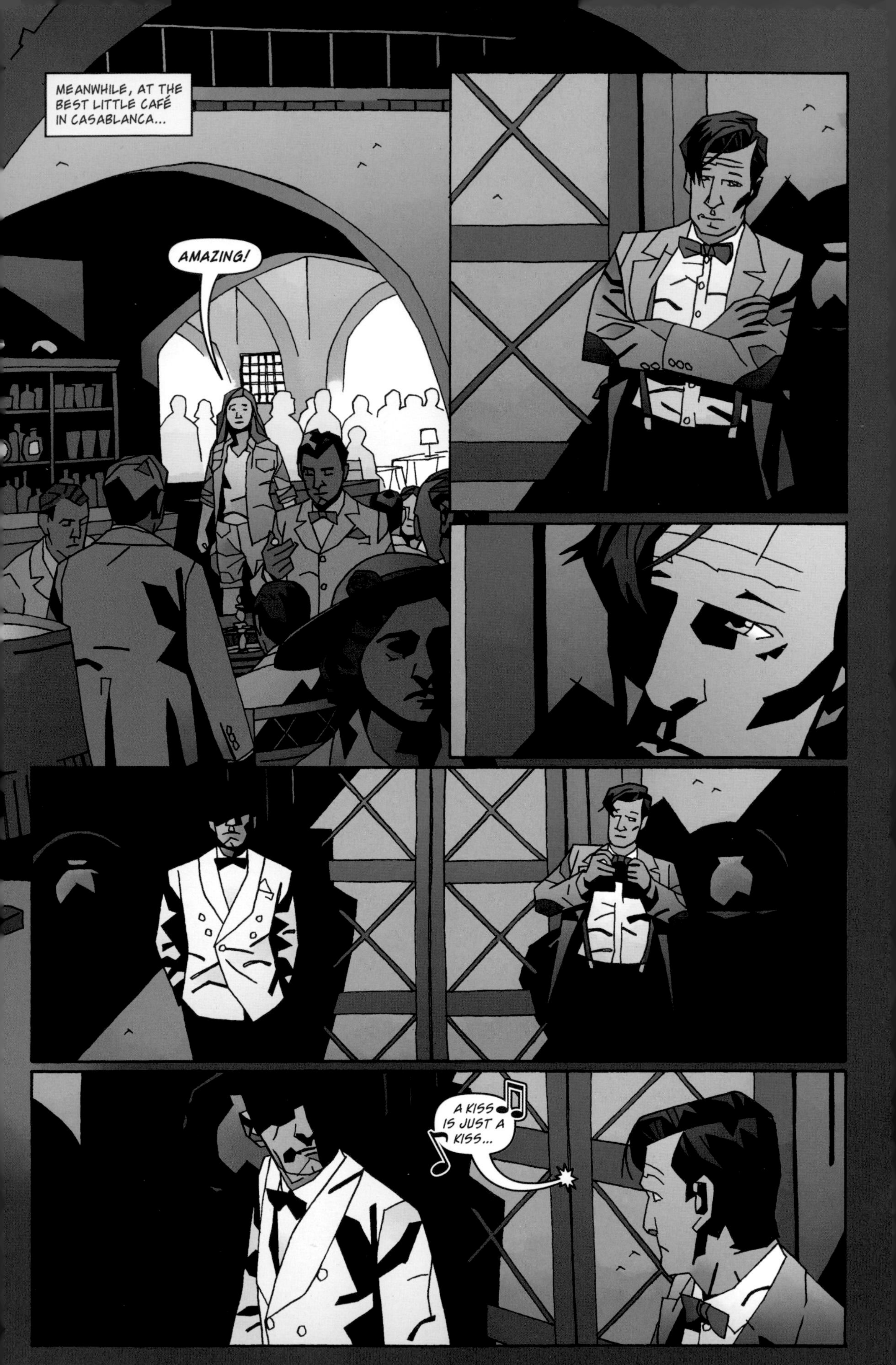
MEANWHILE, AT THE BEST LITTLE CAFÉ IN CASABLANCA...
AMAZING!
A KISS IS JUST A KISS...

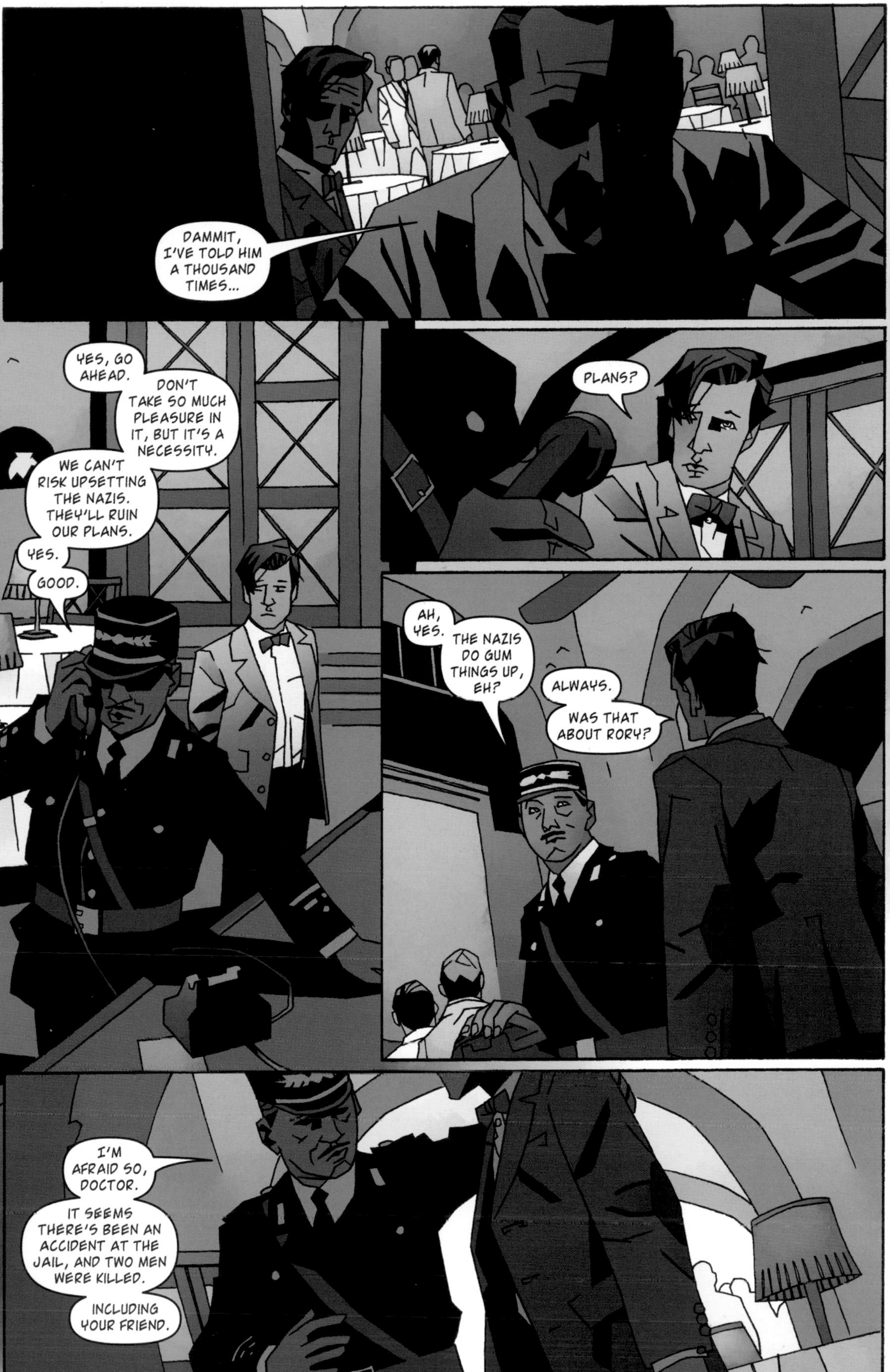
DAMMIT, I'VE TOLD HIM A THOUSAND TIMES...
YES, GO AHEAD.
DON'T TAKE SO MUCH PLEASURE IN IT, BUT IT'S A NECESSITY.
WE CAN'T RISK UPSETTING THE NAZIS. THEY'LL RUIN OUR PLANS.
YES.
GOOD.
PLANS?
AH, YES.
THE NAZIS DO GUM THINGS UP, EH?
ALWAYS.
WAS THAT ABOUT RORY?
I'M AFRAID SO, DOCTOR.
IT SEEMS THERE'S BEEN AN ACCIDENT AT THE JAIL, AND TWO MEN WERE KILLED.
INCLUDING YOUR FRIEND.

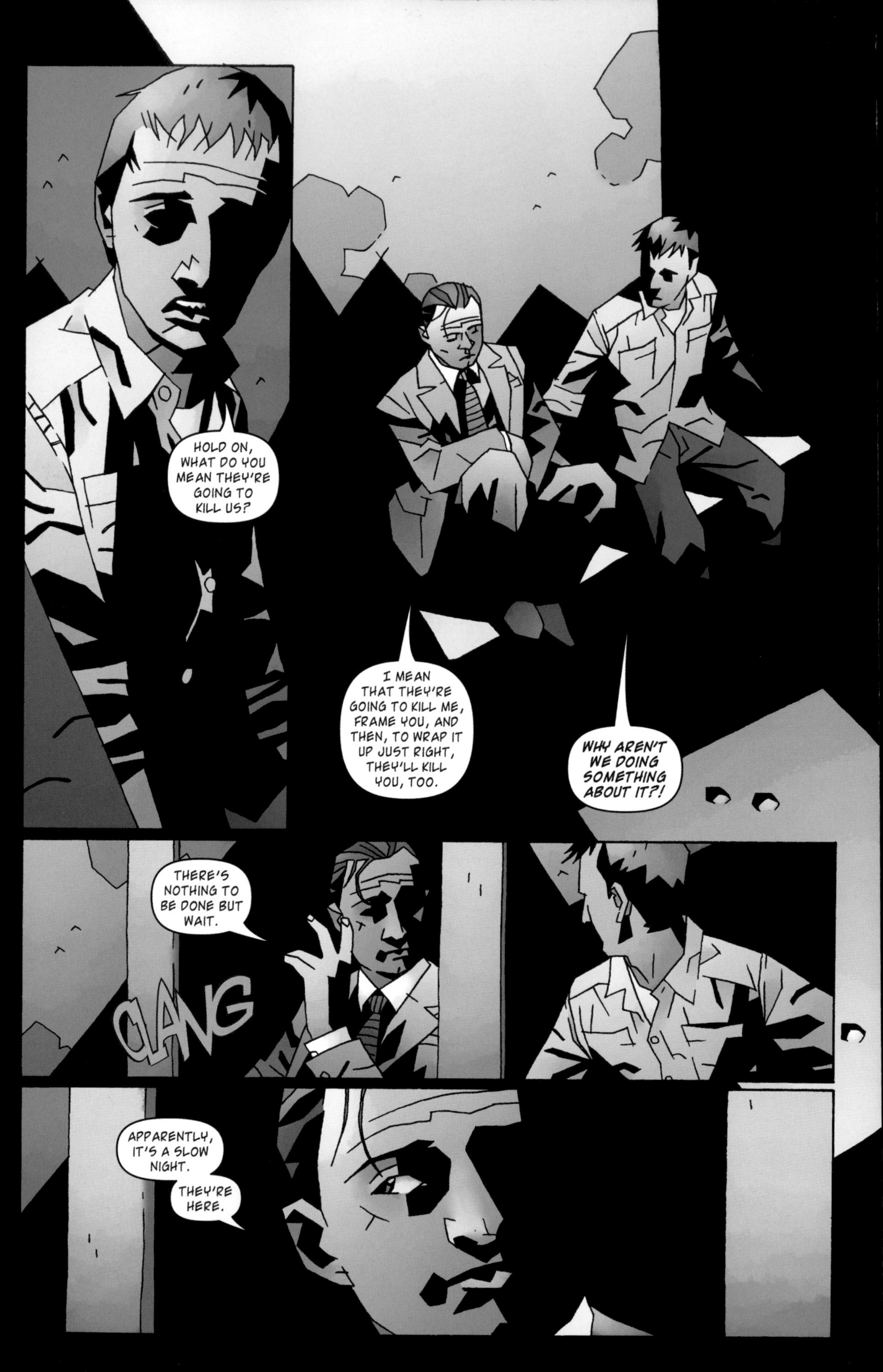
HOLD ON, WHAT DO YOU MEAN THEY'RE GOING TO KILL US?
I MEAN THAT THEY'RE GOING TO KILL ME, FRAME YOU, AND THEN, TO WRAP IT UP JUST RIGHT, THEY'LL KILL YOU, TOO.
WHY AREN'T WE DOING SOMETHING ABOUT IT?!
THERE'S NOTHING TO BE DONE BUT WAIT.
CLANG
APPARENTLY, IT'S A SLOW NIGHT.
THEY'RE HERE.

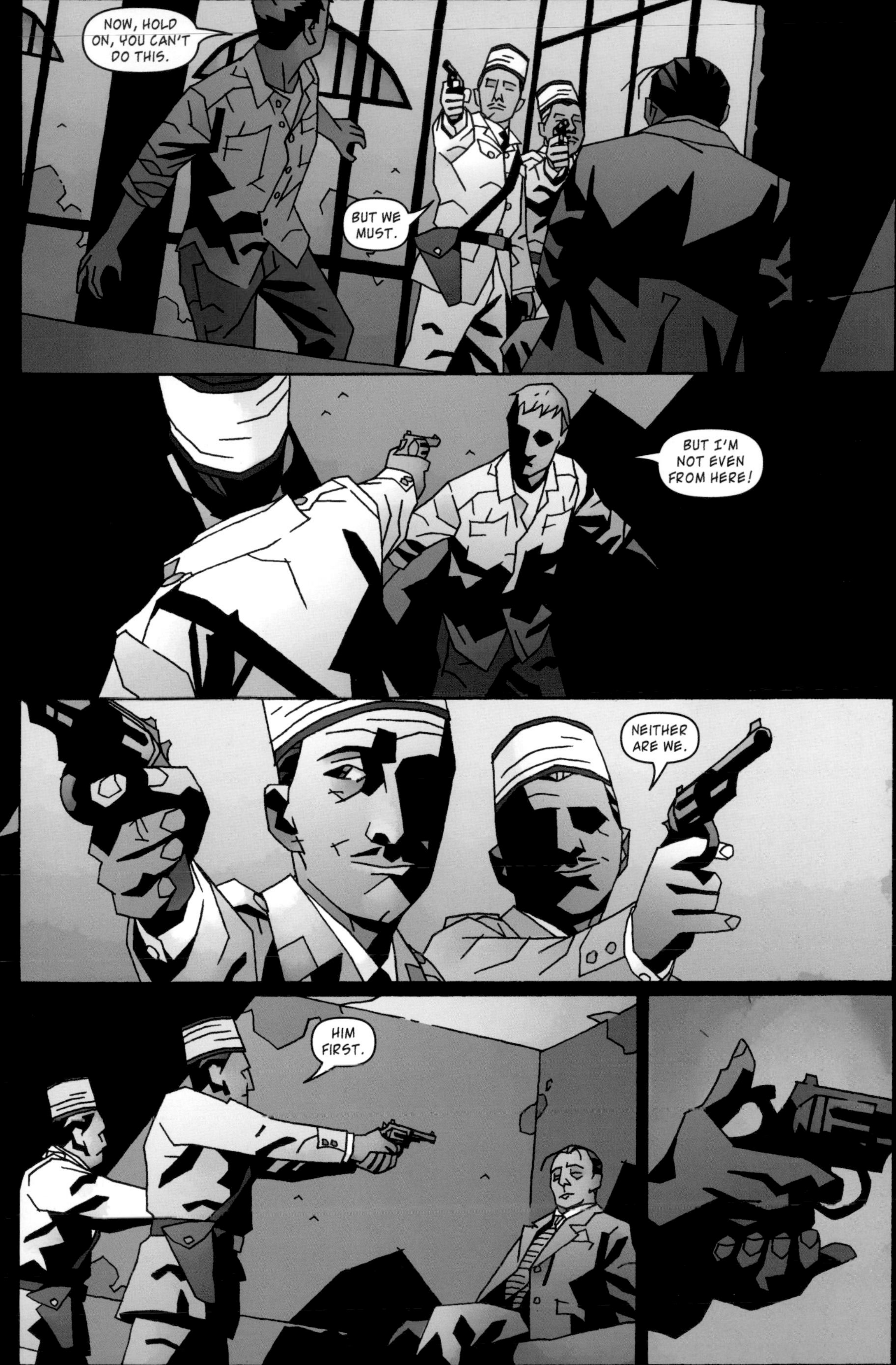
NOW, HOLD ON, YOU CAN'T DO THIS.
BUT WE MUST.
BUT I'M NOT EVEN FROM HERE!
NEITHER ARE WE.
HIM FIRST.

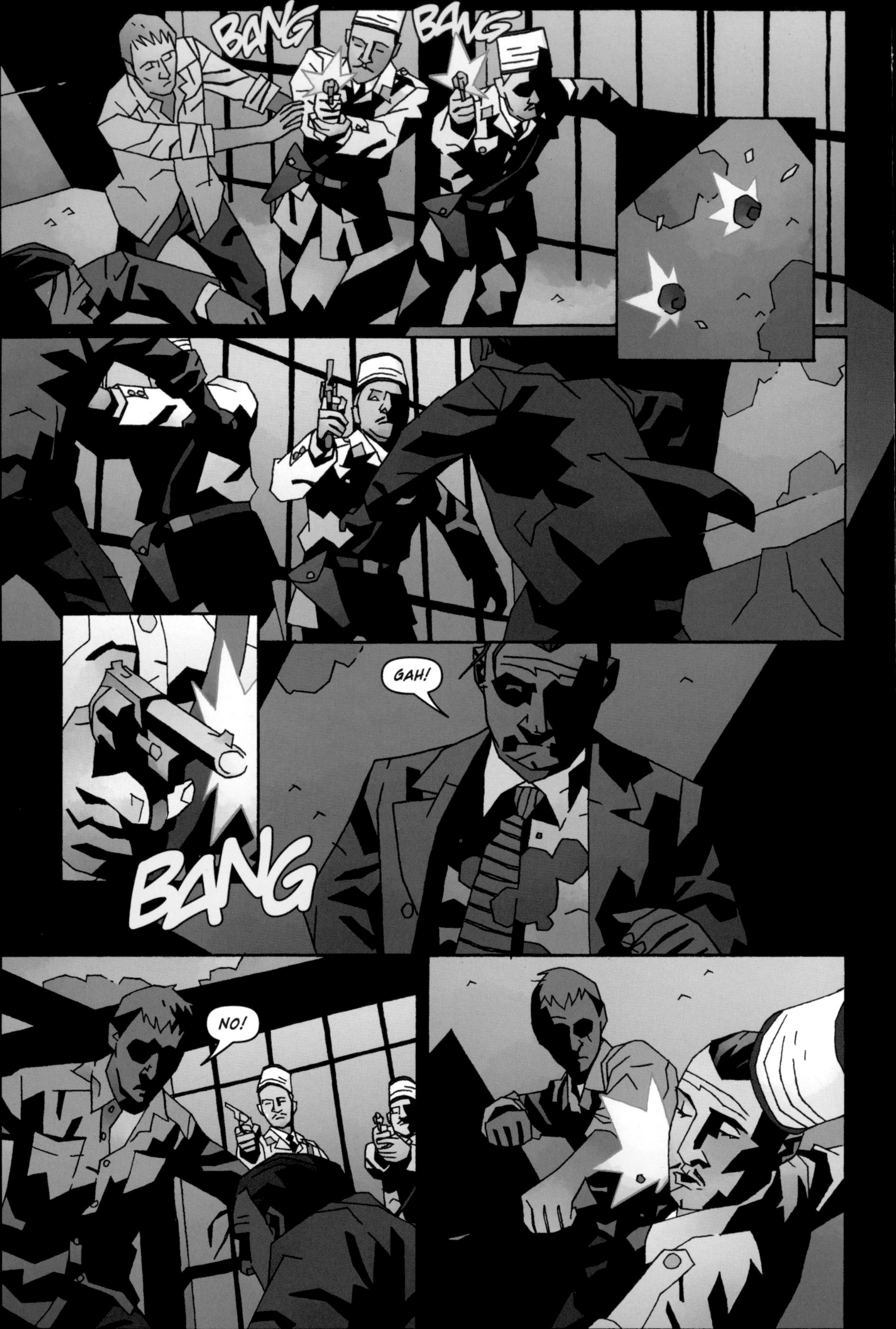
BANG
BANG
GAH!
BANG
NO!

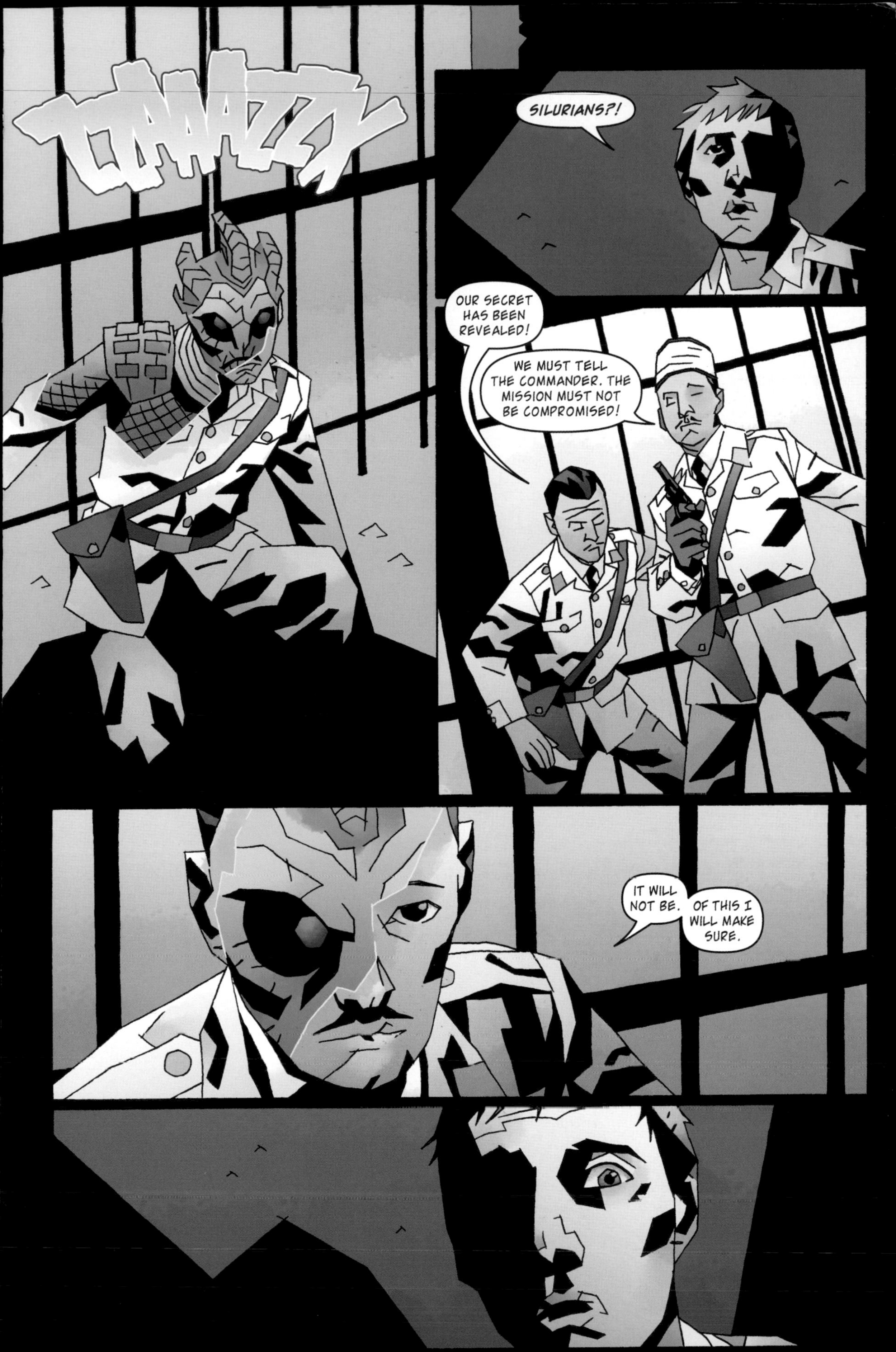
TCHAAZZZ
SILURIANS?!
OUR SECRET HAS BEEN REVEALED!
WE MUST TELL THE COMMANDER. THE MISSION MUST NOT BE COMPROMISED!
IT WILL NOT BE.
OF THIS I WILL MAKE SURE.

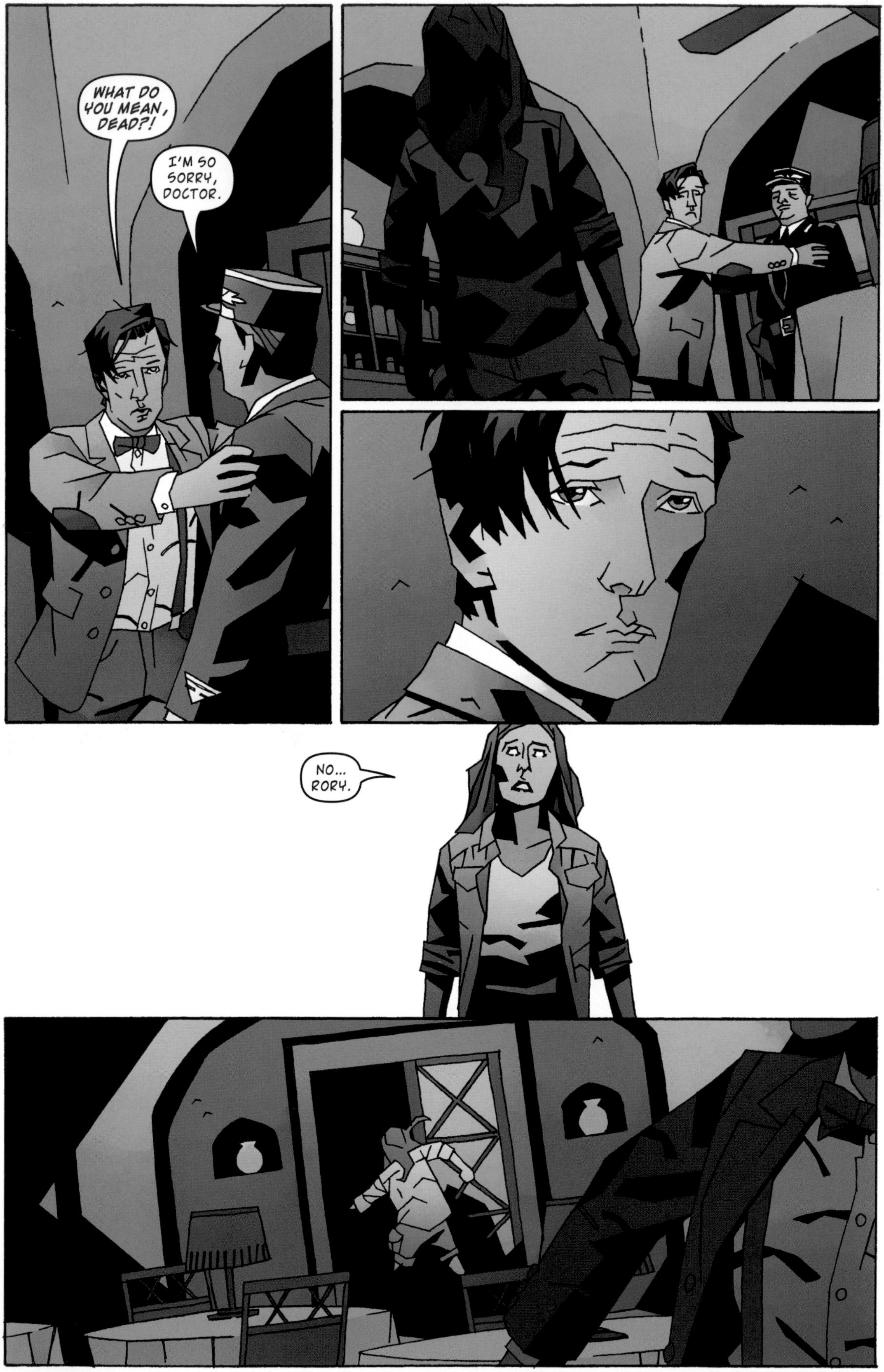
WHAT DO YOU MEAN, DEAD?!
I'M SO SORRY, DOCTOR.
NO... RORY.

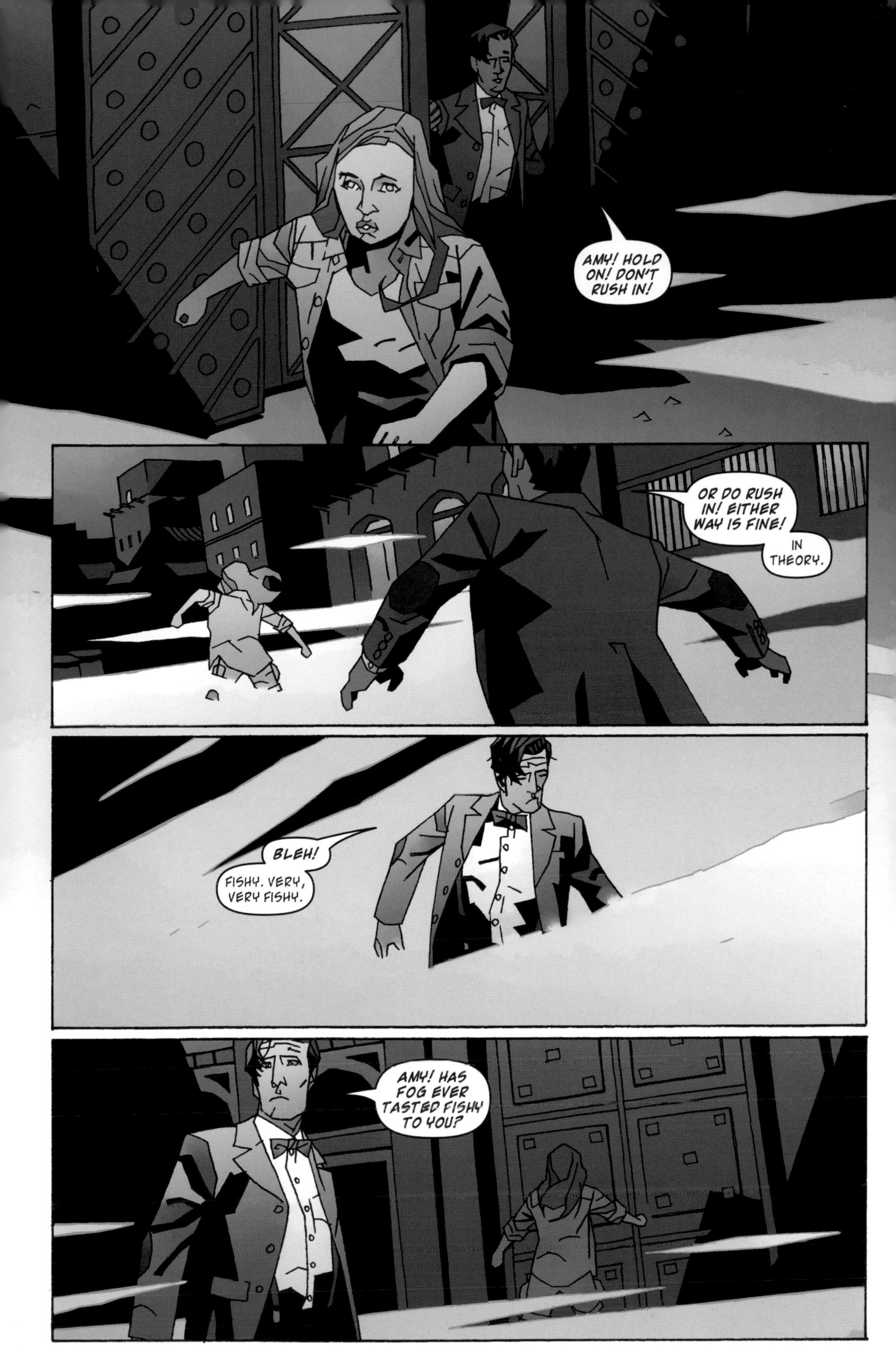

AMY! HOLD ON! DON'T RUSH IN!
OR DO RUSH IN! EITHER WAY IS FINE!
IN THEORY.
BLEH!
FISHY. VERY, VERY FISHY.
AMY! HAS FOG EVER TASTED FISHY TO YOU?

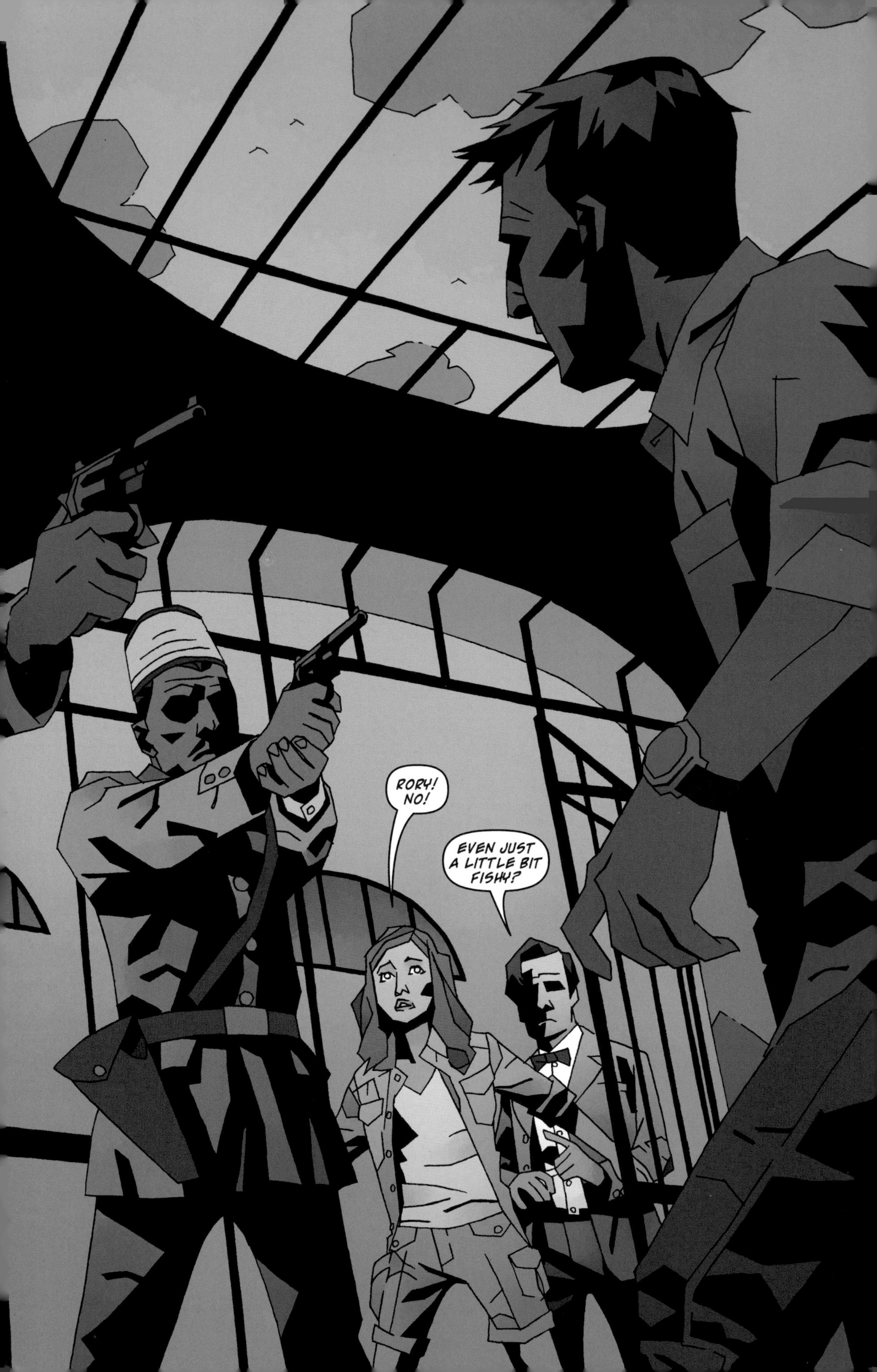
RORY! NO!
EVEN JUST A LITTLE BIT FISHY?

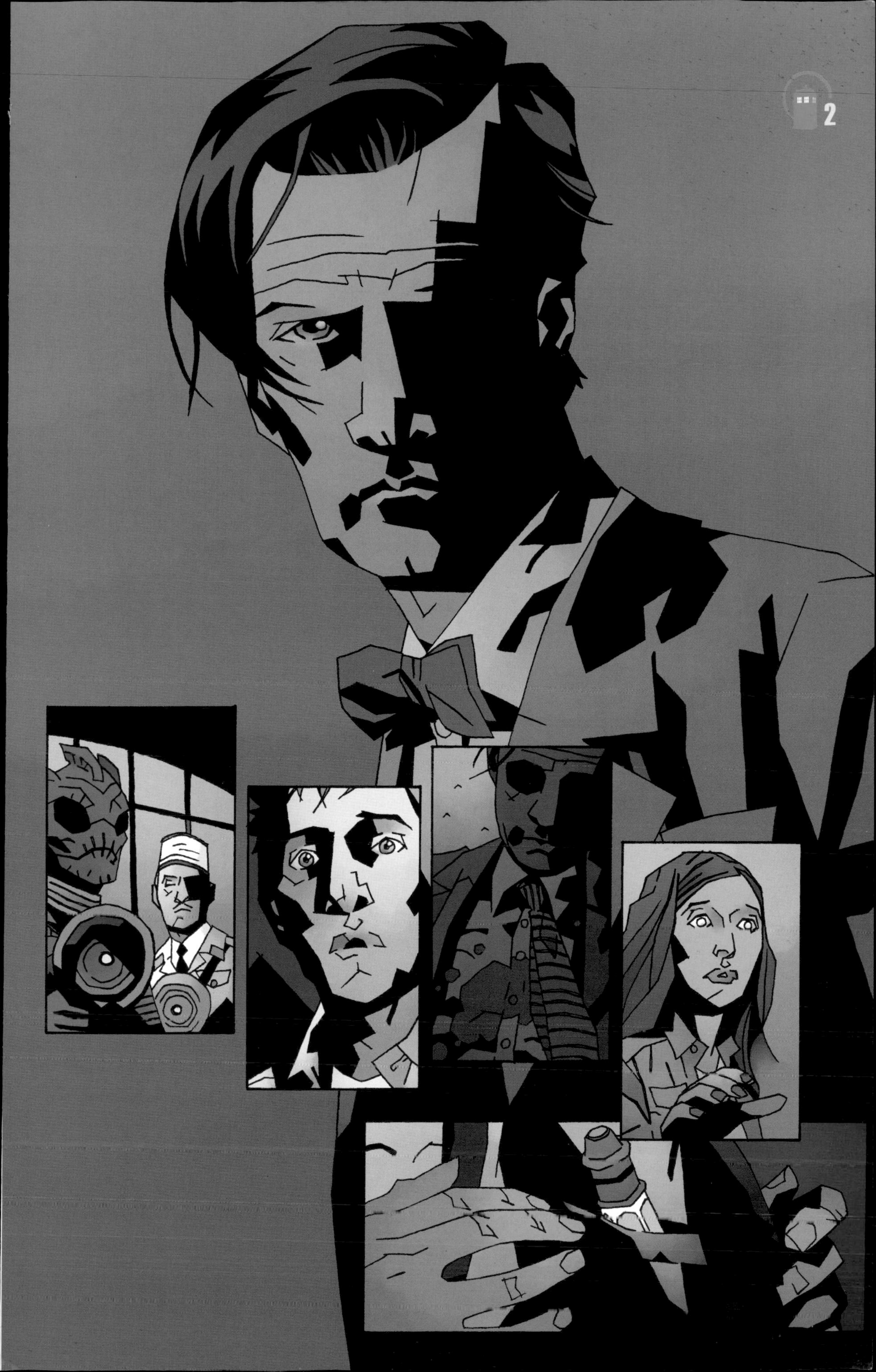

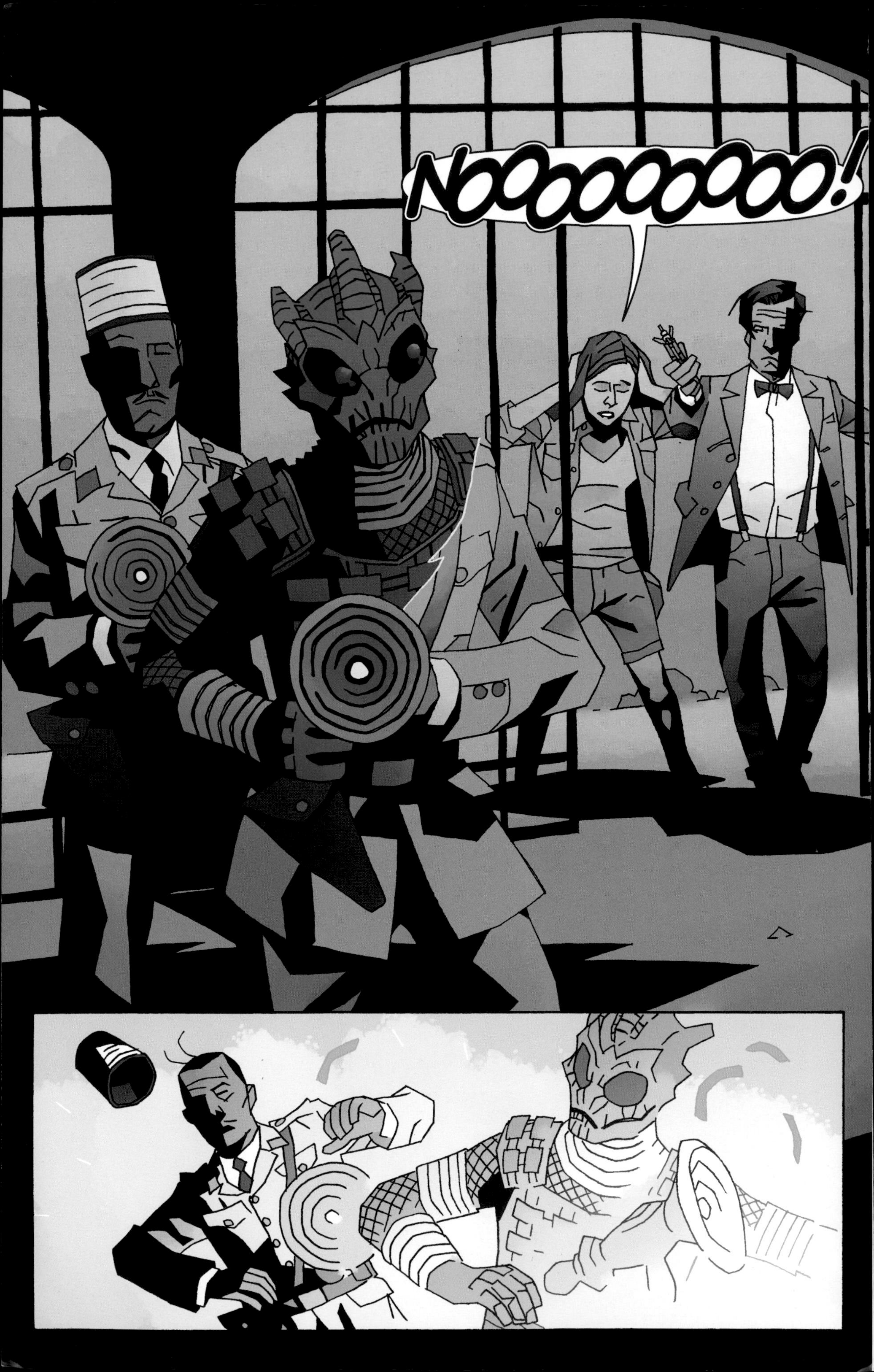
NOOOOOOOO!

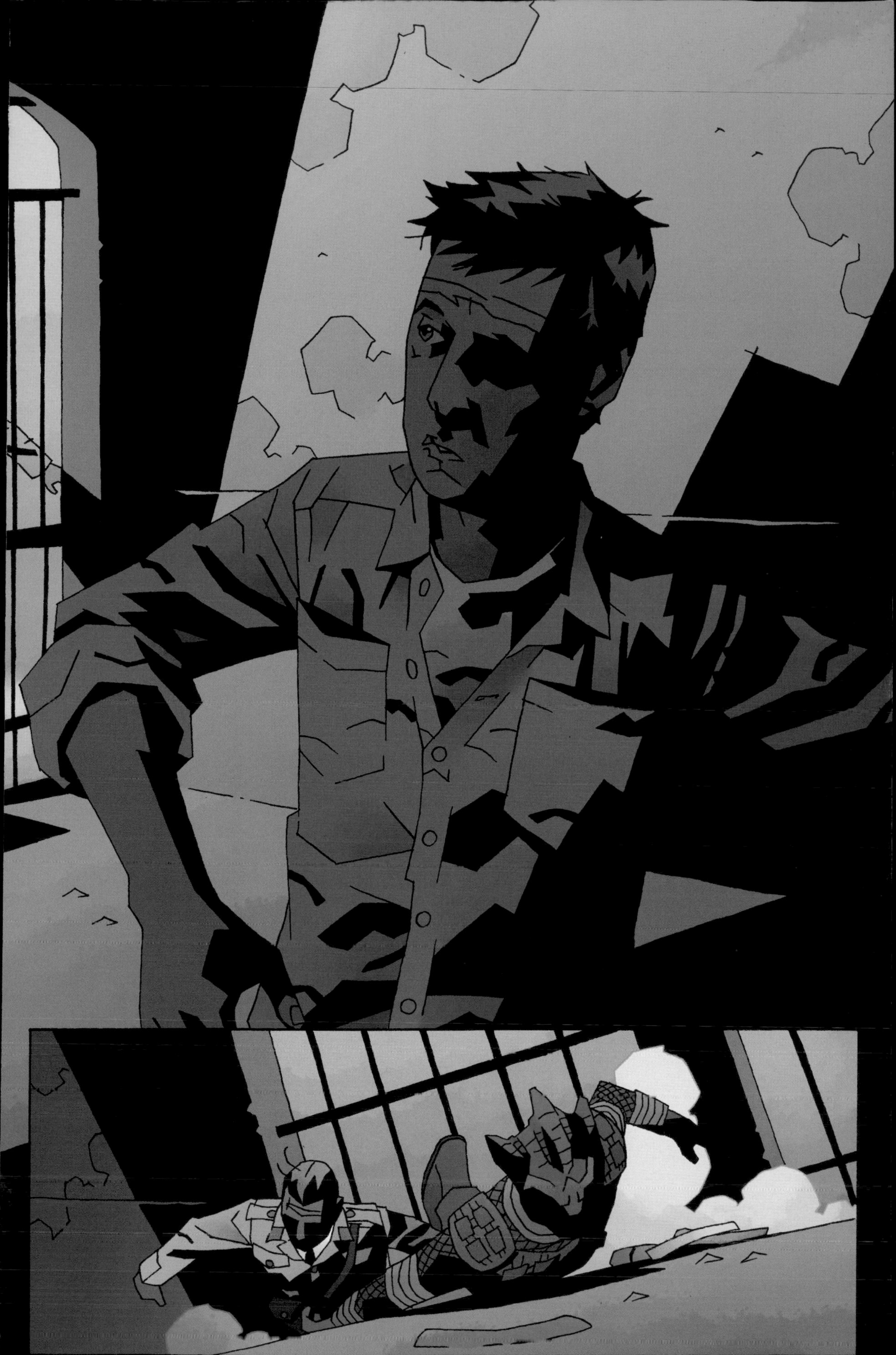

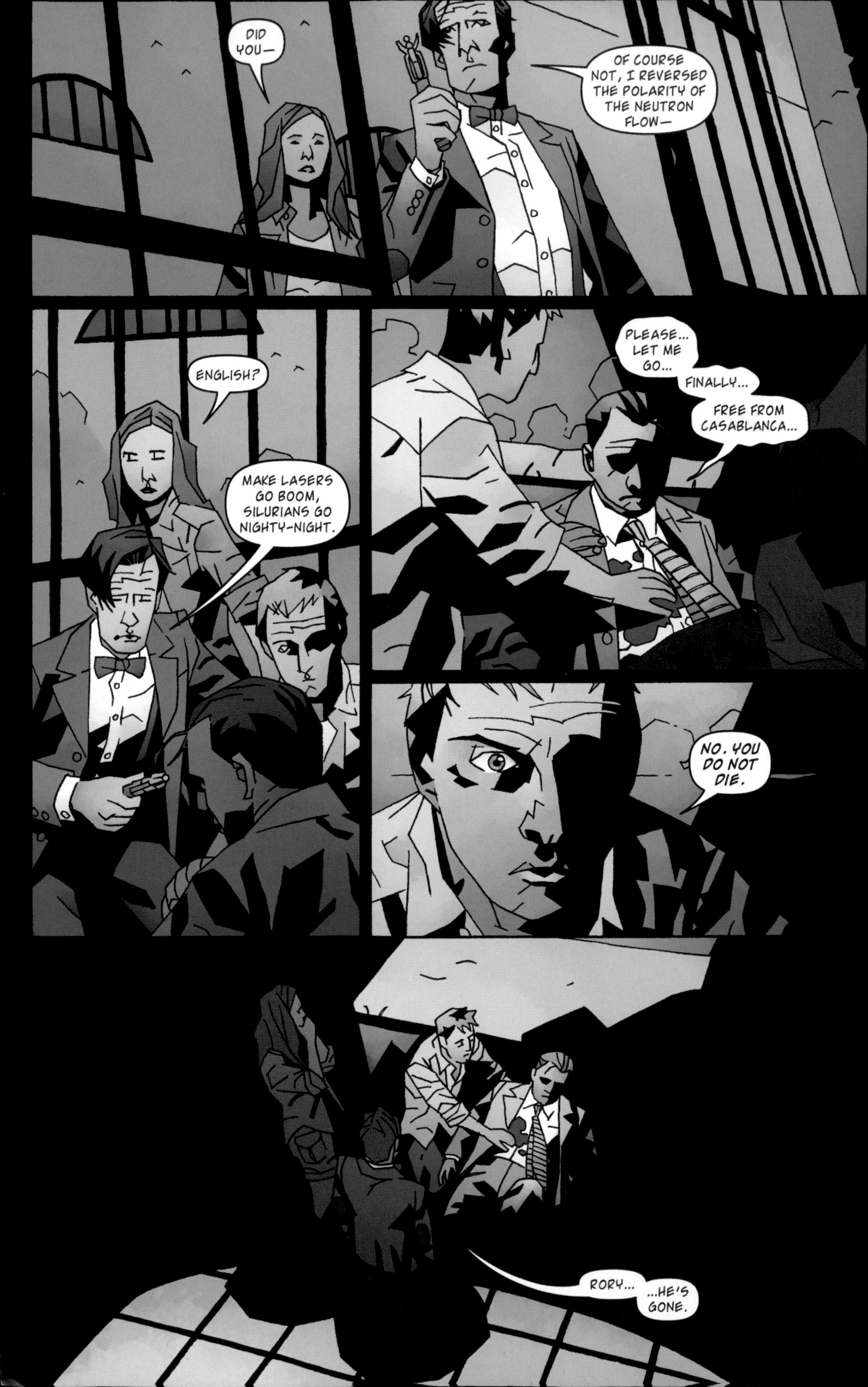
DID YOU—
OF COURSE NOT, I REVERSED THE POLARITY OF THE NEUTRON FLOW—
ENGLISH?
MAKE LASERS GO BOOM, SILURIANS GO NIGHTY-NIGHT.
PLEASE... LET ME GO...
FINALLY...
FREE FROM CASABLANCA...
NO. YOU DO NOT DIE.
RORY...
...HE'S GONE.

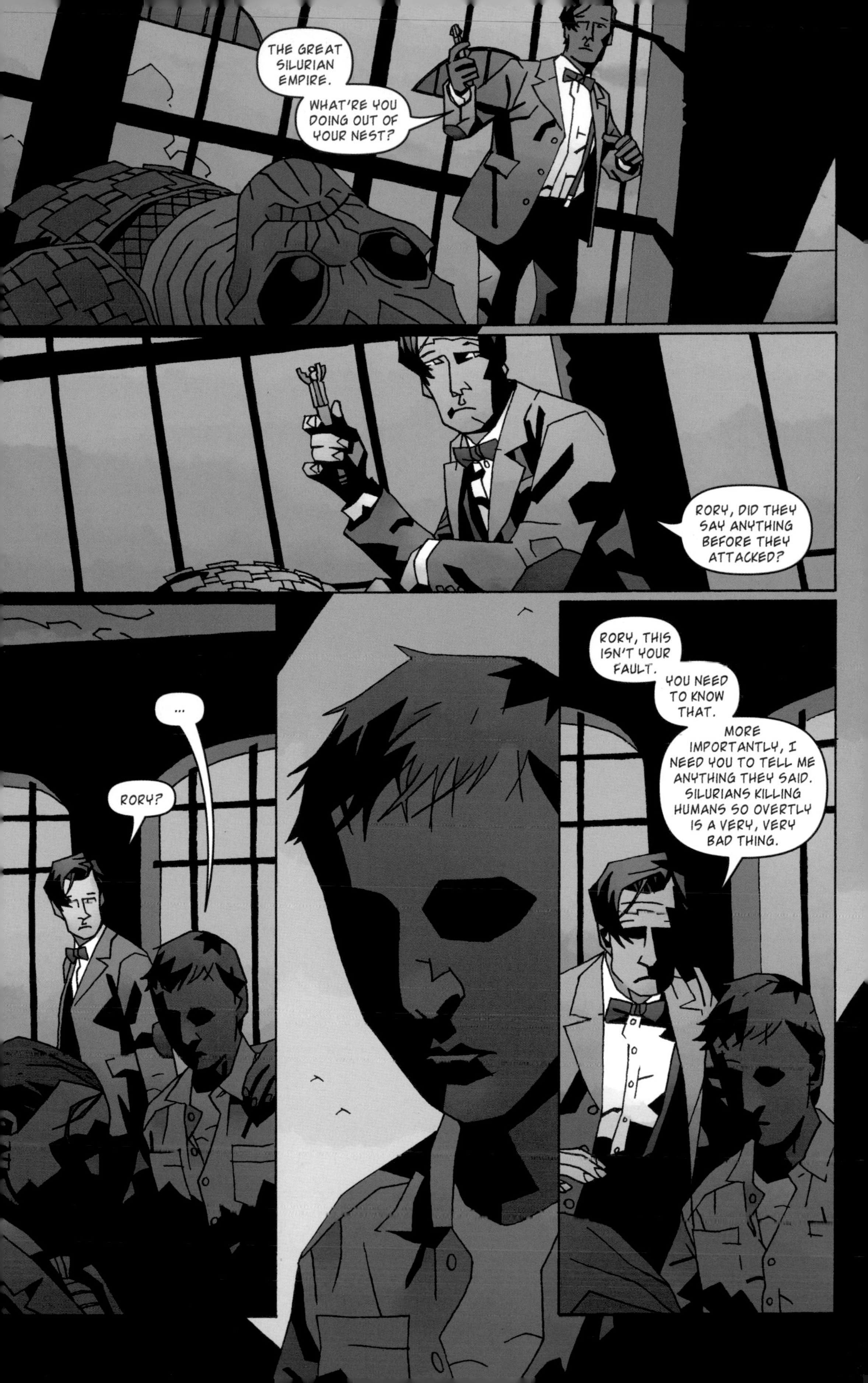
THE GREAT SILURIAN EMPIRE.
WHAT'RE YOU DOING OUT OF YOUR NEST?
RORY, DID THEY SAY ANYTHING BEFORE THEY ATTACKED?
RORY?
...
RORY, THIS ISN'T YOUR FAULT.
YOU NEED TO KNOW THAT.
MORE IMPORTANTLY, I NEED YOU TO TELL ME ANYTHING THEY SAID. SILURIANS KILLING HUMANS SO OVERTLY IS A VERY, VERY BAD THING.

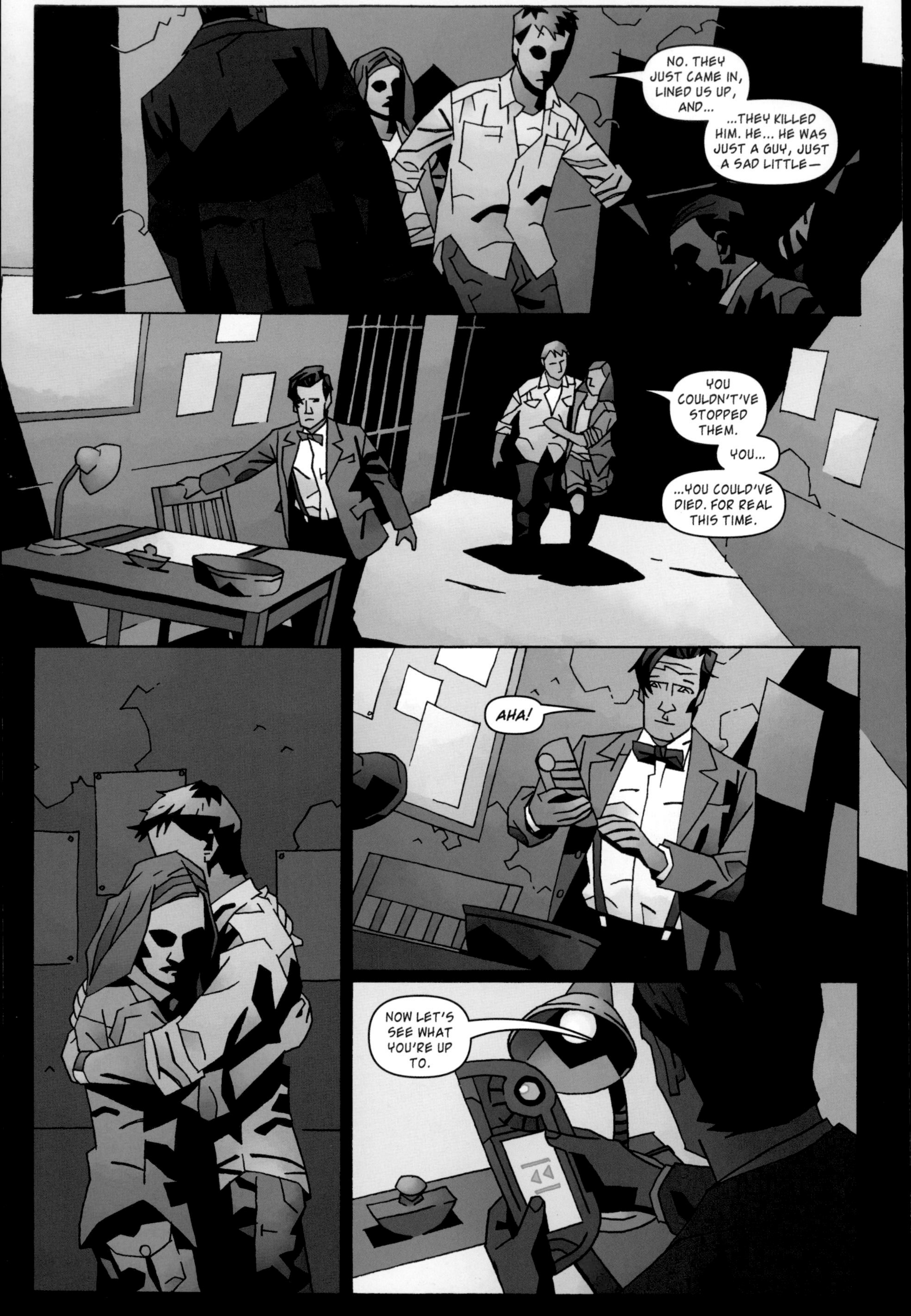
NO. THEY JUST CAME IN, LINED US UP, AND...
...THEY KILLED HIM. HE... HE WAS JUST A GUY, JUST A SAD LITTLE—
YOU COULDN'T'VE STOPPED THEM.
YOU...
...YOU COULD'VE DIED. FOR REAL THIS TIME.
AHA!
NOW LET'S SEE WHAT YOU'RE UP TO.

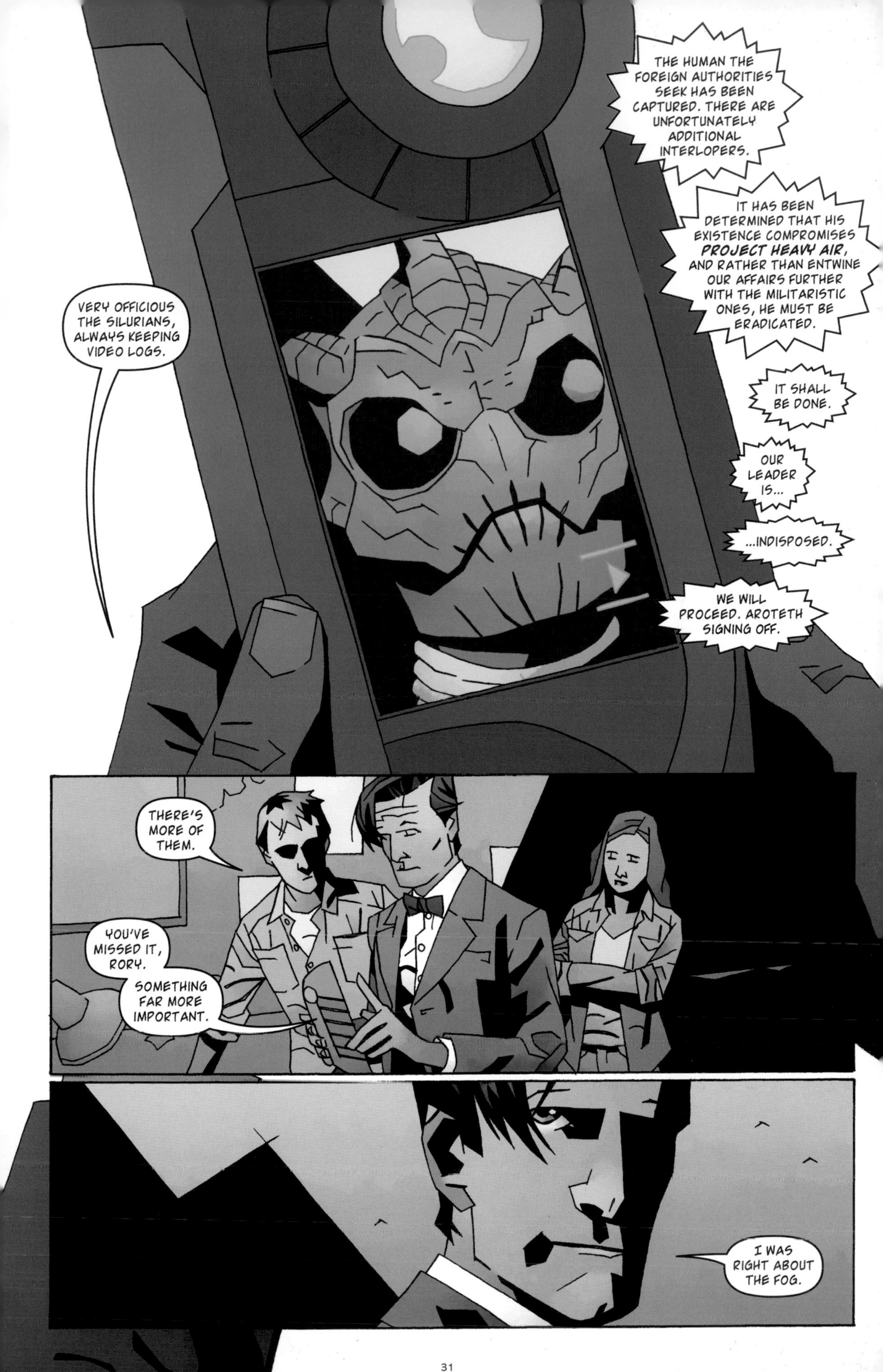
VERY OFFICIOUS THE SILURIANS, ALWAYS KEEPING VIDEO LOGS.
THE HUMAN THE FOREIGN AUTHORITIES SEEK HAS BEEN CAPTURED. THERE ARE UNFORTUNATELY ADDITIONAL INTERLOPERS.
IT HAS BEEN DETERMINED THAT HIS EXISTENCE COMPROMISES ***PROJECT HEAVY AIR***, AND RATHER THAN ENTWINE OUR AFFAIRS FURTHER WITH THE MILITARISTIC ONES, HE MUST BE ERADICATED.
IT SHALL BE DONE.
OUR LEADER IS...
...INDISPOSED.
WE WILL PROCEED. AROTETH SIGNING OFF.
THERE'S MORE OF THEM.
YOU'VE MISSED IT, RORY.
SOMETHING FAR MORE IMPORTANT.
I WAS RIGHT ABOUT THE FOG.

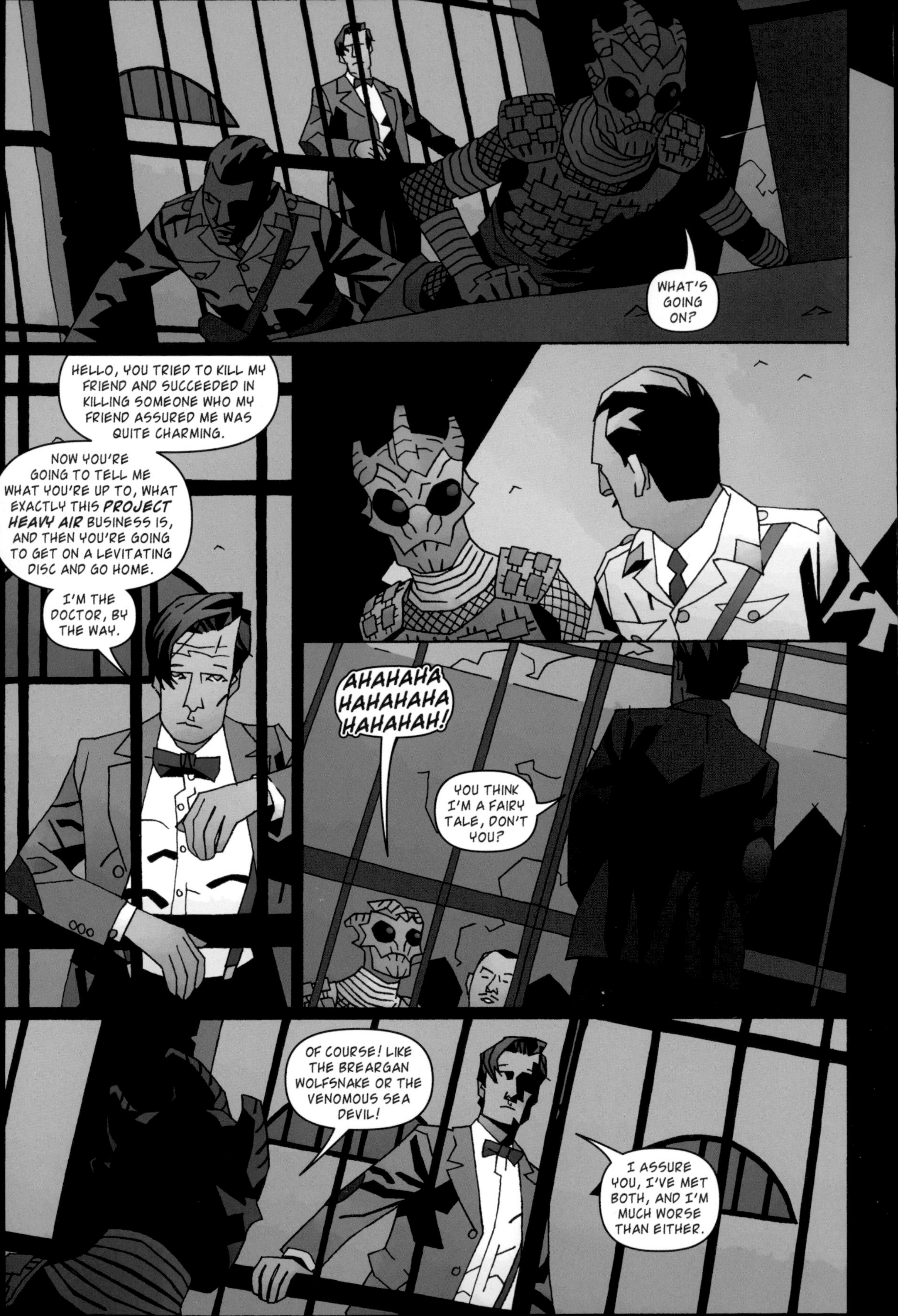
WHAT'S GOING ON?
HELLO, YOU TRIED TO KILL MY FRIEND AND SUCCEEDED IN KILLING SOMEONE WHO MY FRIEND ASSURED ME WAS QUITE CHARMING.
NOW YOU'RE GOING TO TELL ME WHAT YOU'RE UP TO, WHAT EXACTLY THIS *PROJECT HEAVY AIR* BUSINESS IS, AND THEN YOU'RE GOING TO GET ON A LEVITATING DISC AND GO HOME.
I'M THE DOCTOR, BY THE WAY.
AHAHAHA HAHAHAHA HAHAHAH!
YOU THINK I'M A FAIRY TALE, DON'T YOU?
OF COURSE! LIKE THE BREARGAN WOLFSNAKE OR THE VENOMOUS SEA DEVIL!
I ASSURE YOU, I'VE MET BOTH, AND I'M MUCH WORSE THAN EITHER.

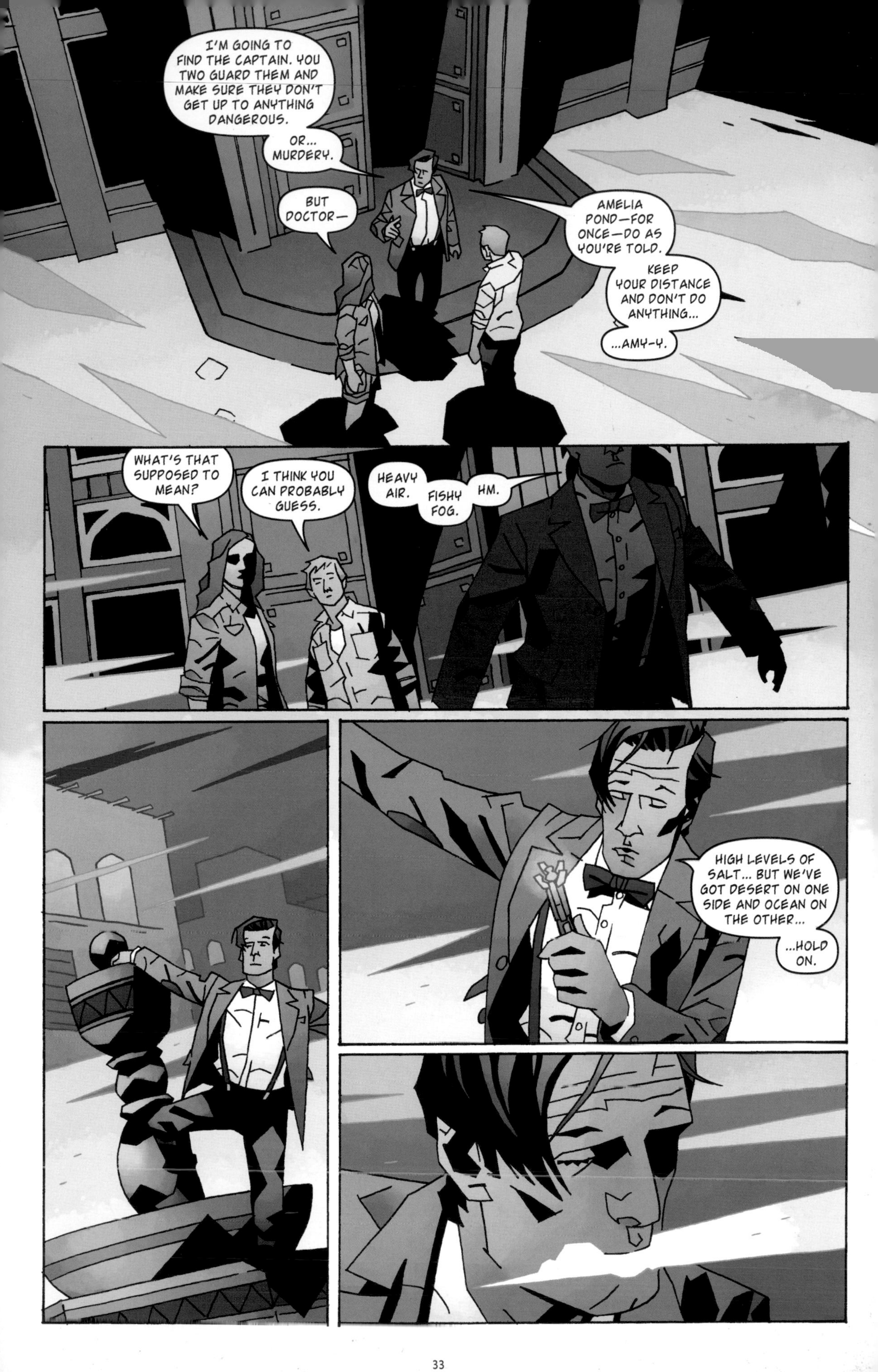
I'M GOING TO FIND THE CAPTAIN. YOU TWO GUARD THEM AND MAKE SURE THEY DON'T GET UP TO ANYTHING DANGEROUS.
OR... MURDERY.
BUT DOCTOR—
AMELIA POND—FOR ONCE—DO AS YOU'RE TOLD.
KEEP YOUR DISTANCE AND DON'T DO ANYTHING...
...AMY-Y.
WHAT'S THAT SUPPOSED TO MEAN?
I THINK YOU CAN PROBABLY GUESS.
HEAVY AIR.
FISHY FOG.
HM.
HIGH LEVELS OF SALT... BUT WE'VE GOT DESERT ON ONE SIDE AND OCEAN ON THE OTHER...
...HOLD ON.

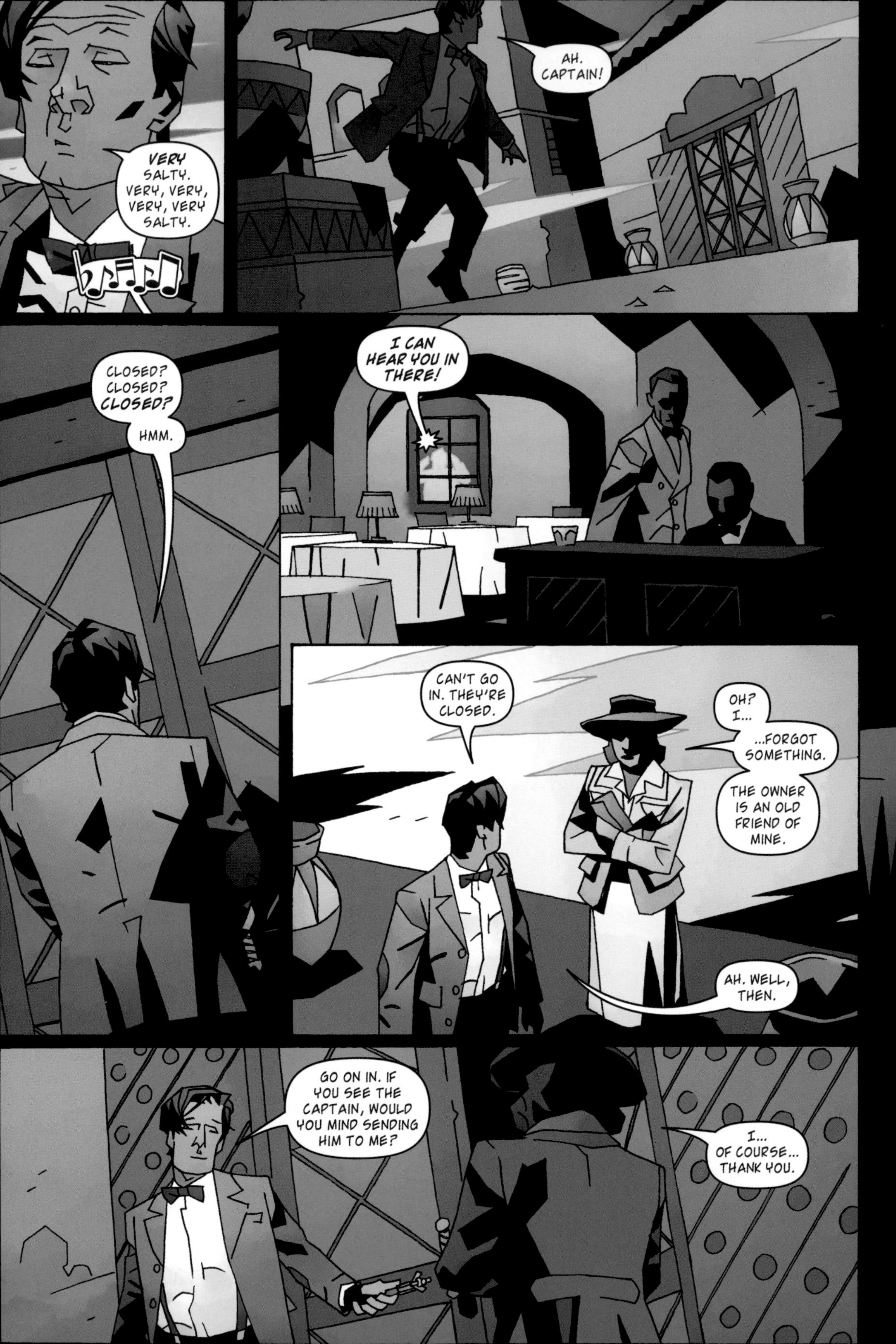
VERY SALTY. VERY, VERY, VERY, VERY SALTY.
AH. CAPTAIN!
CLOSED? CLOSED? CLOSED?
HMM.
I CAN HEAR YOU IN THERE!
CAN'T GO IN. THEY'RE CLOSED.
OH? I...
...FORGOT SOMETHING.
THE OWNER IS AN OLD FRIEND OF MINE.
AH. WELL, THEN.
GO ON IN. IF YOU SEE THE CAPTAIN, WOULD YOU MIND SENDING HIM TO ME?
I... OF COURSE... THANK YOU.

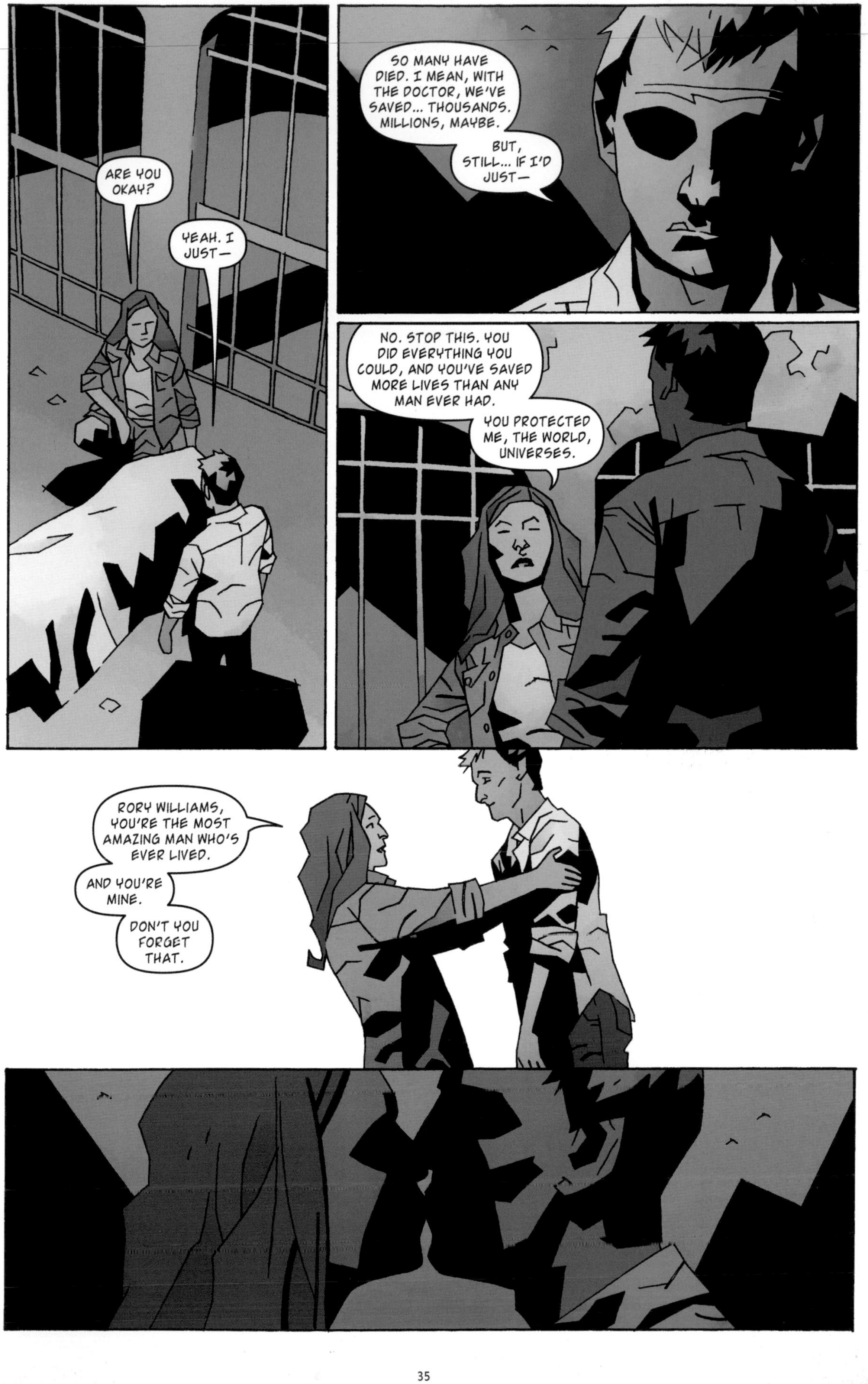
ARE YOU OKAY?
YEAH. I JUST—
SO MANY HAVE DIED. I MEAN, WITH THE DOCTOR, WE'VE SAVED... THOUSANDS. MILLIONS, MAYBE.
BUT, STILL... IF I'D JUST—
NO. STOP THIS. YOU DID EVERYTHING YOU COULD, AND YOU'VE SAVED MORE LIVES THAN ANY MAN EVER HAD.
YOU PROTECTED ME, THE WORLD, UNIVERSES.
RORY WILLIAMS, YOU'RE THE MOST AMAZING MAN WHO'S EVER LIVED.
AND YOU'RE MINE.
DON'T YOU FORGET THAT.

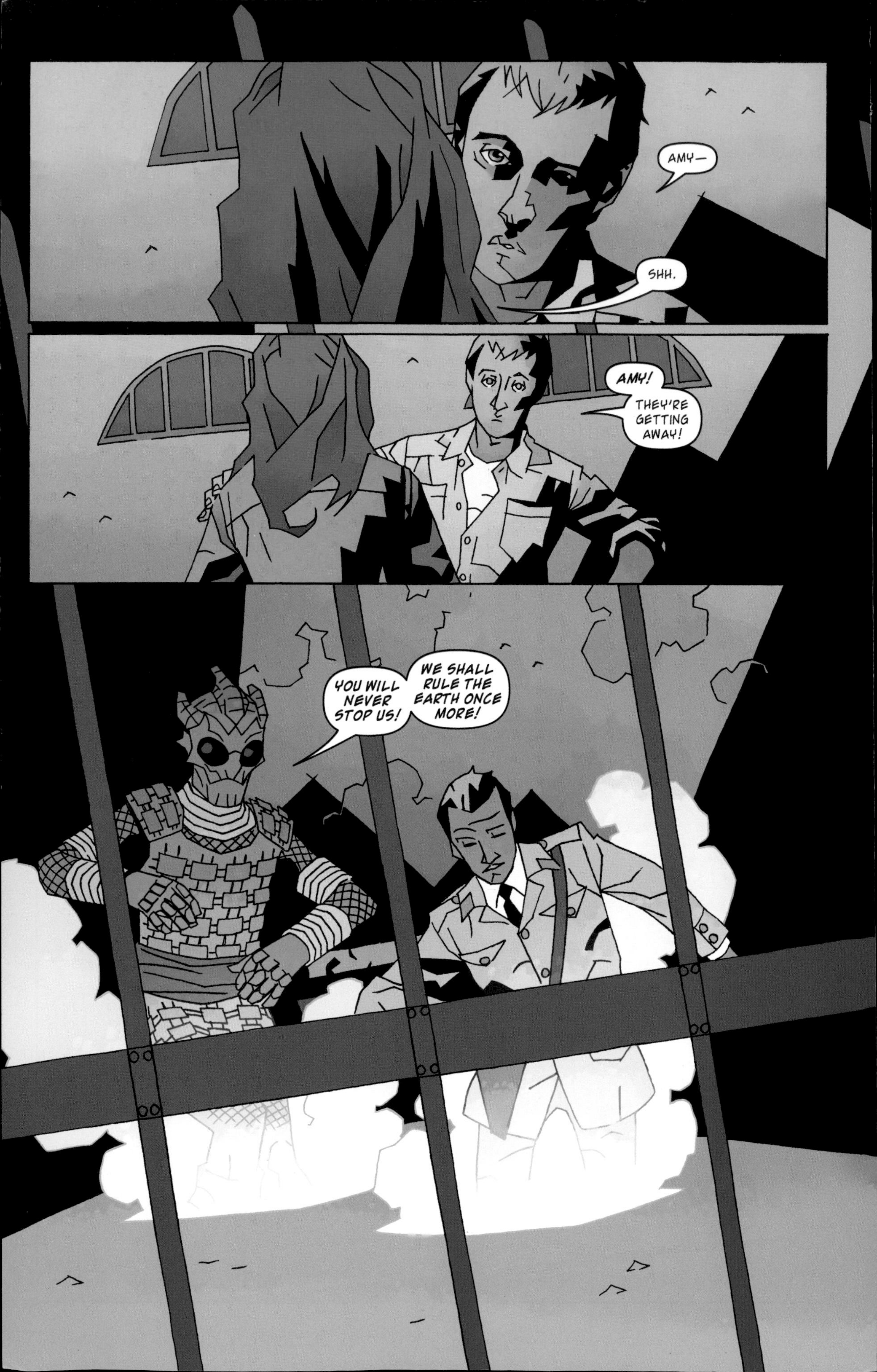
AMY—
SHH.
AMY! THEY'RE GETTING AWAY!
YOU WILL NEVER STOP US!
WE SHALL RULE THE EARTH ONCE MORE!

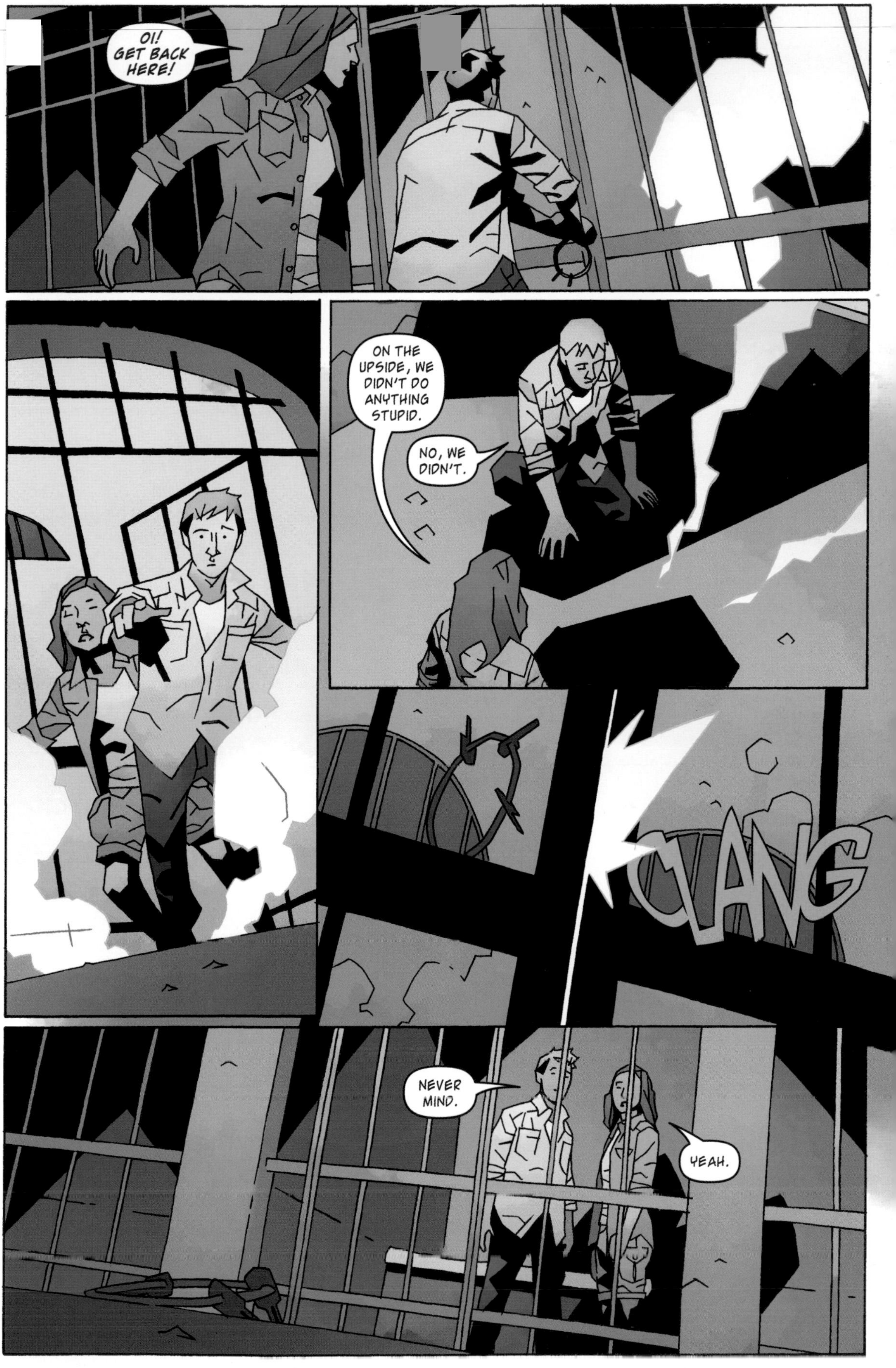
OI! GET BACK HERE!
ON THE UPSIDE, WE DIDN'T DO ANYTHING STUPID.
NO, WE DIDN'T.
CLANG
NEVER MIND.
YEAH.

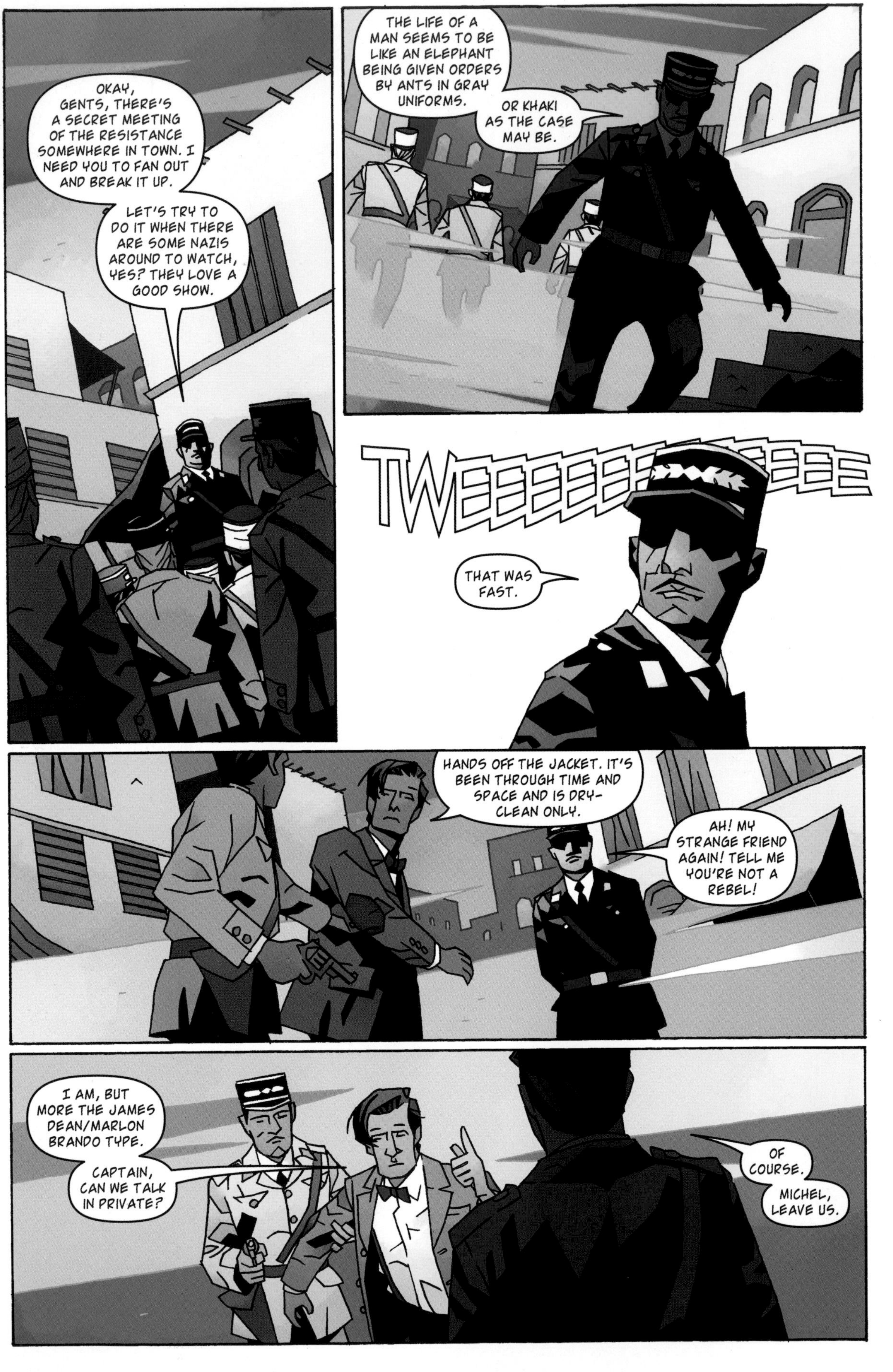
OKAY, GENTS, THERE'S A SECRET MEETING OF THE RESISTANCE SOMEWHERE IN TOWN. I NEED YOU TO FAN OUT AND BREAK IT UP.
LET'S TRY TO DO IT WHEN THERE ARE SOME NAZIS AROUND TO WATCH, YES? THEY LOVE A GOOD SHOW.
THE LIFE OF A MAN SEEMS TO BE LIKE AN ELEPHANT BEING GIVEN ORDERS BY ANTS IN GRAY UNIFORMS.
OR KHAKI AS THE CASE MAY BE.
TWEEEEEEEEEEEEEEE
THAT WAS FAST.
HANDS OFF THE JACKET. IT'S BEEN THROUGH TIME AND SPACE AND IS DRY-CLEAN ONLY.
AH! MY STRANGE FRIEND AGAIN! TELL ME YOU'RE NOT A REBEL!
I AM, BUT MORE THE JAMES DEAN/MARLON BRANDO TYPE.
CAPTAIN, CAN WE TALK IN PRIVATE?
OF COURSE.
MICHEL, LEAVE US.

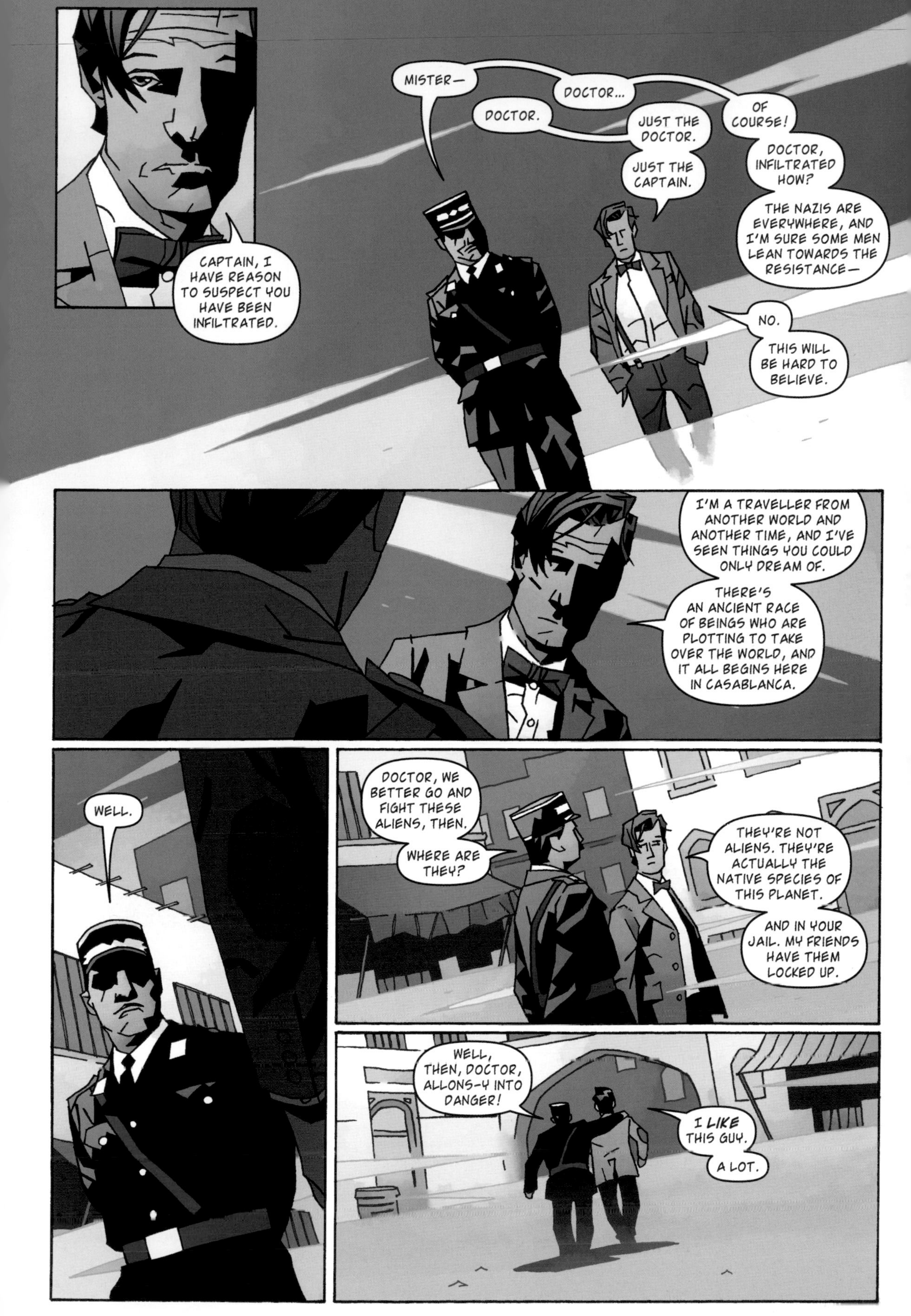
CAPTAIN, I HAVE REASON TO SUSPECT YOU HAVE BEEN INFILTRATED.
MISTER—
DOCTOR...
DOCTOR.
JUST THE DOCTOR.
JUST THE CAPTAIN.
OF COURSE!
DOCTOR, INFILTRATED HOW?
THE NAZIS ARE EVERYWHERE, AND I'M SURE SOME MEN LEAN TOWARDS THE RESISTANCE—
NO.
THIS WILL BE HARD TO BELIEVE.
I'M A TRAVELLER FROM ANOTHER WORLD AND ANOTHER TIME, AND I'VE SEEN THINGS YOU COULD ONLY DREAM OF.
THERE'S AN ANCIENT RACE OF BEINGS WHO ARE PLOTTING TO TAKE OVER THE WORLD, AND IT ALL BEGINS HERE IN CASABLANCA.
WELL.
DOCTOR, WE BETTER GO AND FIGHT THESE ALIENS, THEN.
WHERE ARE THEY?
THEY'RE NOT ALIENS. THEY'RE ACTUALLY THE NATIVE SPECIES OF THIS PLANET.
AND IN YOUR JAIL. MY FRIENDS HAVE THEM LOCKED UP.
WELL, THEN, DOCTOR, ALLONS-Y INTO DANGER!
I LIKE THIS GUY.
A LOT.

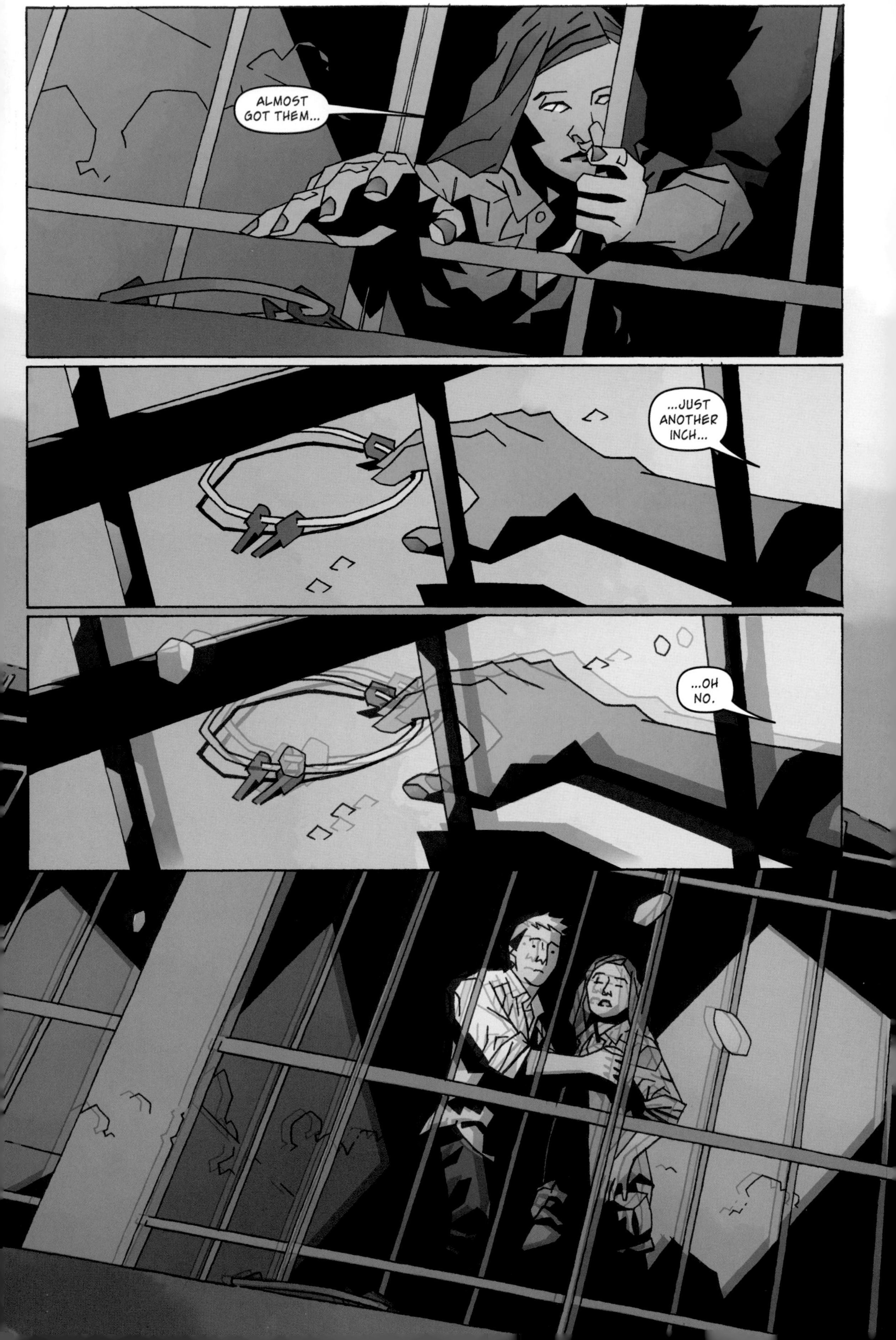
ALMOST GOT THEM...
...JUST ANOTHER INCH...
...OH NO.

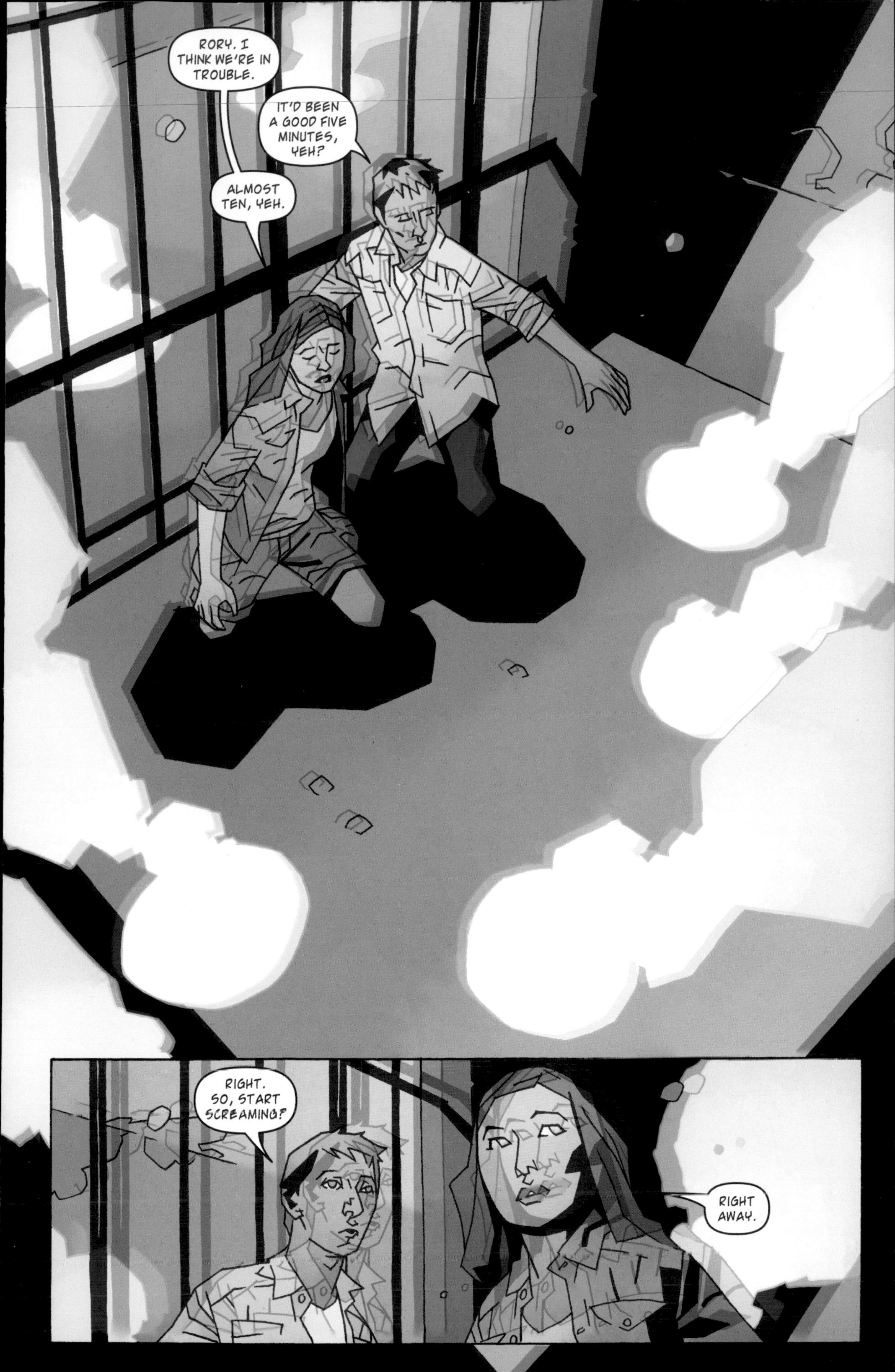
RORY. I THINK WE'RE IN TROUBLE.
IT'D BEEN A GOOD FIVE MINUTES, YEH?
ALMOST TEN, YEH.
RIGHT. SO, START SCREAMING?
RIGHT AWAY.

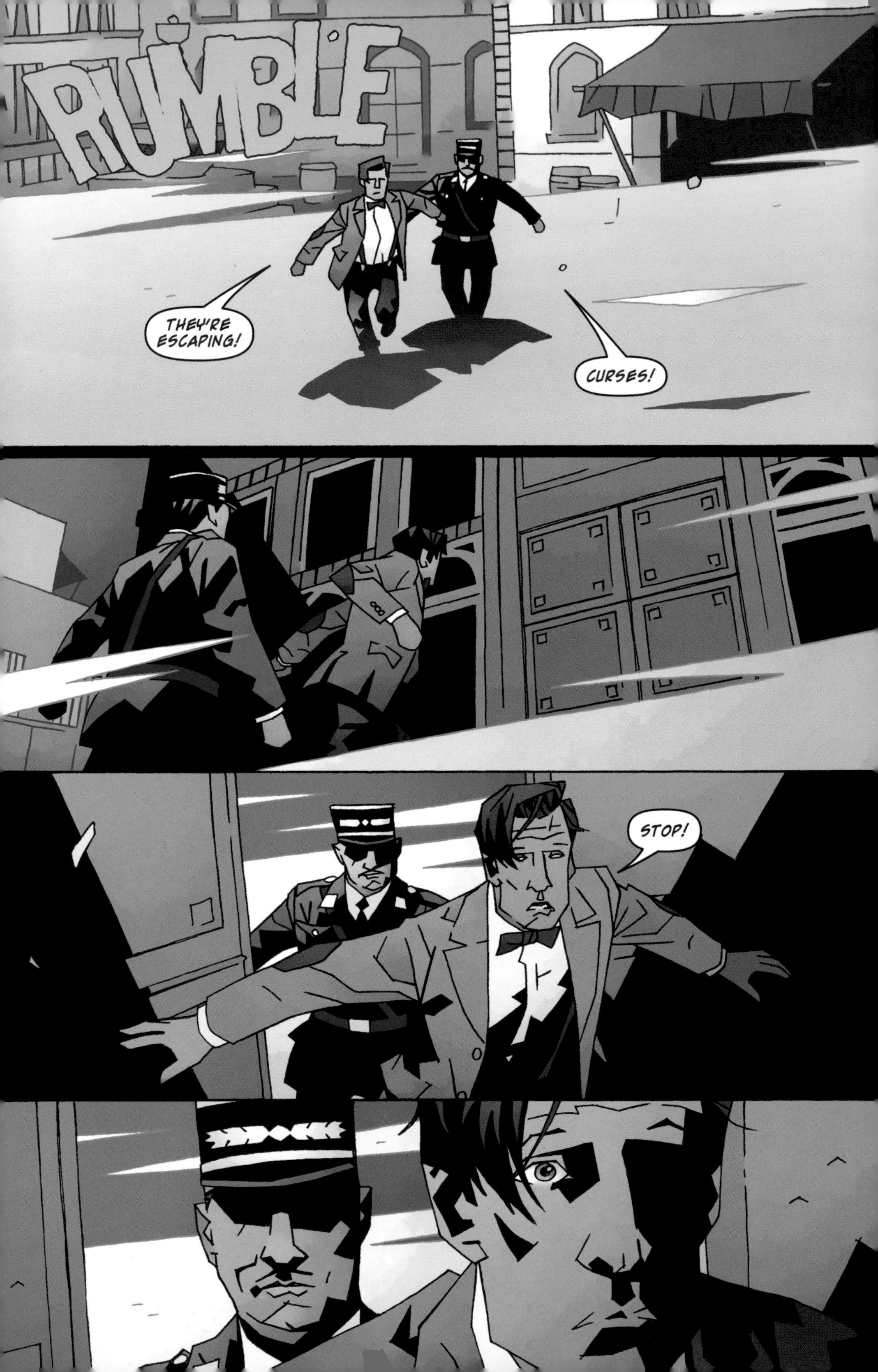
RUMBLE
THEY'RE ESCAPING!
CURSES!
STOP!

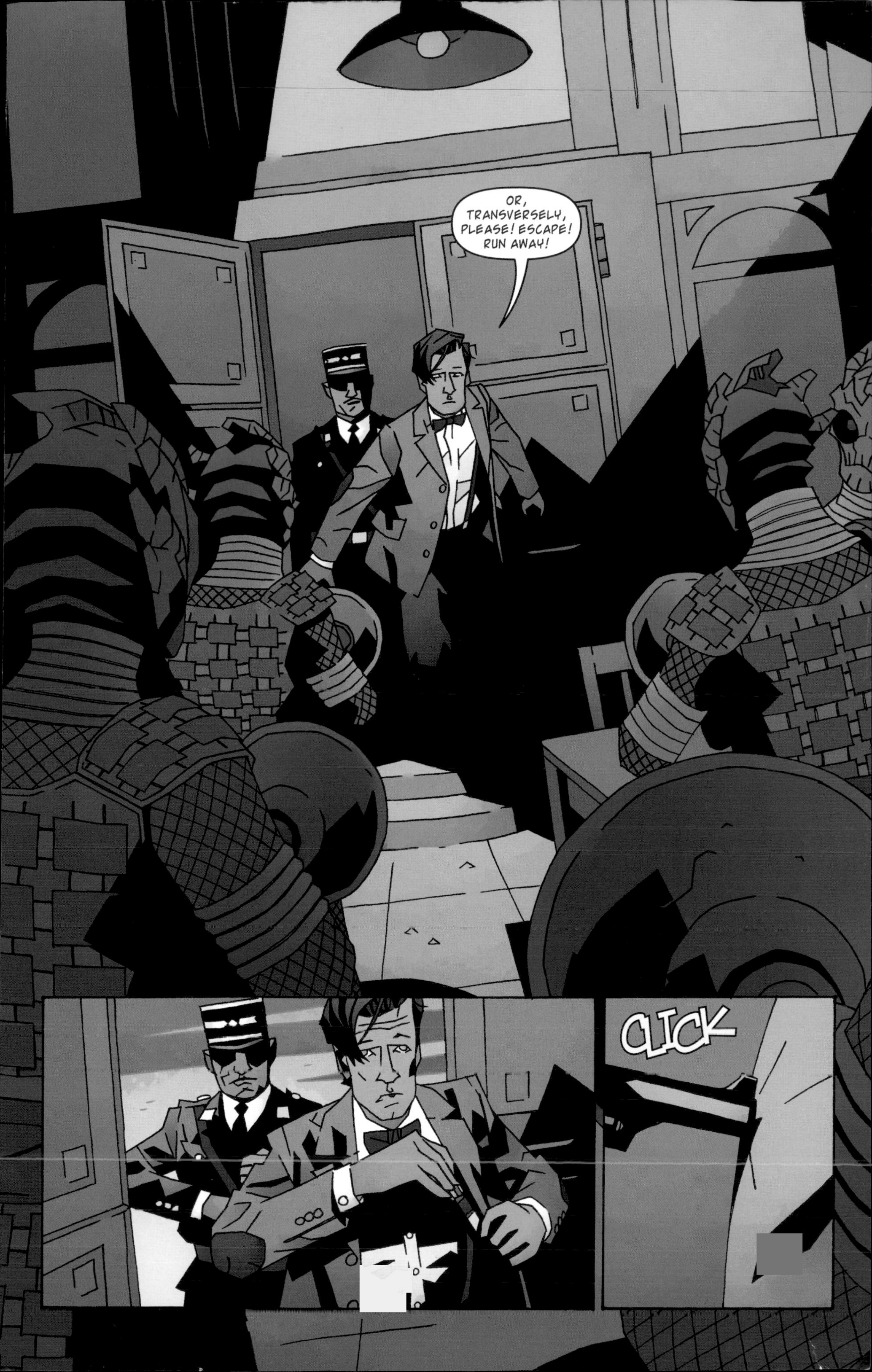
OR, TRANSVERSELY, PLEASE! ESCAPE! RUN AWAY!
CLICK

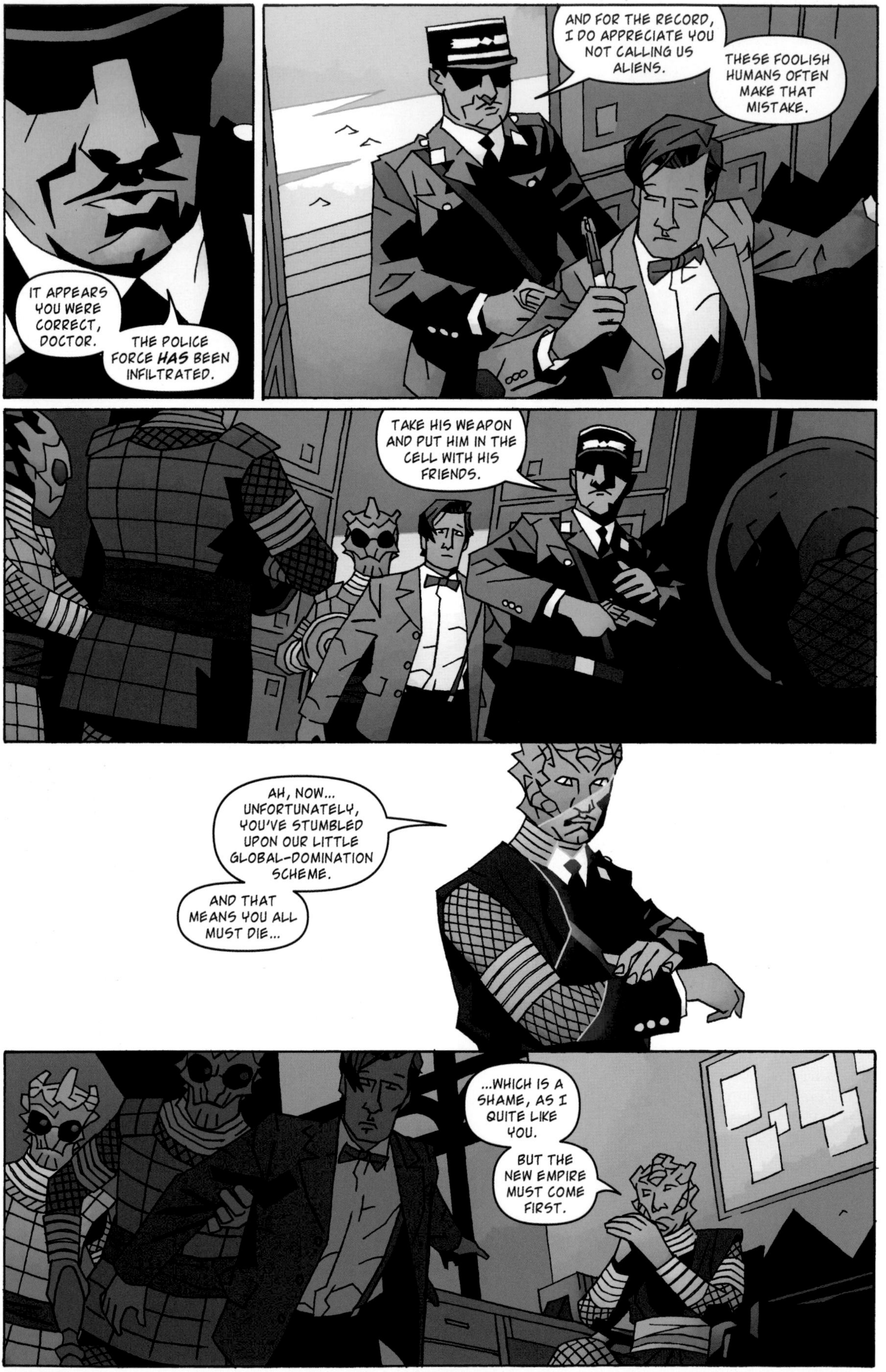
IT APPEARS YOU WERE CORRECT, DOCTOR.
THE POLICE FORCE HAS BEEN INFILTRATED.
AND FOR THE RECORD, I DO APPRECIATE YOU NOT CALLING US ALIENS.
THESE FOOLISH HUMANS OFTEN MAKE THAT MISTAKE.
TAKE HIS WEAPON AND PUT HIM IN THE CELL WITH HIS FRIENDS.
AH, NOW... UNFORTUNATELY, YOU'VE STUMBLED UPON OUR LITTLE GLOBAL-DOMINATION SCHEME.
AND THAT MEANS YOU ALL MUST DIE...
...WHICH IS A SHAME, AS I QUITE LIKE YOU.
BUT THE NEW EMPIRE MUST COME FIRST.

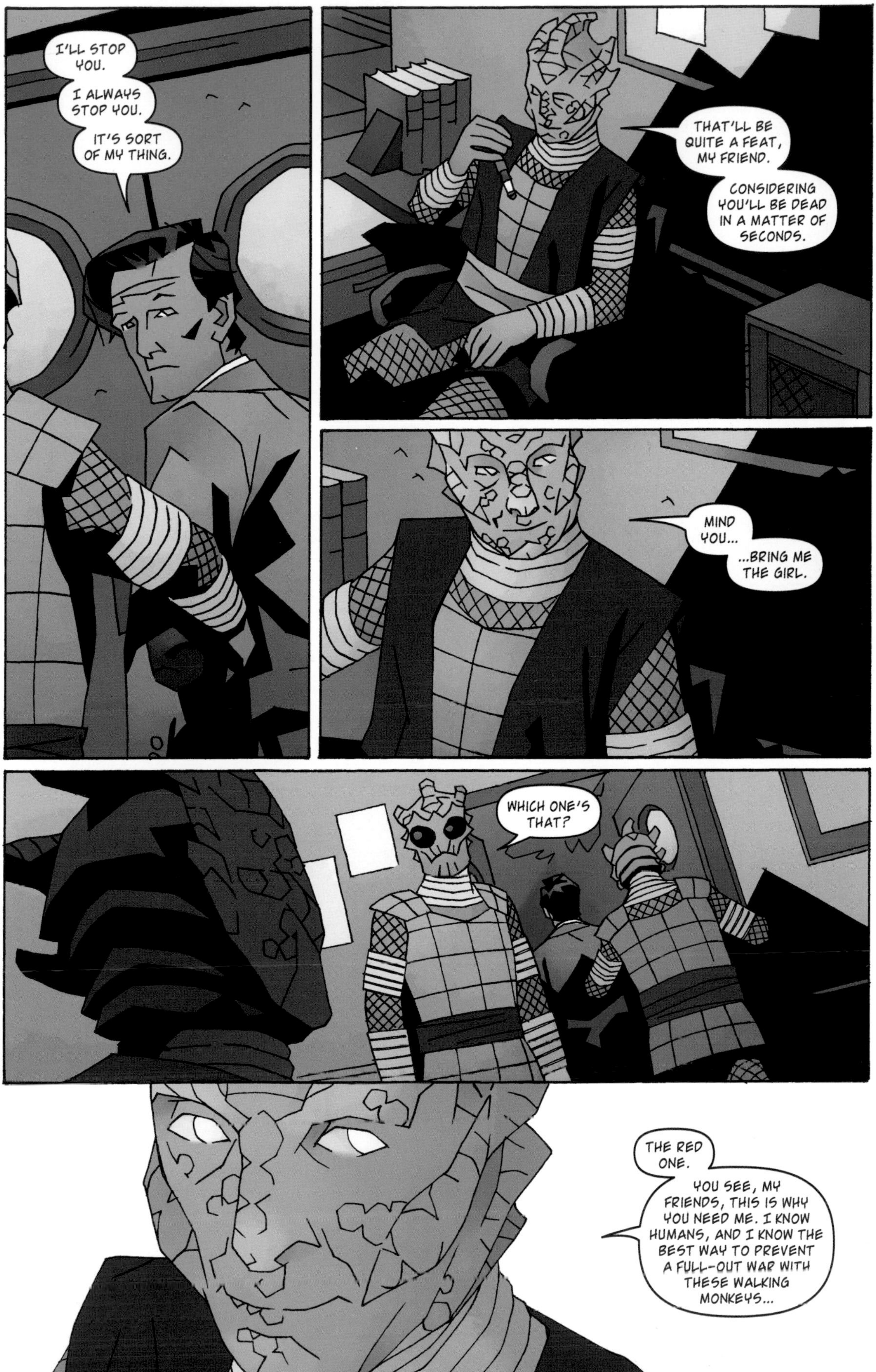
I'LL STOP YOU.
I ALWAYS STOP YOU.
IT'S SORT OF MY THING.
THAT'LL BE QUITE A FEAT, MY FRIEND.
CONSIDERING YOU'LL BE DEAD IN A MATTER OF SECONDS.
MIND YOU...
...BRING ME THE GIRL.
WHICH ONE'S THAT?
THE RED ONE.
YOU SEE, MY FRIENDS, THIS IS WHY YOU NEED ME. I KNOW HUMANS, AND I KNOW THE BEST WAY TO PREVENT A FULL-OUT WAR WITH THESE WALKING MONKEYS...

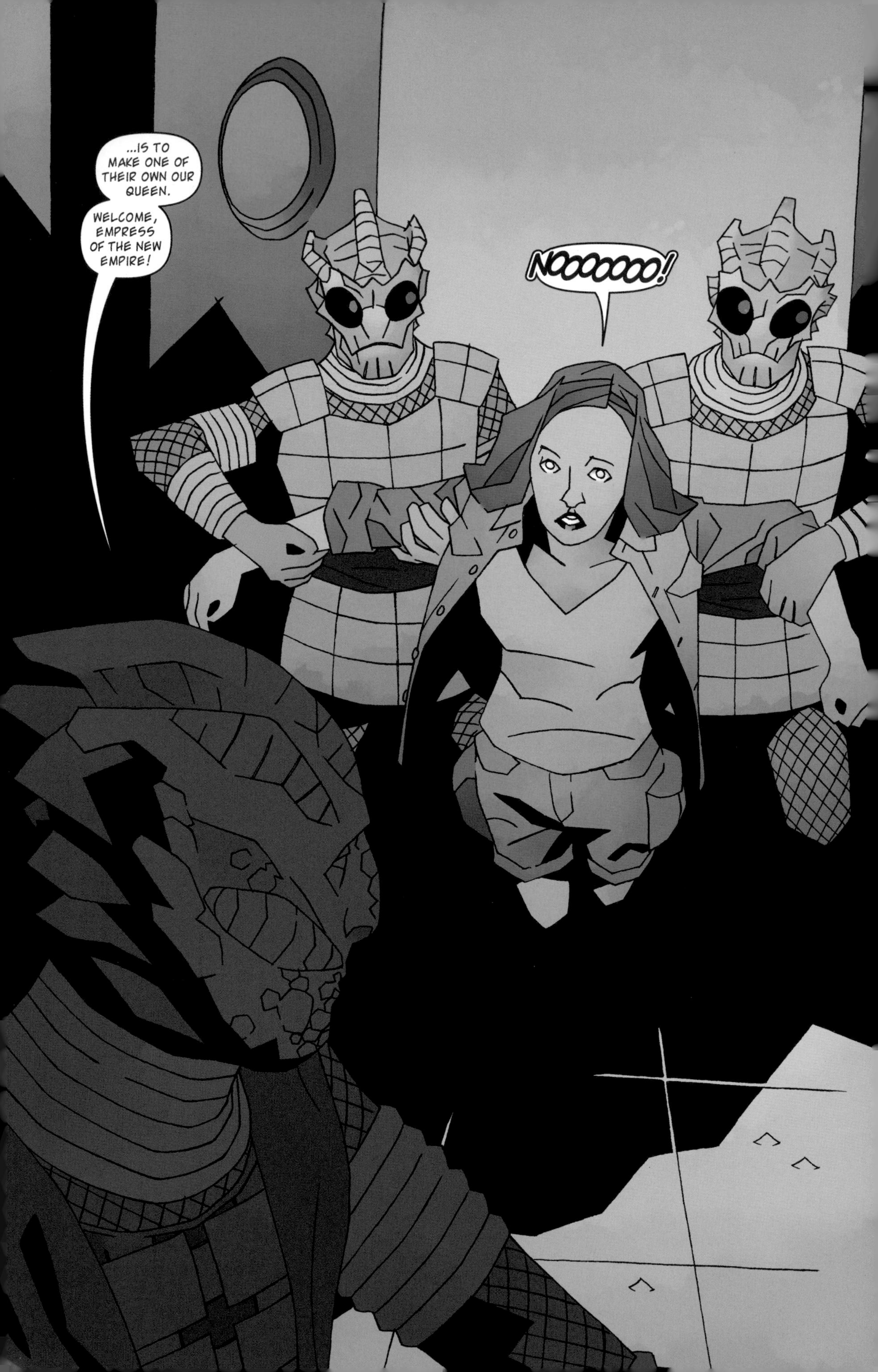
...IS TO MAKE ONE OF THEIR OWN OUR QUEEN.
WELCOME, EMPRESS OF THE NEW EMPIRE!
NOOOOOOO!

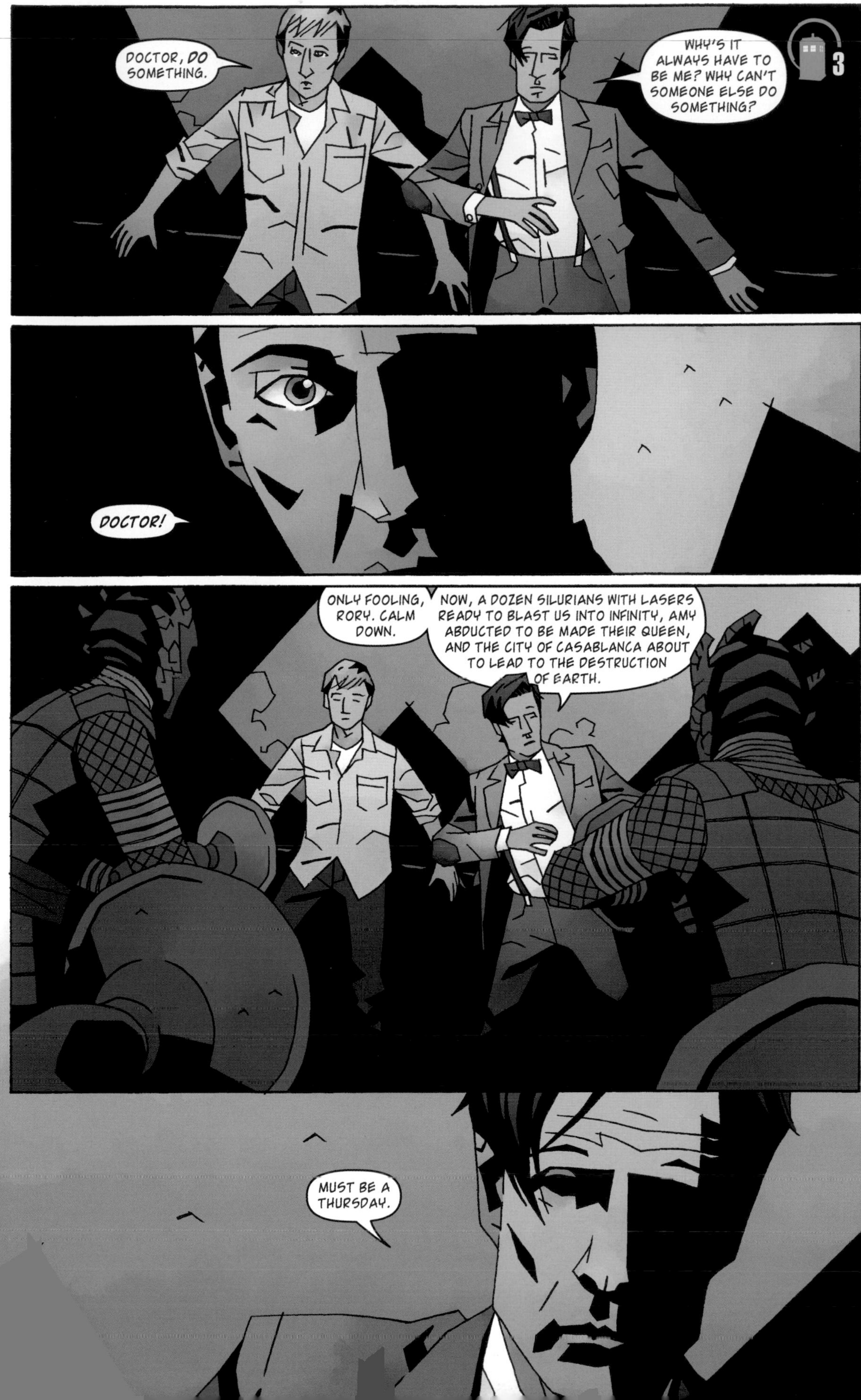
DOCTOR, DO SOMETHING.
WHY'S IT ALWAYS HAVE TO BE ME? WHY CAN'T SOMEONE ELSE DO SOMETHING?
DOCTOR!
ONLY FOOLING, RORY. CALM DOWN.
NOW, A DOZEN SILURIANS WITH LASERS READY TO BLAST US INTO INFINITY, AMY ABDUCTED TO BE MADE THEIR QUEEN, AND THE CITY OF CASABLANCA ABOUT TO LEAD TO THE DESTRUCTION OF EARTH.
MUST BE A THURSDAY.

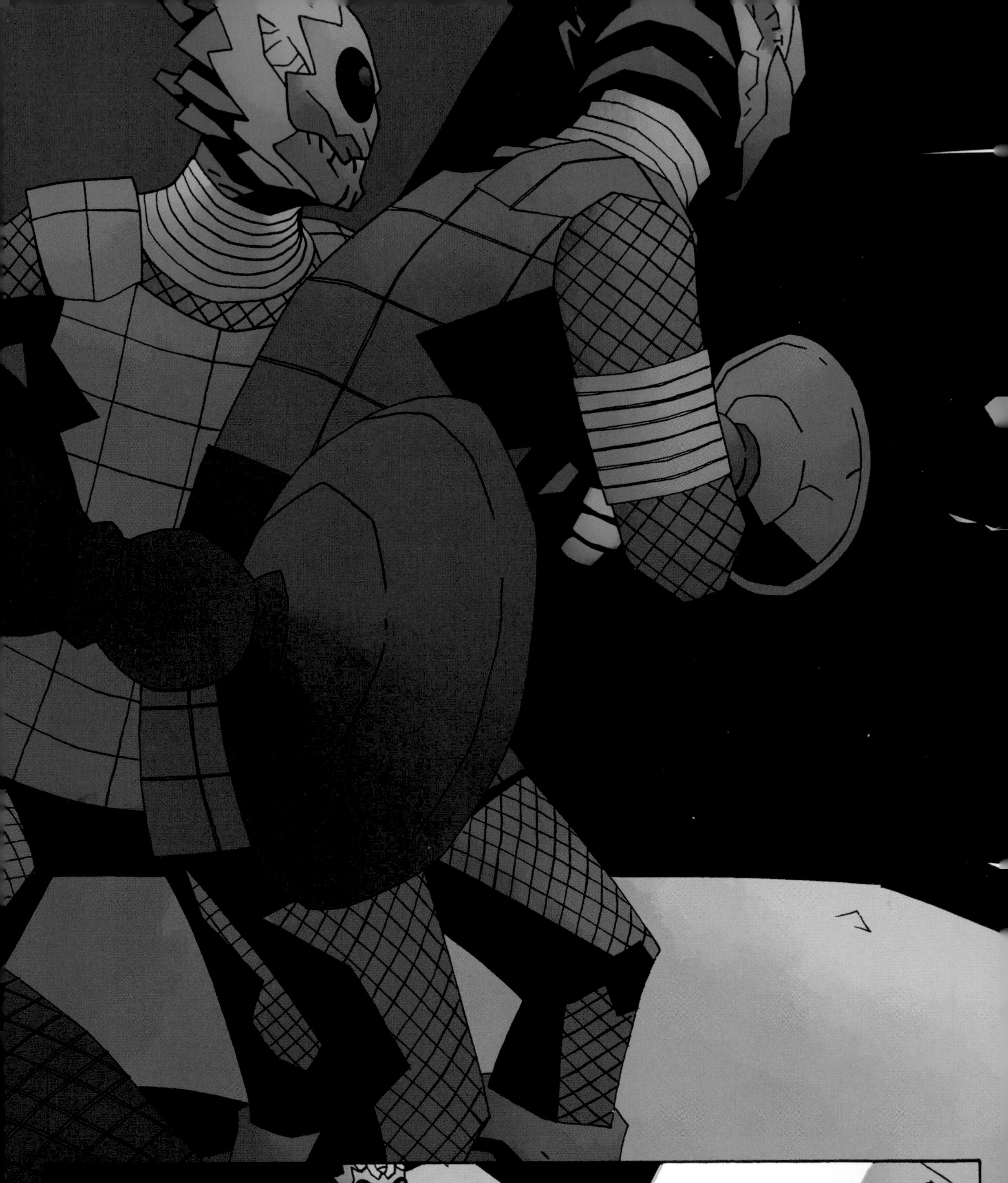
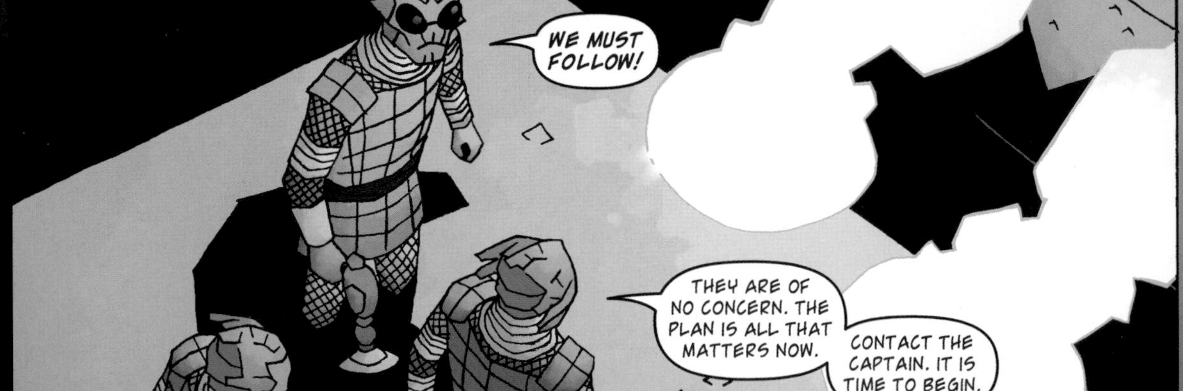
WE MUST FOLLOW!
THEY ARE OF NO CONCERN. THE PLAN IS ALL THAT MATTERS NOW.
CONTACT THE CAPTAIN. IT IS TIME TO BEGIN.

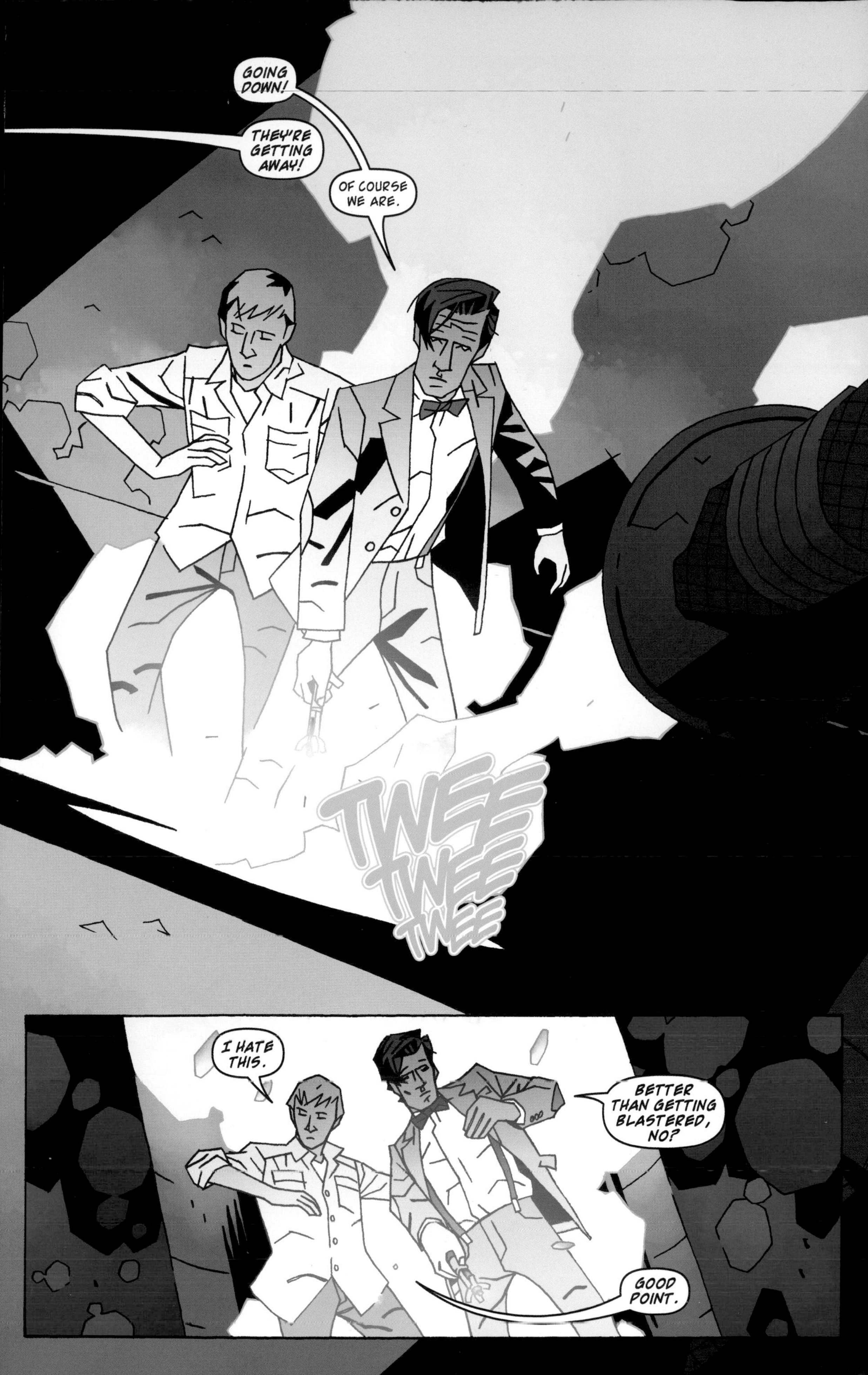
GOING DOWN!
THEY'RE GETTING AWAY!
OF COURSE WE ARE.
TWEE TWEE TWEE
I HATE THIS.
BETTER THAN GETTING BLASTERED, NO?
GOOD POINT.

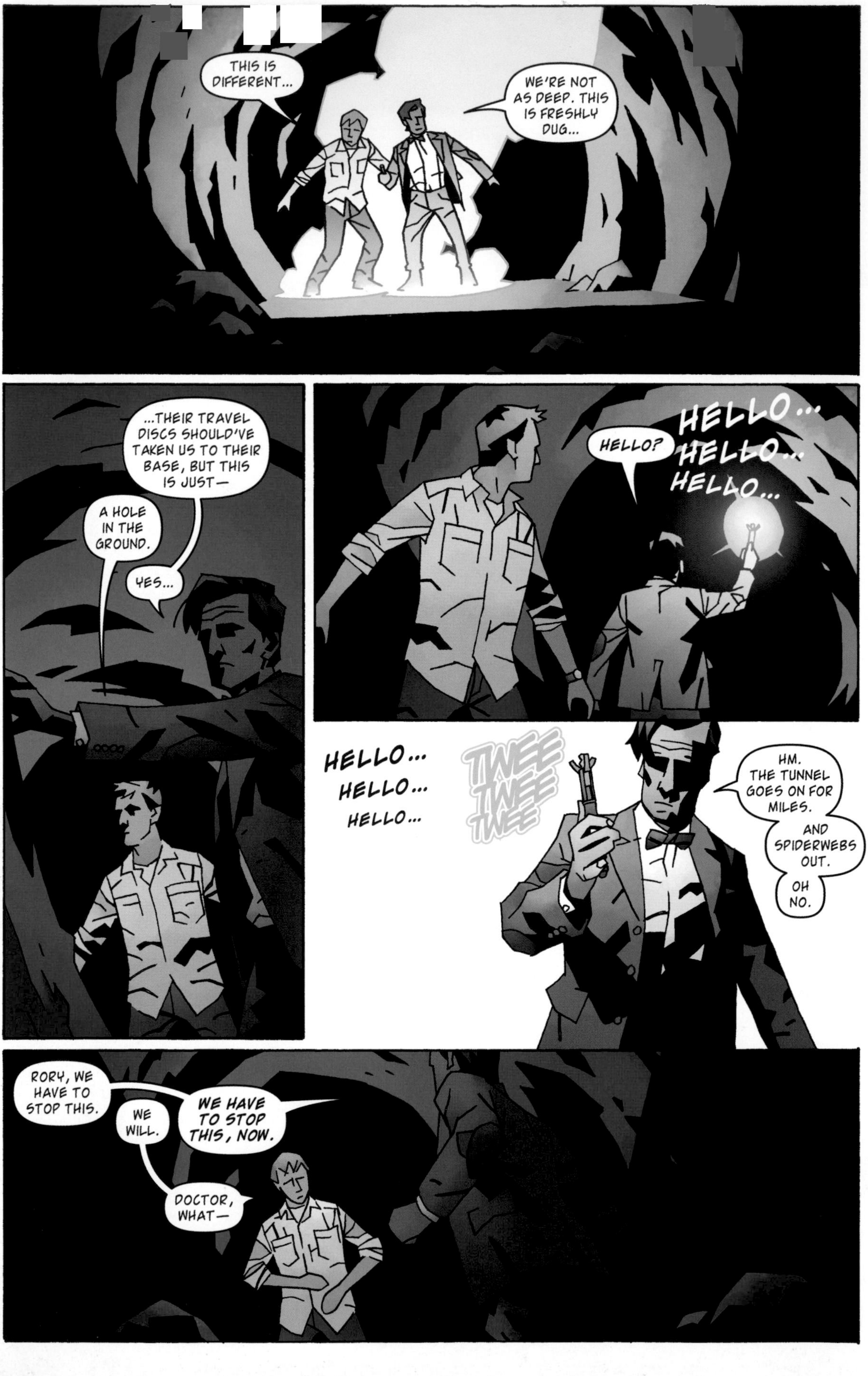
THIS IS DIFFERENT...
WE'RE NOT AS DEEP. THIS IS FRESHLY DUG...
...THEIR TRAVEL DISCS SHOULD'VE TAKEN US TO THEIR BASE, BUT THIS IS JUST—
A HOLE IN THE GROUND.
YES...
HELLO?
HELLO... HELLO... HELLO...
HELLO... HELLO... HELLO...
TWEE TWEE TWEE
HM. THE TUNNEL GOES ON FOR MILES.
AND SPIDERWEBS OUT.
OH NO.
RORY, WE HAVE TO STOP THIS.
WE WILL.
WE HAVE TO STOP THIS, NOW.
DOCTOR, WHAT—

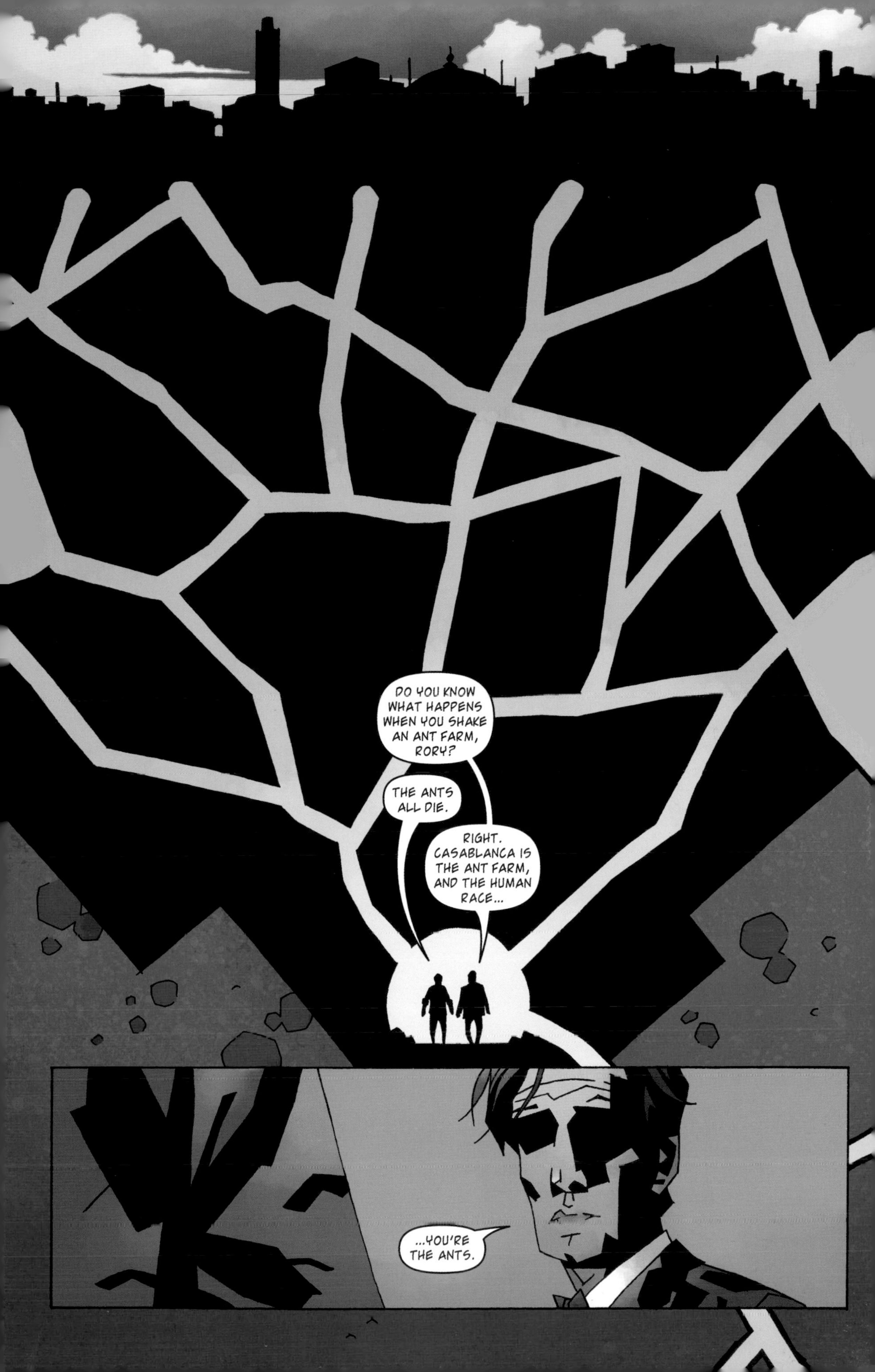
DO YOU KNOW WHAT HAPPENS WHEN YOU SHAKE AN ANT FARM, RORY?
THE ANTS ALL DIE.
RIGHT. CASABLANCA IS THE ANT FARM, AND THE HUMAN RACE...
...YOU'RE THE ANTS.

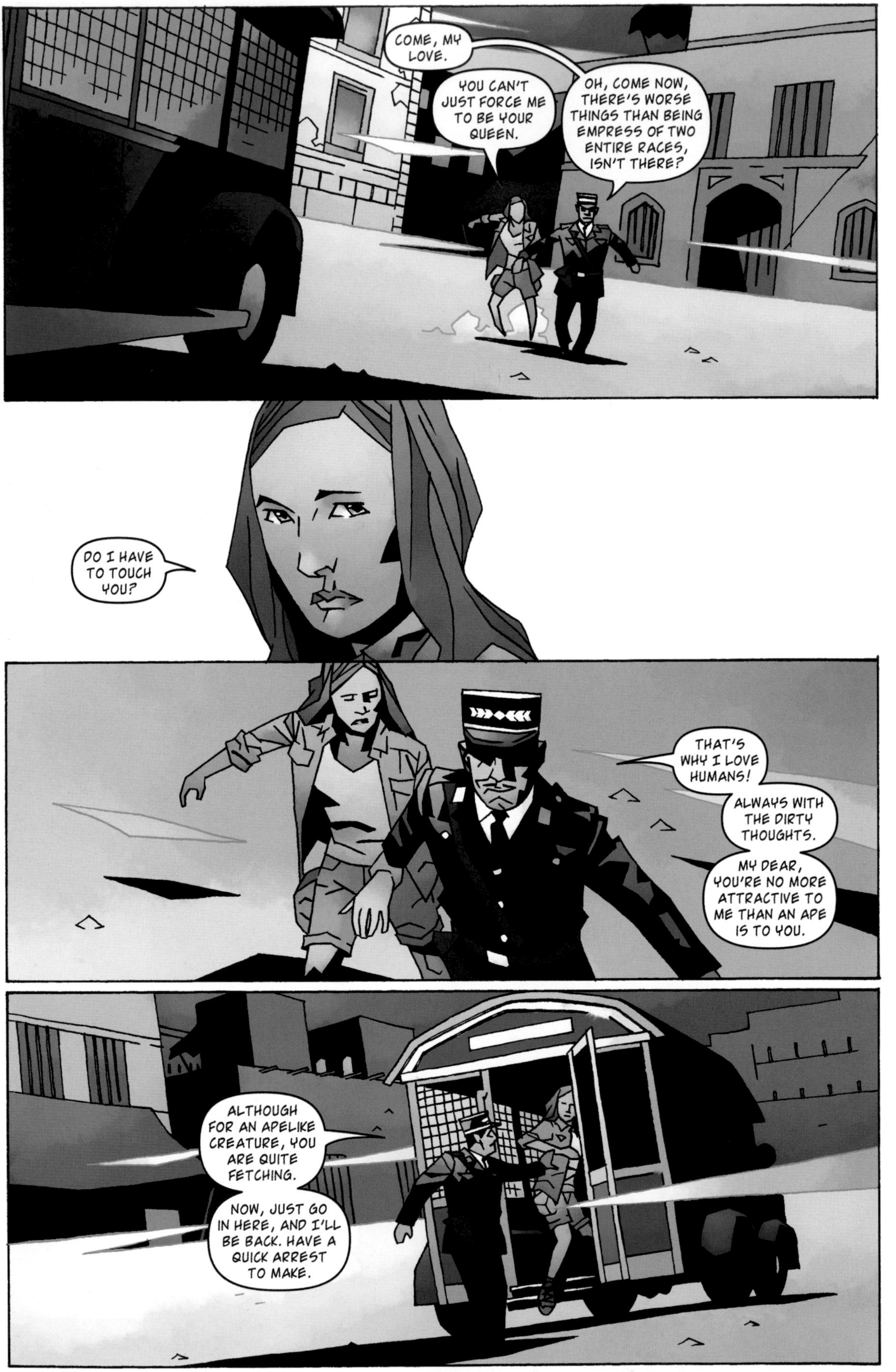
COME, MY LOVE.
YOU CAN'T JUST FORCE ME TO BE YOUR QUEEN.
OH, COME NOW, THERE'S WORSE THINGS THAN BEING EMPRESS OF TWO ENTIRE RACES, ISN'T THERE?
DO I HAVE TO TOUCH YOU?
THAT'S WHY I LOVE HUMANS!
ALWAYS WITH THE DIRTY THOUGHTS.
MY DEAR, YOU'RE NO MORE ATTRACTIVE TO ME THAN AN APE IS TO YOU.
ALTHOUGH FOR AN APELIKE CREATURE, YOU ARE QUITE FETCHING.
NOW, JUST GO IN HERE, AND I'LL BE BACK. HAVE A QUICK ARREST TO MAKE.

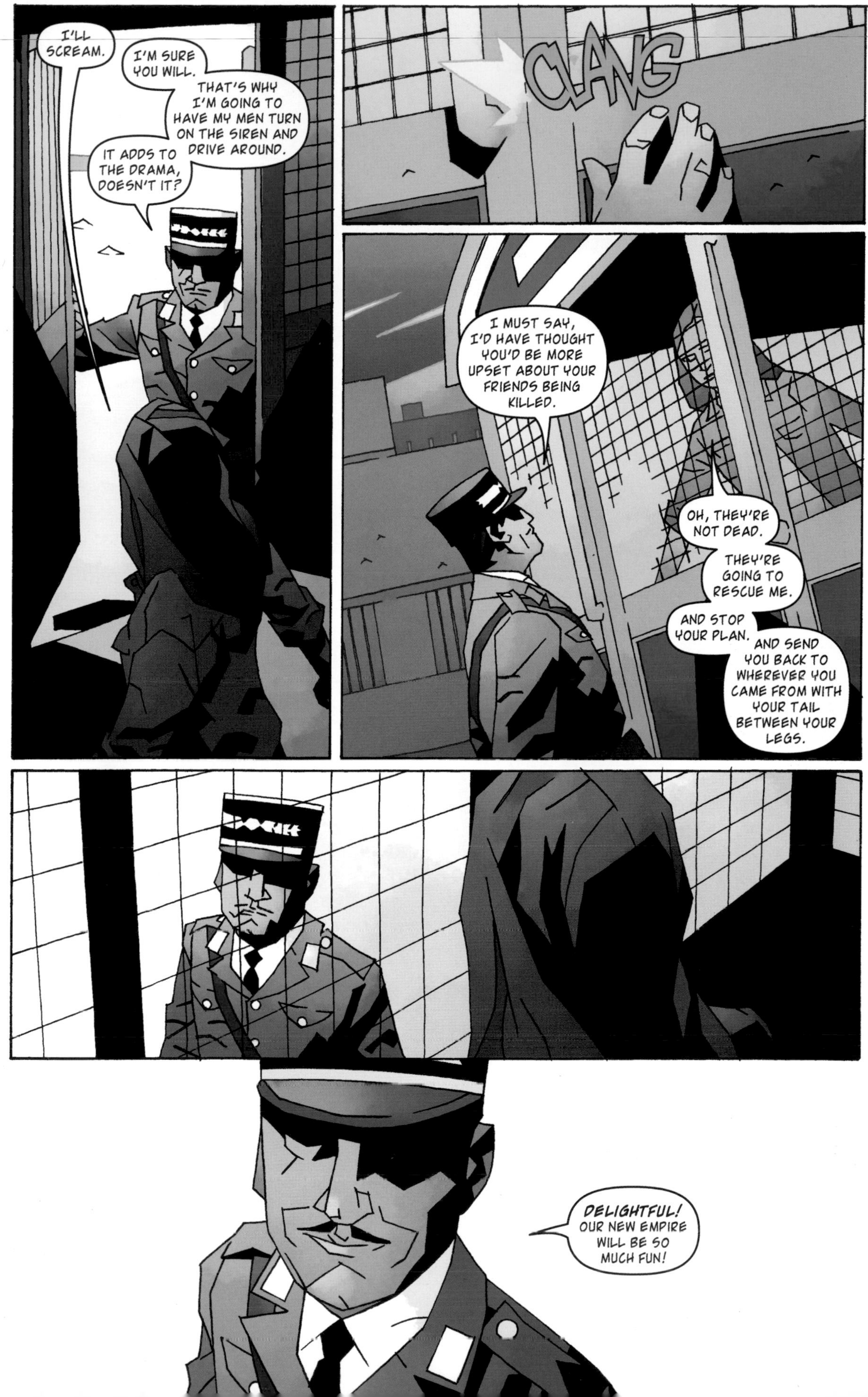

I'LL SCREAM.
I'M SURE YOU WILL.
THAT'S WHY I'M GOING TO HAVE MY MEN TURN ON THE SIREN AND DRIVE AROUND.
IT ADDS TO THE DRAMA, DOESN'T IT?
CLANG
I MUST SAY, I'D HAVE THOUGHT YOU'D BE MORE UPSET ABOUT YOUR FRIENDS BEING KILLED.
OH, THEY'RE NOT DEAD.
THEY'RE GOING TO RESCUE ME.
AND STOP YOUR PLAN.
AND SEND YOU BACK TO WHEREVER YOU CAME FROM WITH YOUR TAIL BETWEEN YOUR LEGS.
DELIGHTFUL! OUR NEW EMPIRE WILL BE SO MUCH FUN!

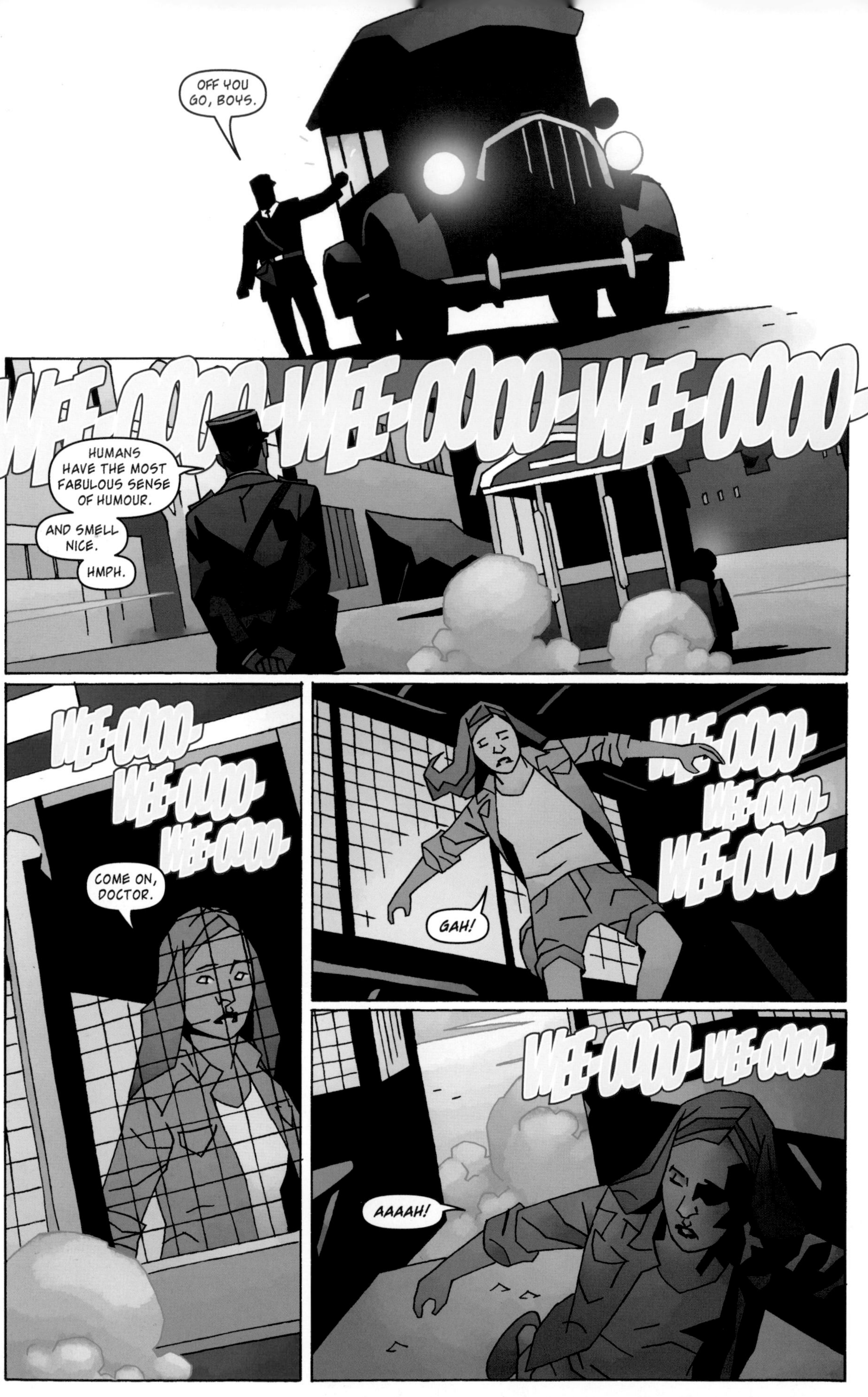
OFF YOU GO, BOYS.
WEE-OOOO-WEE-OOOO-WEE-OOOO-
HUMANS HAVE THE MOST FABULOUS SENSE OF HUMOUR.
AND SMELL NICE.
HMPH.
WEE-OOOO-
WEE-OOOO-
WEE-OOOO-
COME ON, DOCTOR.
WEE-OOOO-
WEE-OOOO-
WEE-OOOO-
GAH!
WEE-OOOO-WEE-OOOO-
AAAAH!

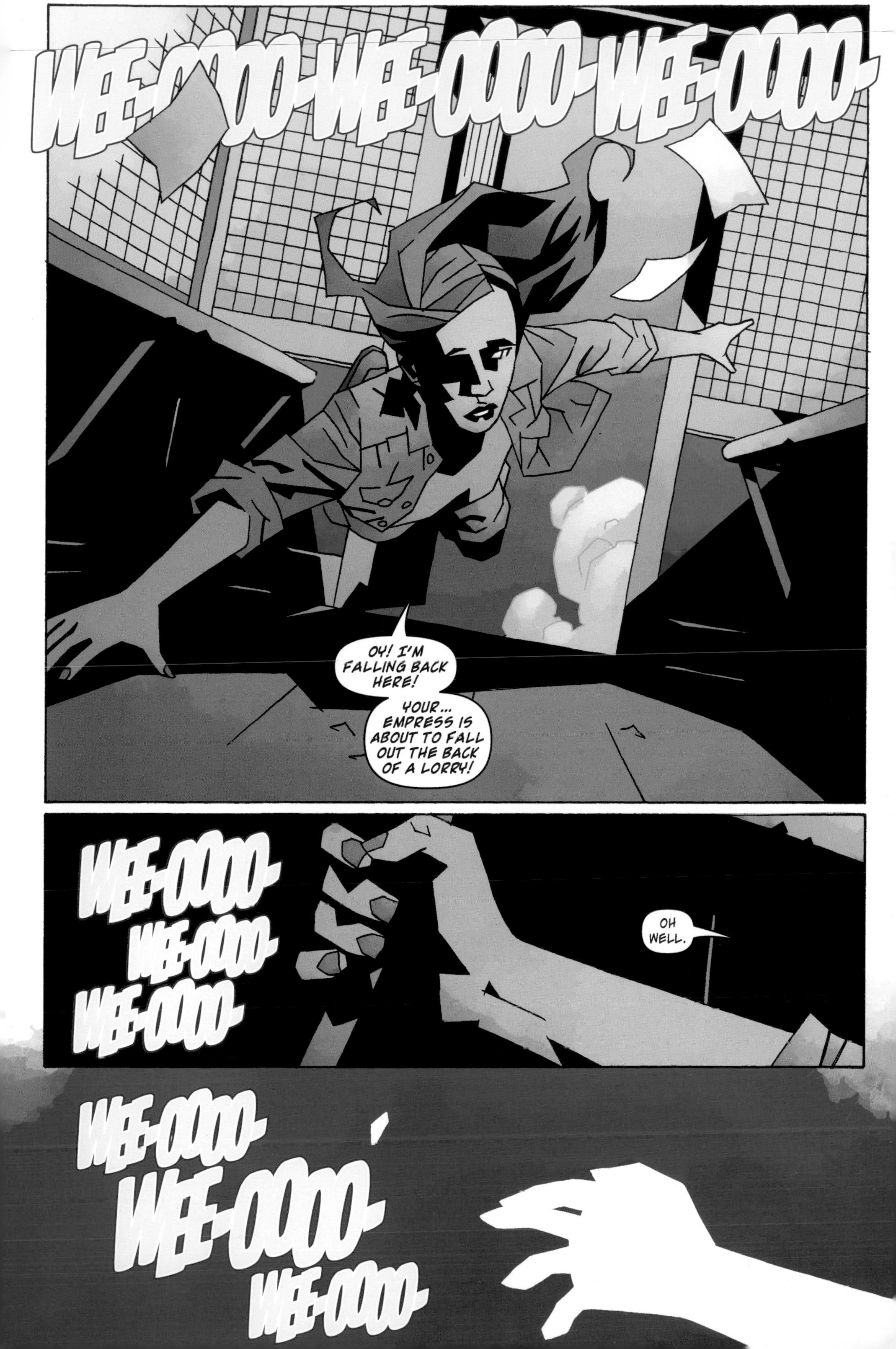
WEE-OOOO-WEE-OOOO-WEE-OOOO-
OY! I'M FALLING BACK HERE!
YOUR... EMPRESS IS ABOUT TO FALL OUT THE BACK OF A LORRY!
WEE-OOOO-
WEE-OOOO-
WEE-OOOO-
OH WELL.
WEE-OOOO-
WEE-OOOO-
WEE-OOOO-

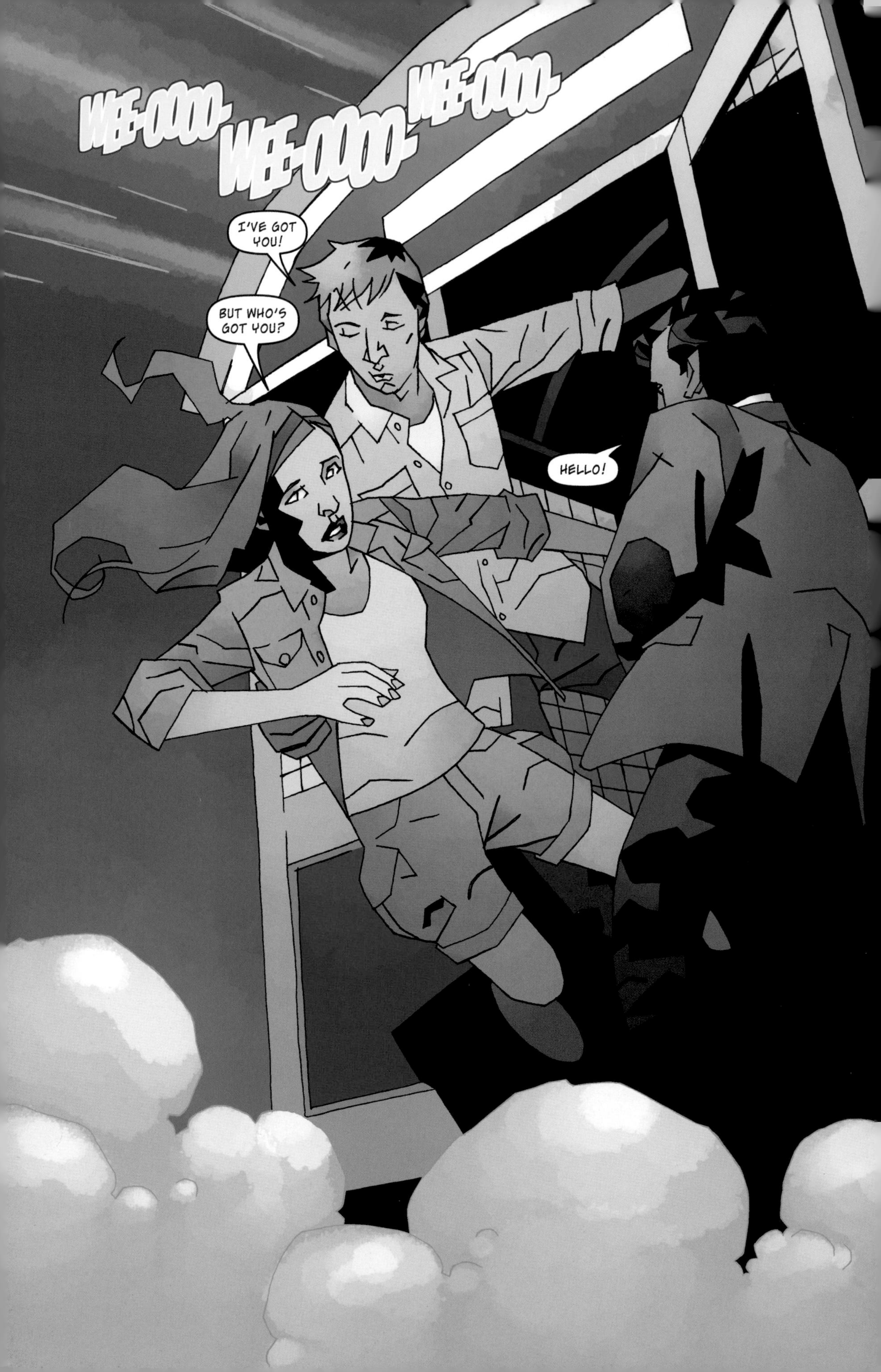
WEE-OOOO-
WEE-OOOO-
WEE-OOOO-
I'VE GOT YOU!
BUT WHO'S GOT YOU?
HELLO!

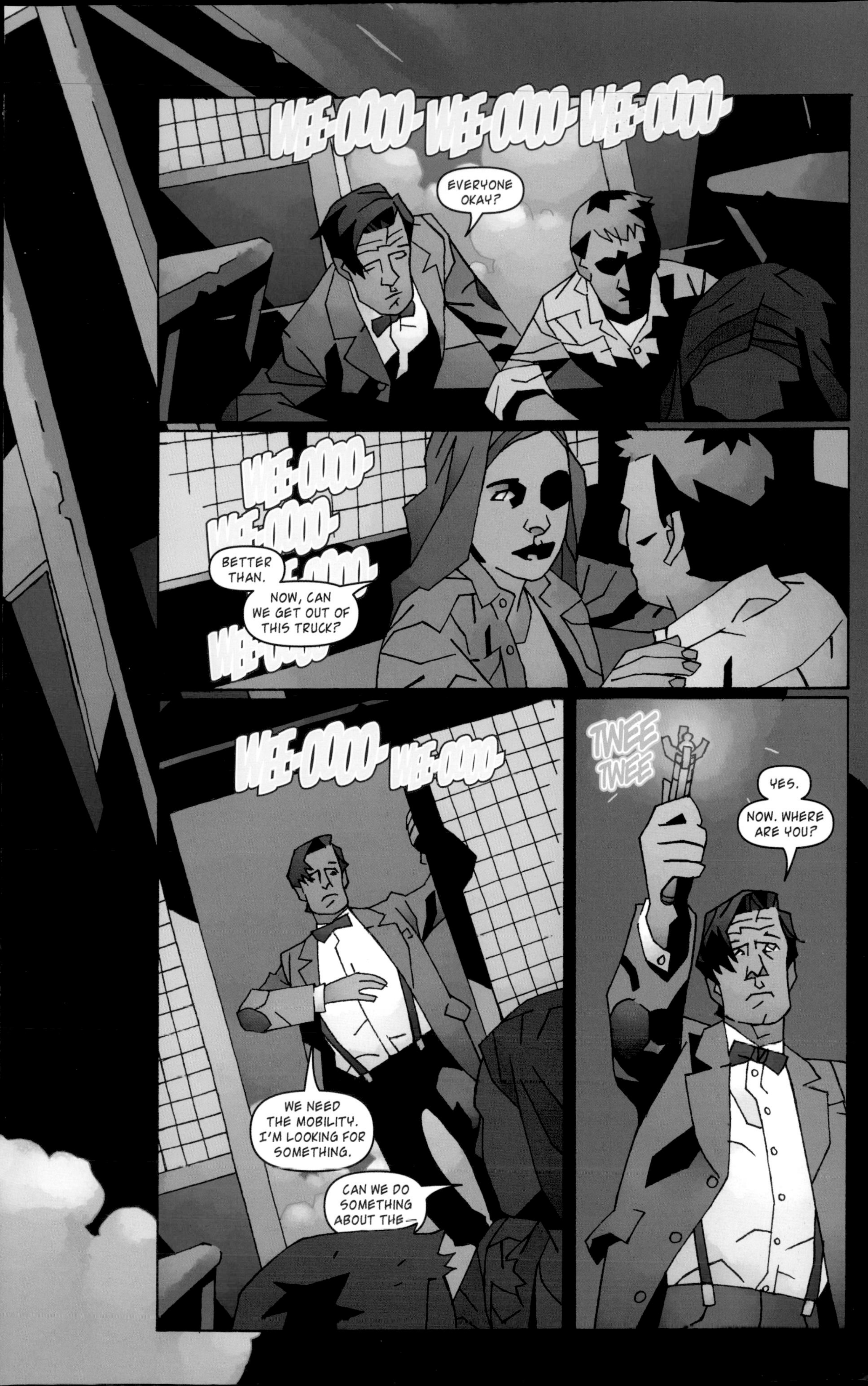

WEE-OOOO-WEE-OOOO-WEE-OOOO-
EVERYONE OKAY?
WEE-OOOO-
WEE-OOOO-
BETTER THAN.
NOW, CAN WE GET OUT OF THIS TRUCK?
WEE-OOOO-WEE-OOOO-
WE NEED THE MOBILITY. I'M LOOKING FOR SOMETHING.
CAN WE DO SOMETHING ABOUT THE—
TWEE TWEE
YES.
NOW. WHERE ARE YOU?

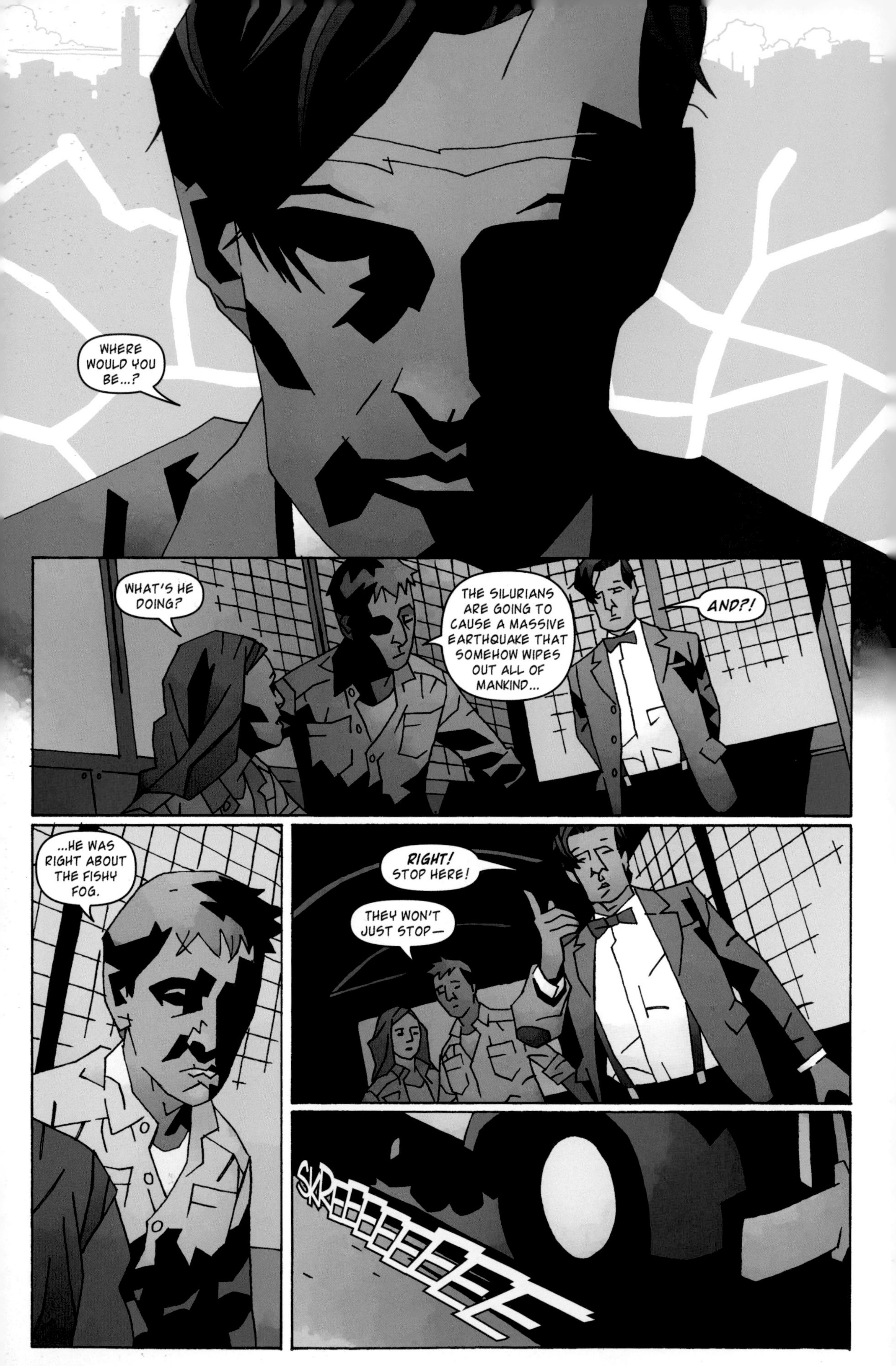
WHERE WOULD YOU BE...?
WHAT'S HE DOING?
THE SILURIANS ARE GOING TO CAUSE A MASSIVE EARTHQUAKE THAT SOMEHOW WIPES OUT ALL OF MANKIND...
AND?!
...HE WAS RIGHT ABOUT THE FISHY FOG.
RIGHT! STOP HERE!
THEY WON'T JUST STOP—
SKREEEEEEEEEEE

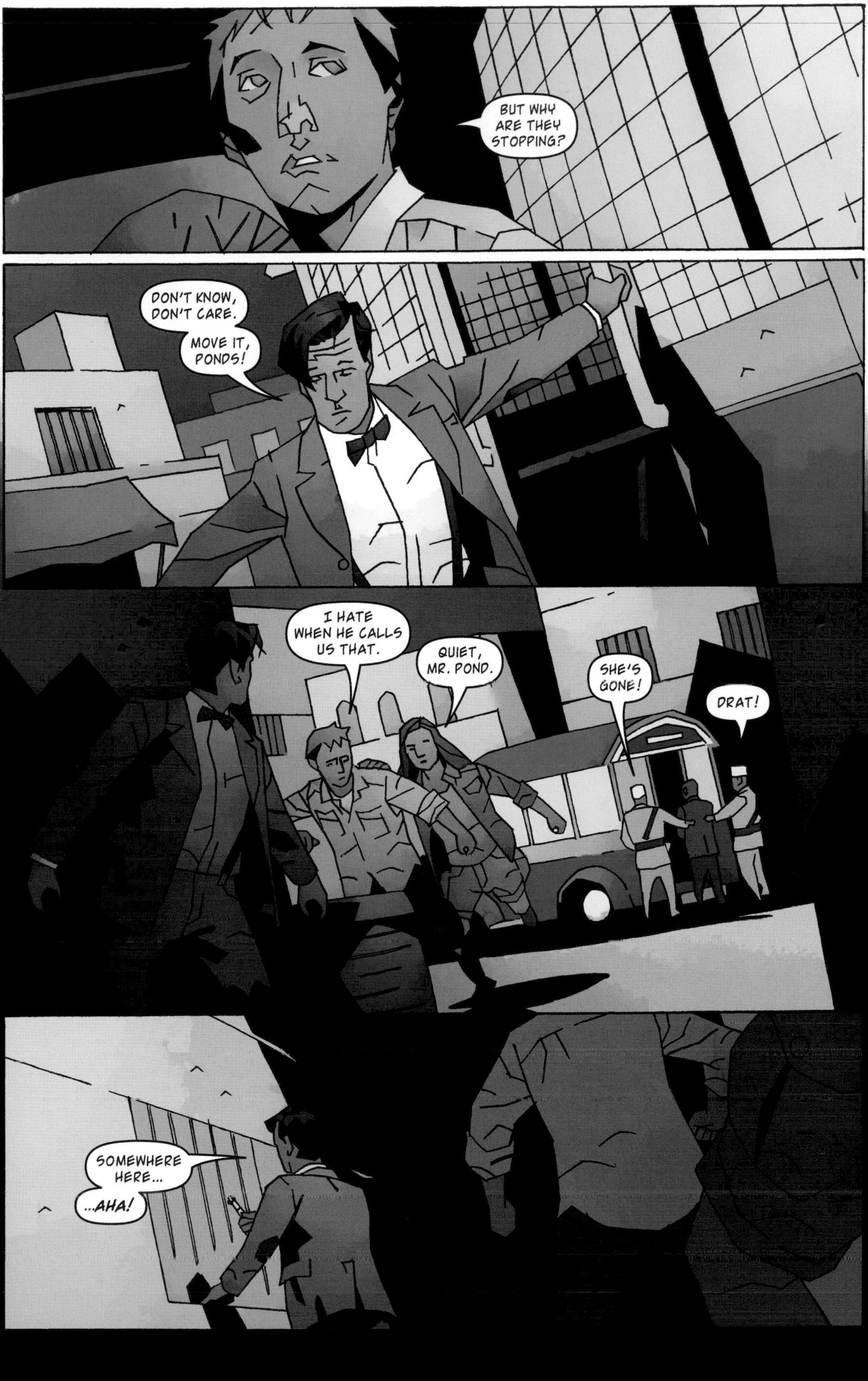
BUT WHY ARE THEY STOPPING?
DON'T KNOW, DON'T CARE.
MOVE IT, PONDS!
I HATE WHEN HE CALLS US THAT.
QUIET, MR. POND.
SHE'S GONE!
DRAT!
SOMEWHERE HERE...
...AHA!

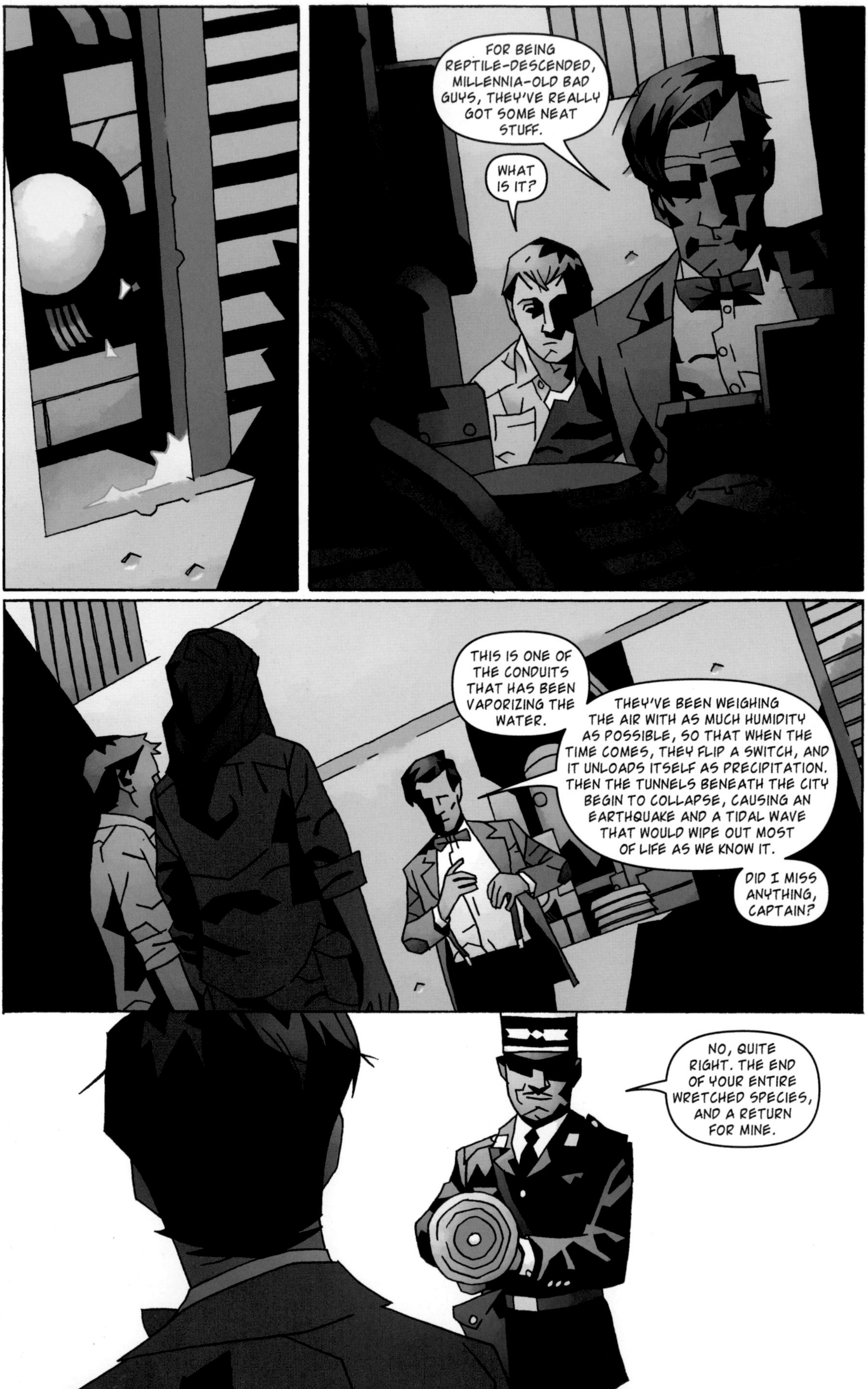
FOR BEING REPTILE-DESCENDED, MILLENNIA-OLD BAD GUYS, THEY'VE REALLY GOT SOME NEAT STUFF.
WHAT IS IT?
THIS IS ONE OF THE CONDUITS THAT HAS BEEN VAPORIZING THE WATER.
THEY'VE BEEN WEIGHING THE AIR WITH AS MUCH HUMIDITY AS POSSIBLE, SO THAT WHEN THE TIME COMES, THEY FLIP A SWITCH, AND IT UNLOADS ITSELF AS PRECIPITATION. THEN THE TUNNELS BENEATH THE CITY BEGIN TO COLLAPSE, CAUSING AN EARTHQUAKE AND A TIDAL WAVE THAT WOULD WIPE OUT MOST OF LIFE AS WE KNOW IT.
DID I MISS ANYTHING, CAPTAIN?
NO, QUITE RIGHT. THE END OF YOUR ENTIRE WRETCHED SPECIES, AND A RETURN FOR MINE.

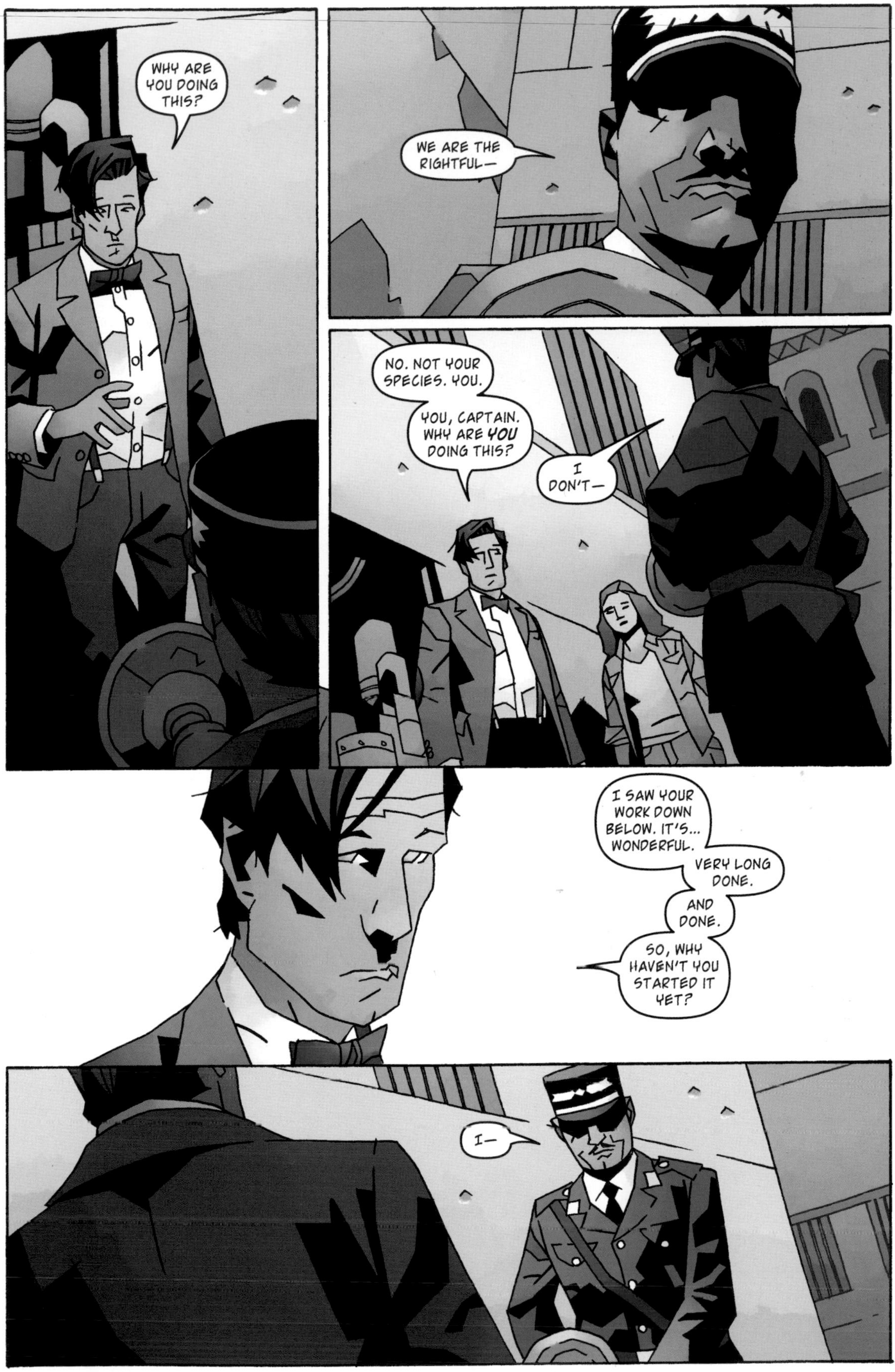
WHY ARE YOU DOING THIS?
WE ARE THE RIGHTFUL—
NO. NOT YOUR SPECIES. YOU.
YOU, CAPTAIN. WHY ARE YOU DOING THIS?
I DON'T—
I SAW YOUR WORK DOWN BELOW. IT'S... WONDERFUL.
VERY LONG DONE.
AND DONE.
SO, WHY HAVEN'T YOU STARTED IT YET?
I—

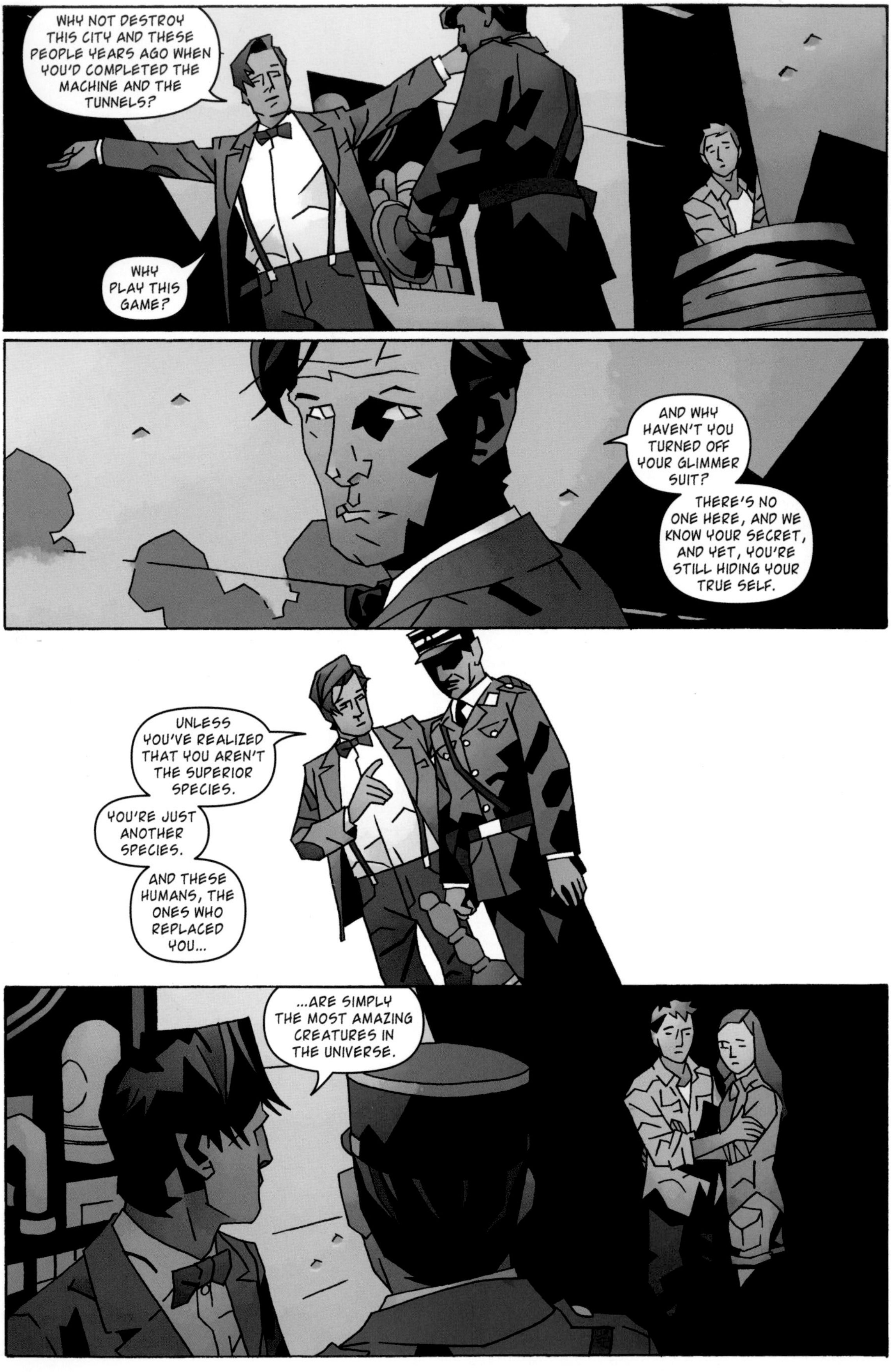
WHY NOT DESTROY THIS CITY AND THESE PEOPLE YEARS AGO WHEN YOU'D COMPLETED THE MACHINE AND THE TUNNELS?
WHY PLAY THIS GAME?
AND WHY HAVEN'T YOU TURNED OFF YOUR GLIMMER SUIT?
THERE'S NO ONE HERE, AND WE KNOW YOUR SECRET, AND YET, YOU'RE STILL HIDING YOUR TRUE SELF.
UNLESS YOU'VE REALIZED THAT YOU AREN'T THE SUPERIOR SPECIES.
YOU'RE JUST ANOTHER SPECIES.
AND THESE HUMANS, THE ONES WHO REPLACED YOU...
...ARE SIMPLY THE MOST AMAZING CREATURES IN THE UNIVERSE.

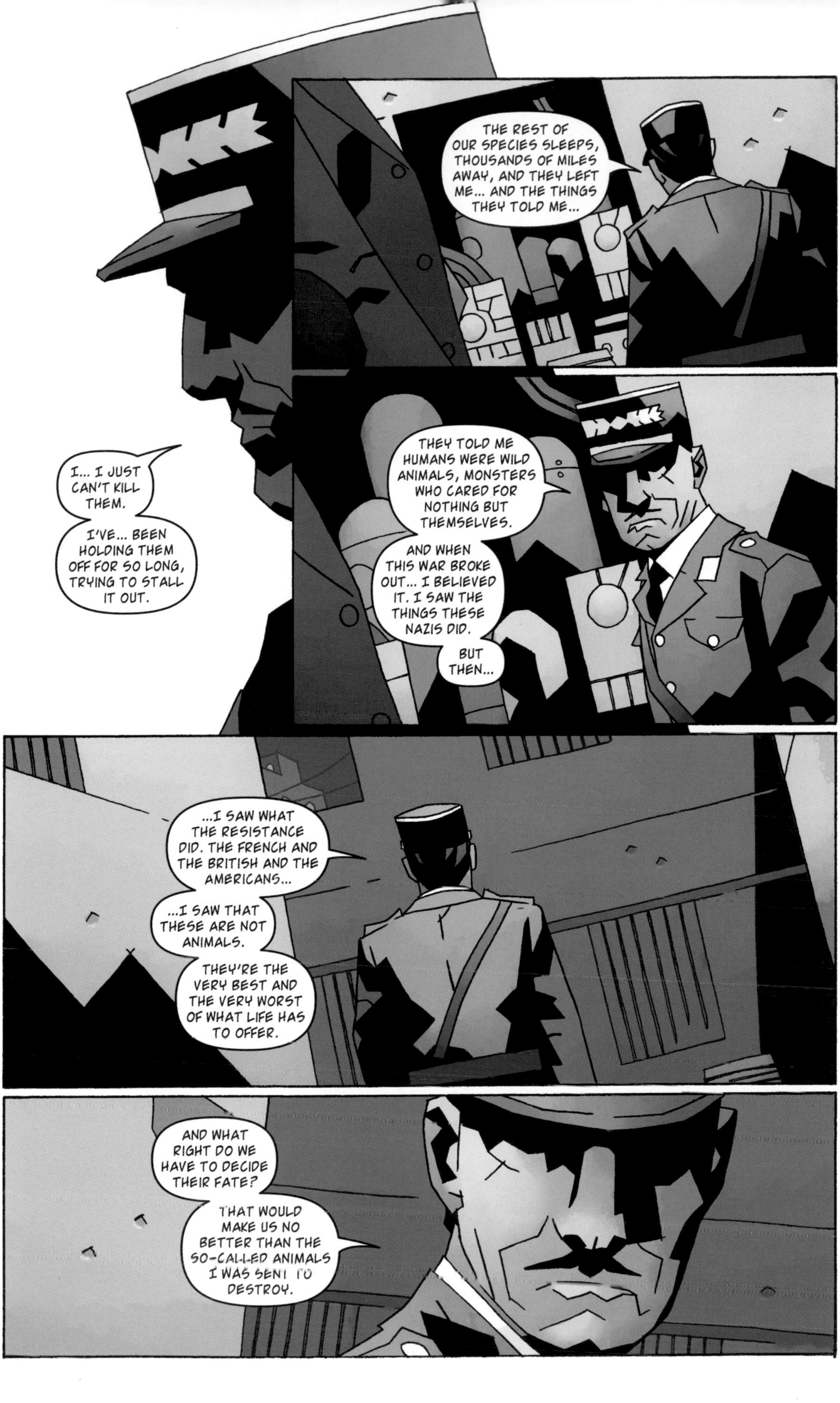
THE REST OF OUR SPECIES SLEEPS, THOUSANDS OF MILES AWAY, AND THEY LEFT ME... AND THE THINGS THEY TOLD ME...
I... I JUST CAN'T KILL THEM.
I'VE... BEEN HOLDING THEM OFF FOR SO LONG, TRYING TO STALL IT OUT.
THEY TOLD ME HUMANS WERE WILD ANIMALS, MONSTERS WHO CARED FOR NOTHING BUT THEMSELVES.
AND WHEN THIS WAR BROKE OUT... I BELIEVED IT. I SAW THE THINGS THESE NAZIS DID.
BUT THEN...
...I SAW WHAT THE RESISTANCE DID. THE FRENCH AND THE BRITISH AND THE AMERICANS...
...I SAW THAT THESE ARE NOT ANIMALS.
THEY'RE THE VERY BEST AND THE VERY WORST OF WHAT LIFE HAS TO OFFER.
AND WHAT RIGHT DO WE HAVE TO DECIDE THEIR FATE?
THAT WOULD MAKE US NO BETTER THAN THE SO-CALLED ANIMALS I WAS SENT TO DESTROY.

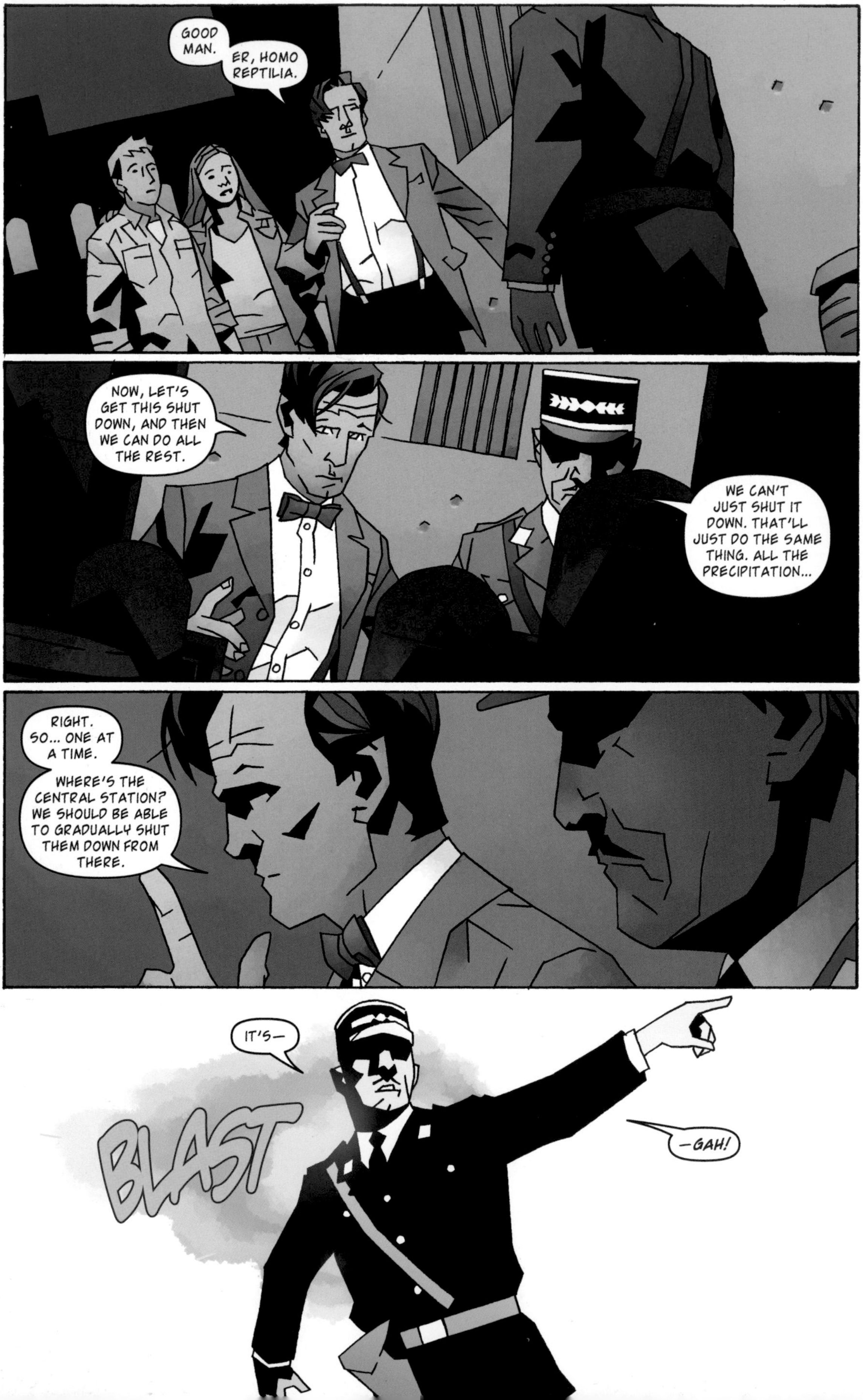
GOOD MAN.
ER, HOMO REPTILIA.
NOW, LET'S GET THIS SHUT DOWN, AND THEN WE CAN DO ALL THE REST.
WE CAN'T JUST SHUT IT DOWN. THAT'LL JUST DO THE SAME THING. ALL THE PRECIPITATION...
RIGHT. SO... ONE AT A TIME.
WHERE'S THE CENTRAL STATION? WE SHOULD BE ABLE TO GRADUALLY SHUT THEM DOWN FROM THERE.
IT'S—
BLAST
—GAH!

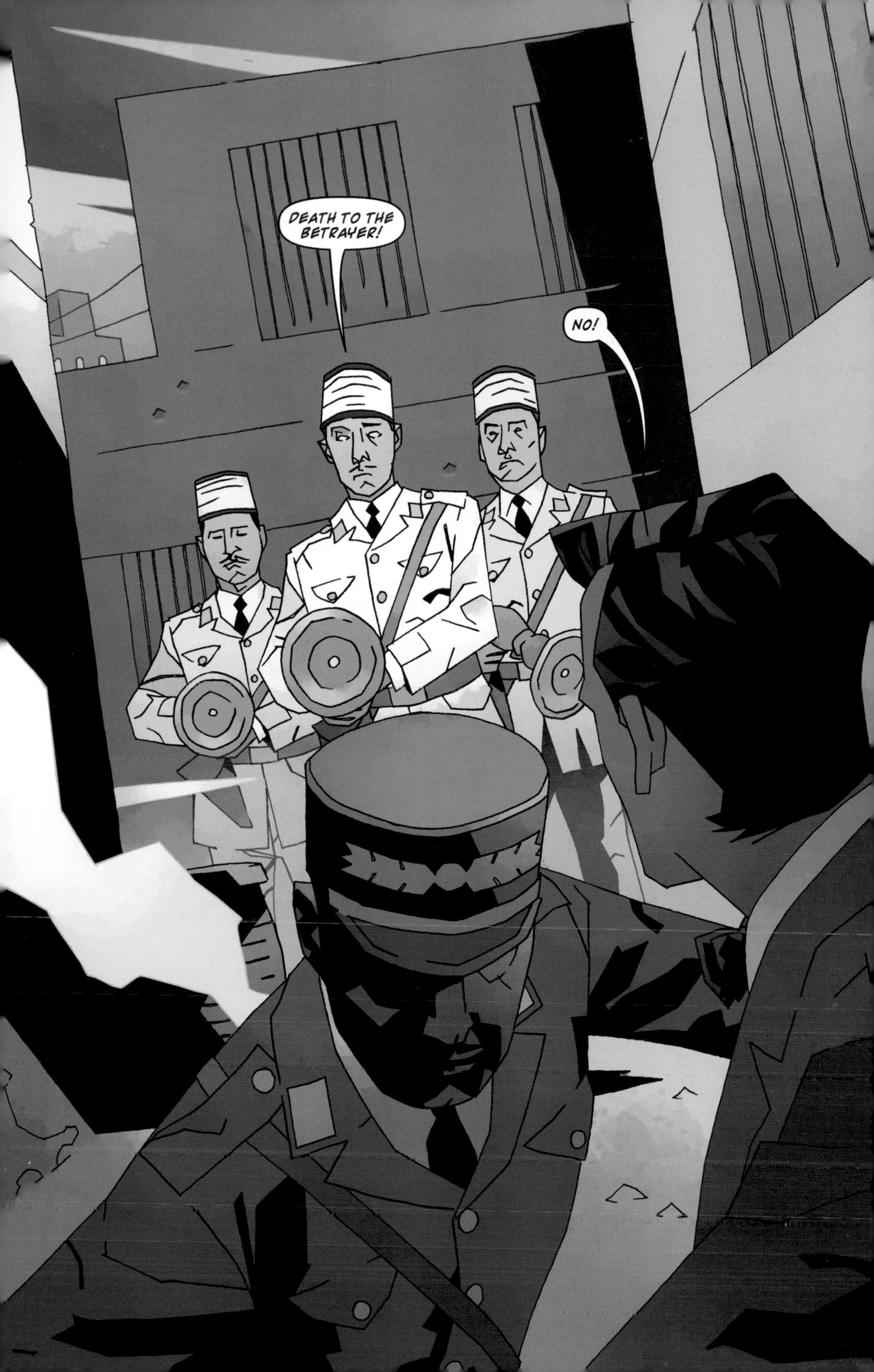
DEATH TO THE BETRAYER!
NO!

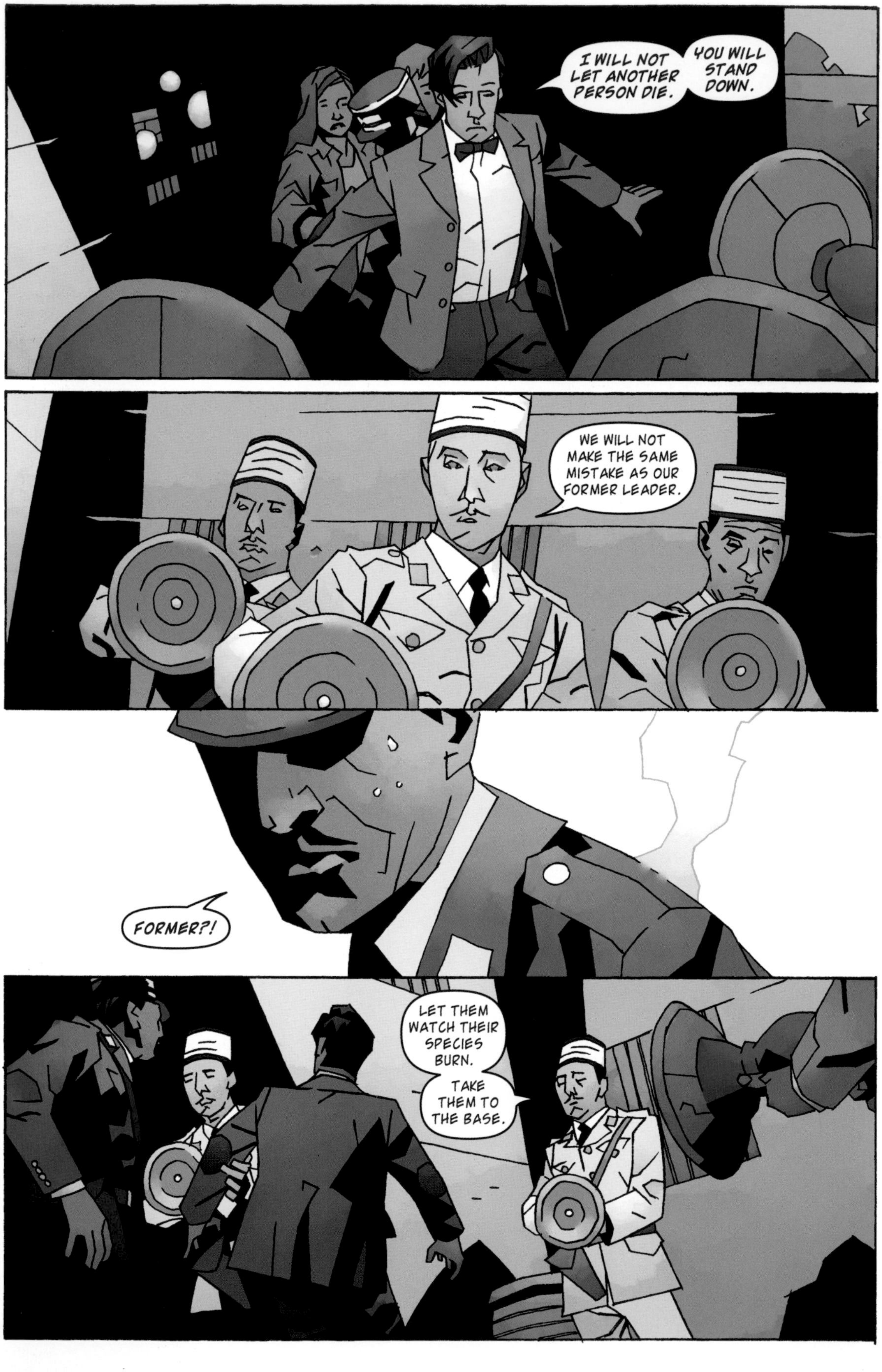
I WILL NOT LET ANOTHER PERSON DIE.
YOU WILL STAND DOWN.
WE WILL NOT MAKE THE SAME MISTAKE AS OUR FORMER LEADER.
FORMER?!
LET THEM WATCH THEIR SPECIES BURN.
TAKE THEM TO THE BASE.

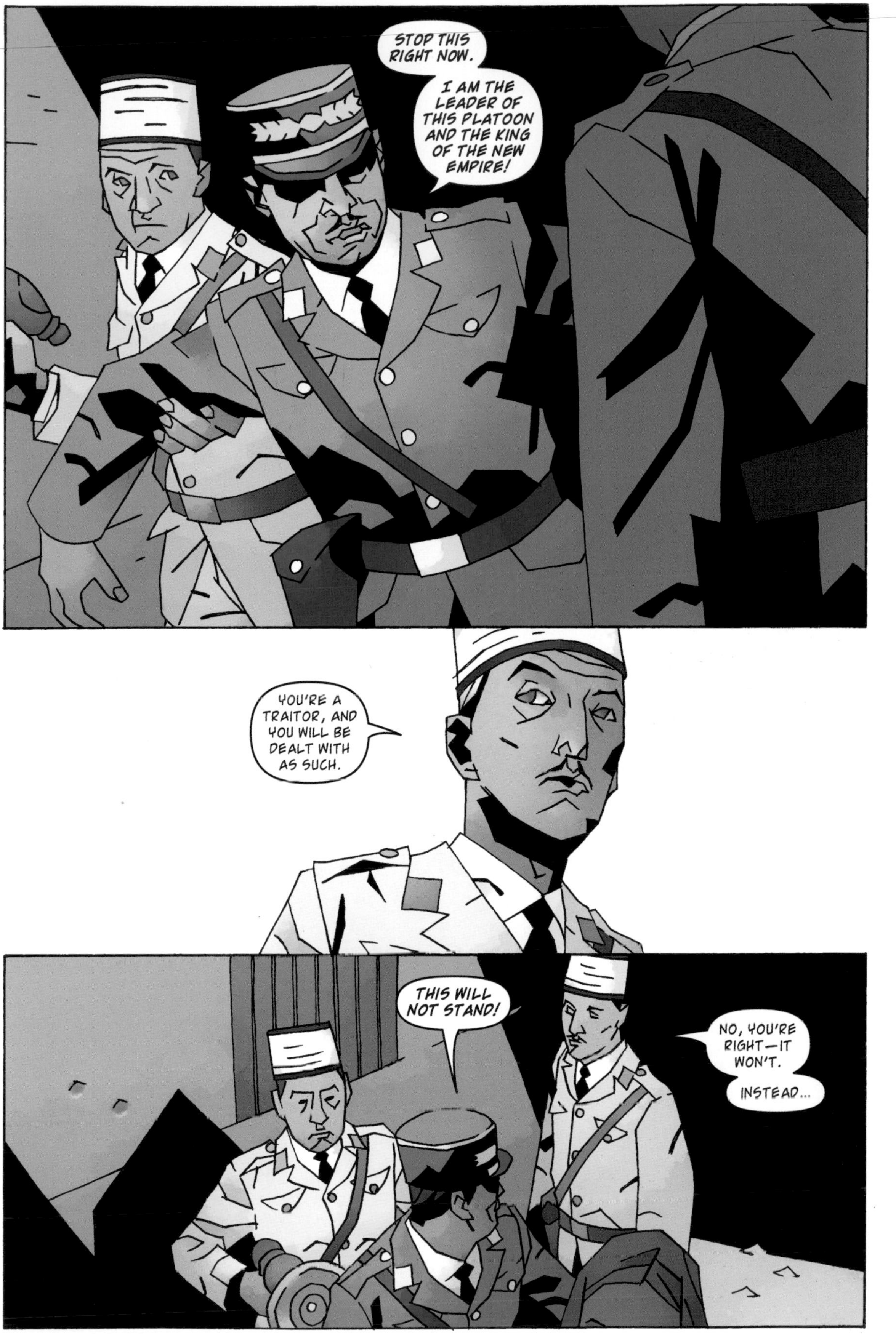
STOP THIS RIGHT NOW.
I AM THE LEADER OF THIS PLATOON AND THE KING OF THE NEW EMPIRE!
YOU'RE A TRAITOR, AND YOU WILL BE DEALT WITH AS SUCH.
THIS WILL NOT STAND!
NO, YOU'RE RIGHT—IT WON'T.
INSTEAD...

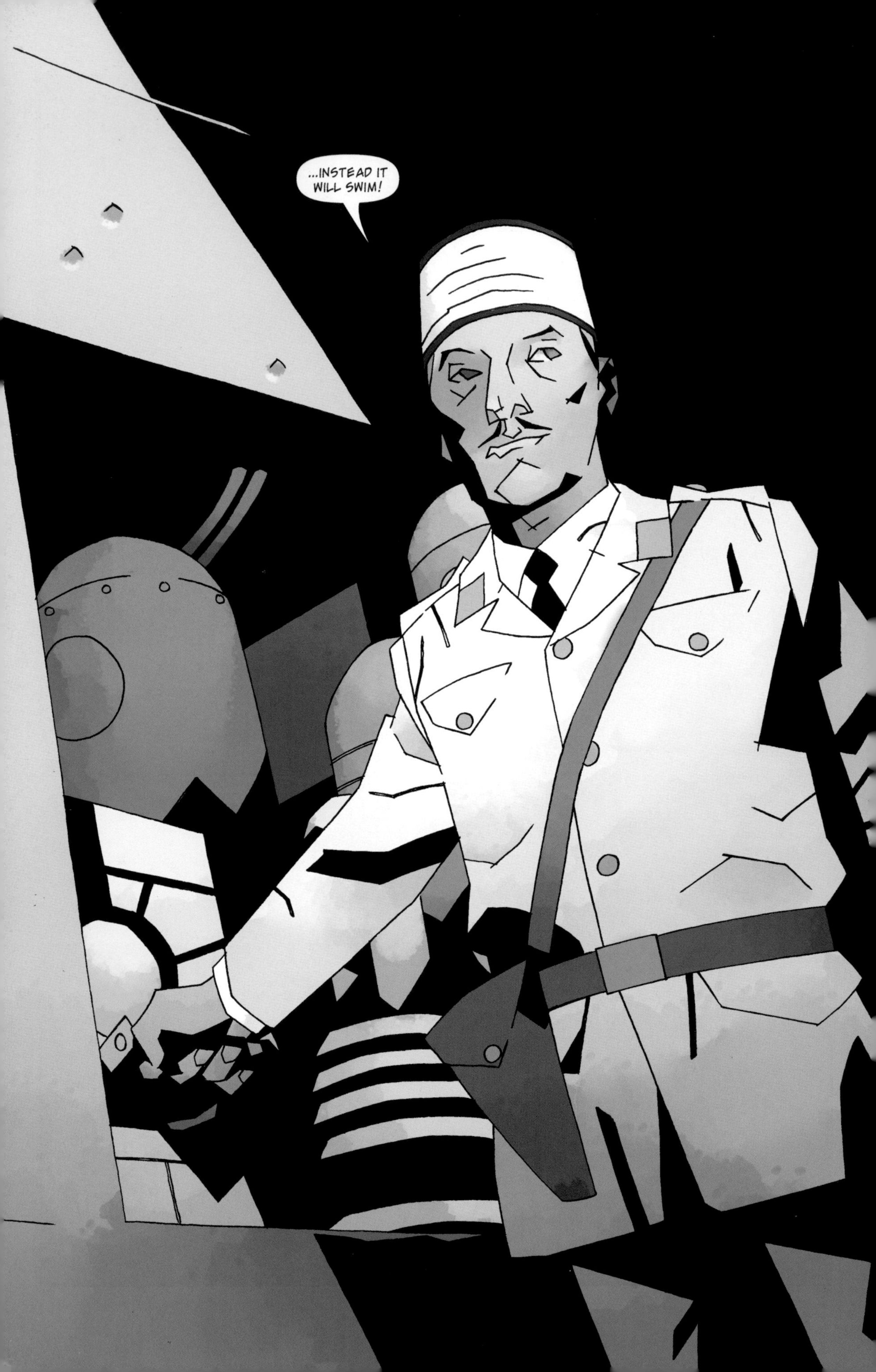
...INSTEAD IT WILL SWIM!

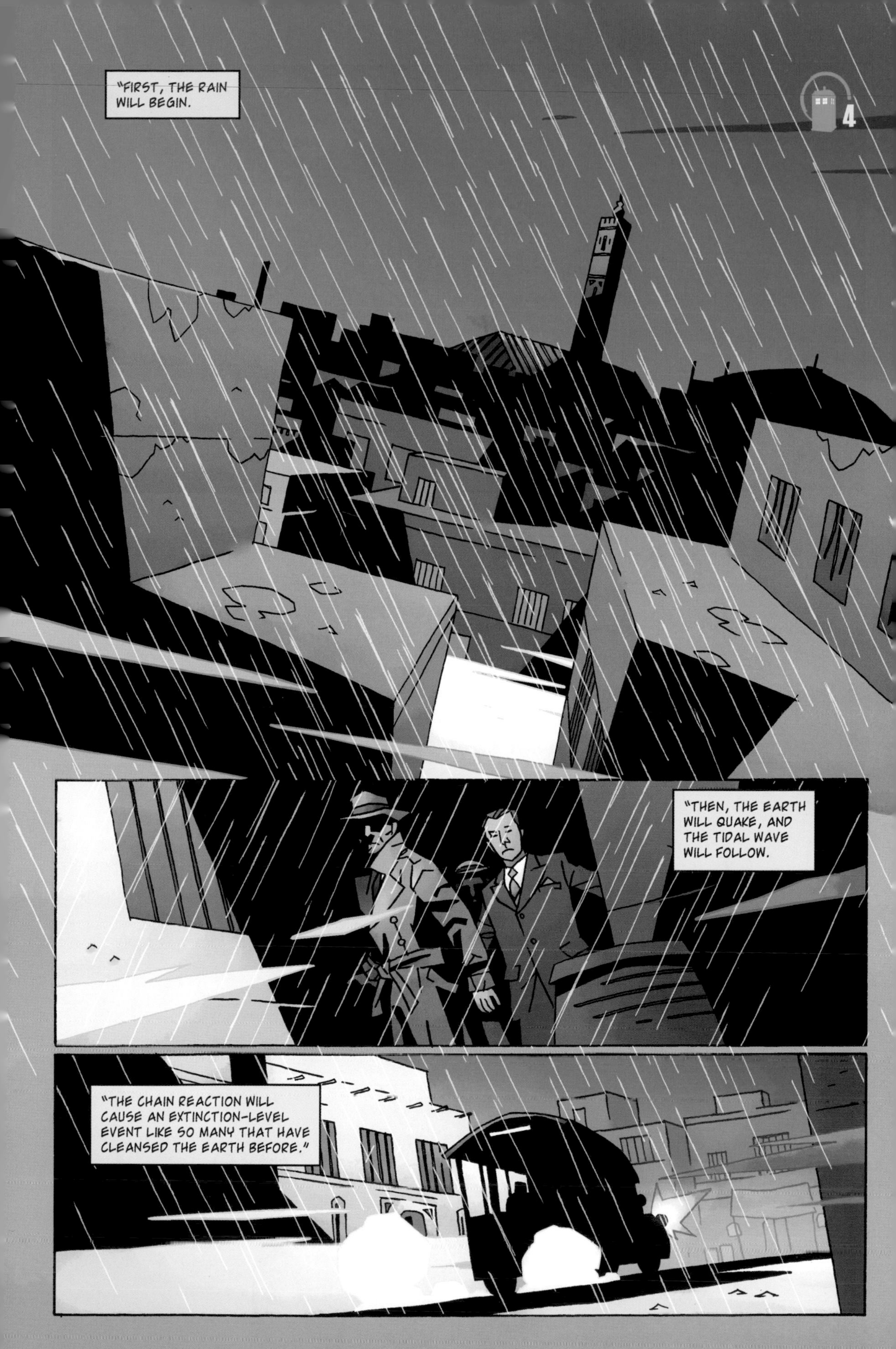
"FIRST, THE RAIN WILL BEGIN.
4
"THEN, THE EARTH WILL QUAKE, AND THE TIDAL WAVE WILL FOLLOW.
"THE CHAIN REACTION WILL CAUSE AN EXTINCTION-LEVEL EVENT LIKE SO MANY THAT HAVE CLEANSED THE EARTH BEFORE."

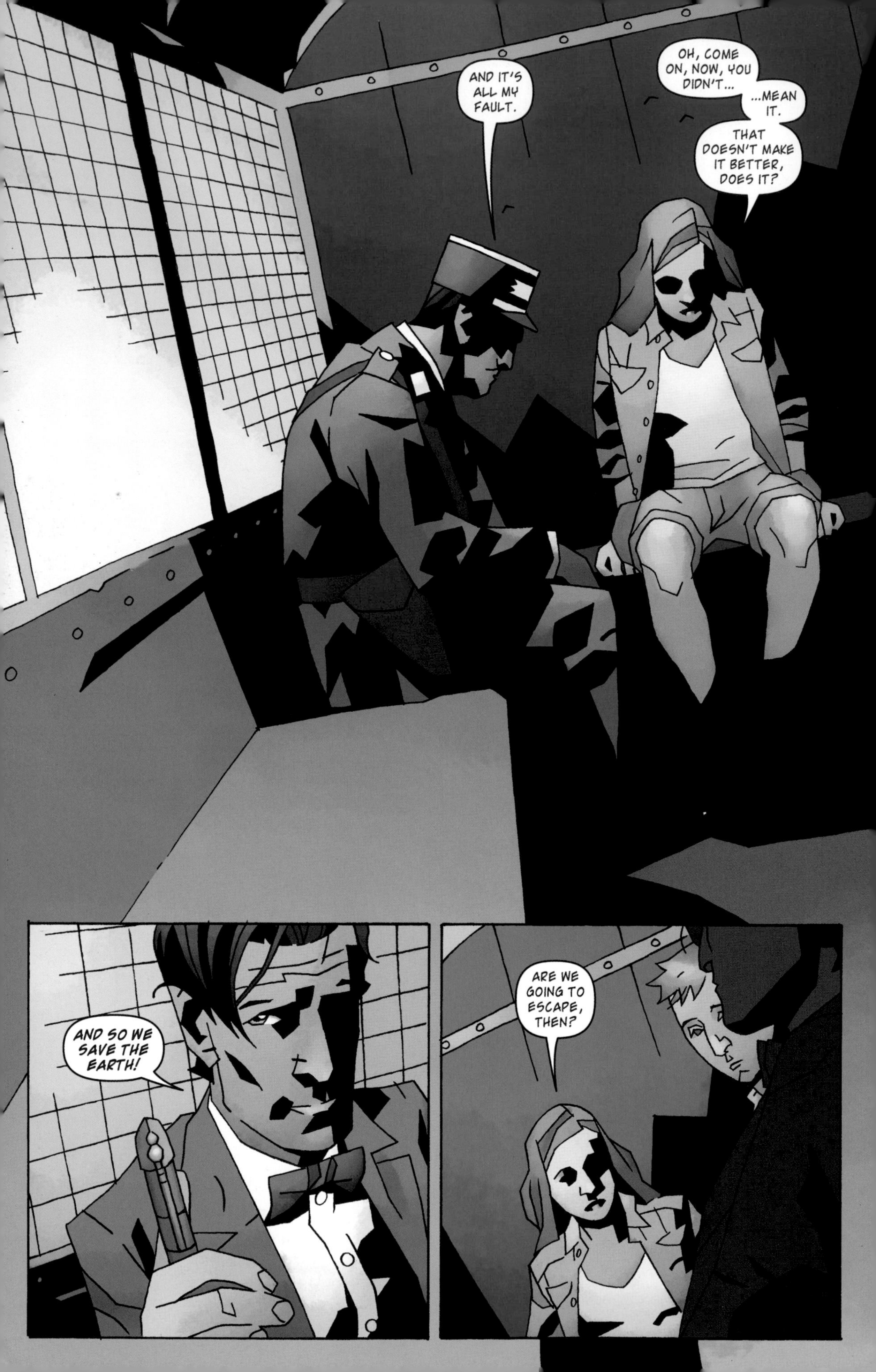
AND IT'S ALL MY FAULT.
OH, COME ON, NOW, YOU DIDN'T...
...MEAN IT.
THAT DOESN'T MAKE IT BETTER, DOES IT?
AND SO WE SAVE THE EARTH!
ARE WE GOING TO ESCAPE, THEN?

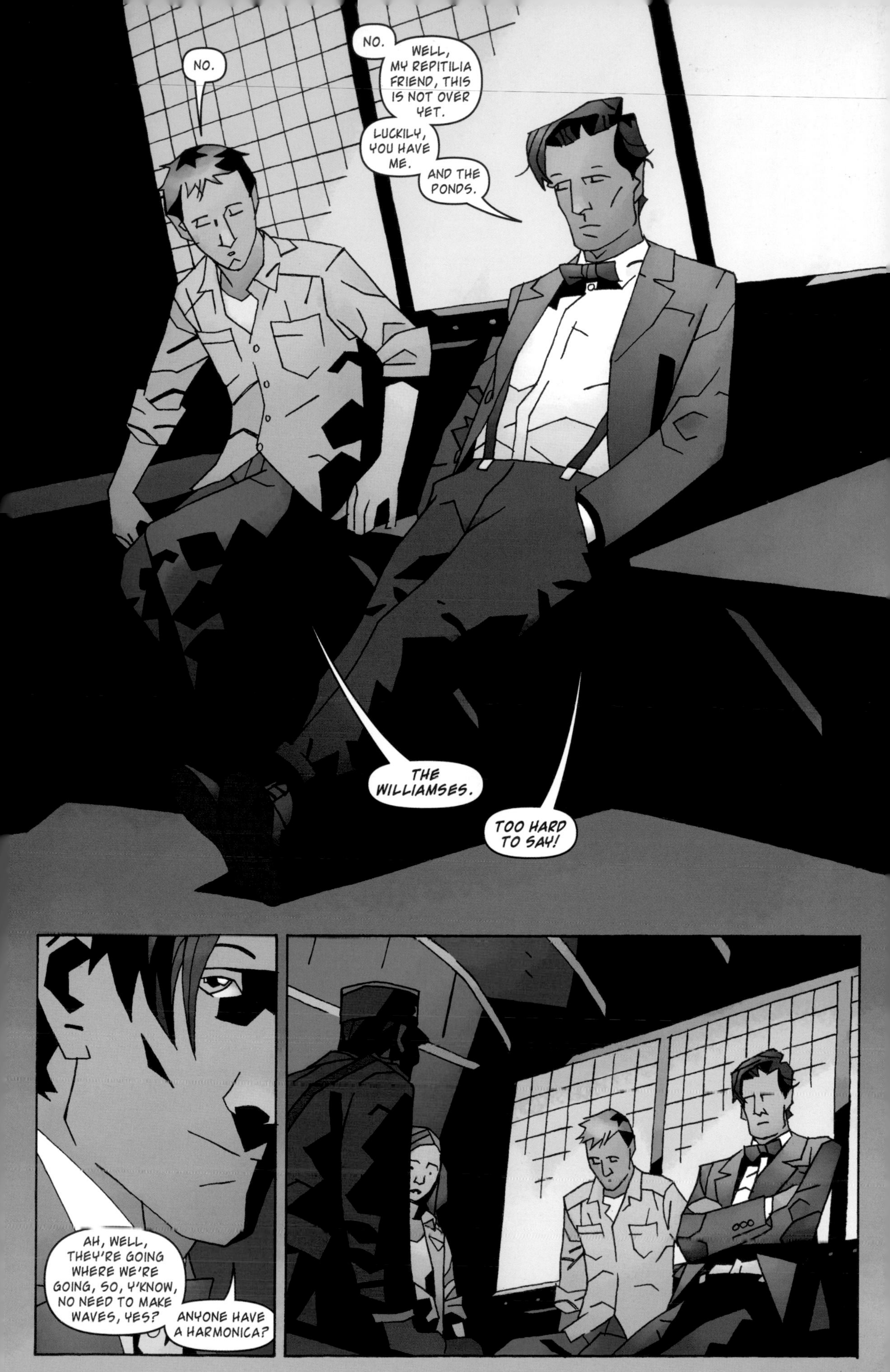
NO.
NO.
WELL, MY REPITILIA FRIEND, THIS IS NOT OVER YET.
LUCKILY, YOU HAVE ME.
AND THE PONDS.
THE WILLIAMSES.
TOO HARD TO SAY!
AH, WELL, THEY'RE GOING WHERE WE'RE GOING, SO, Y'KNOW, NO NEED TO MAKE WAVES, YES?
ANYONE HAVE A HARMONICA?

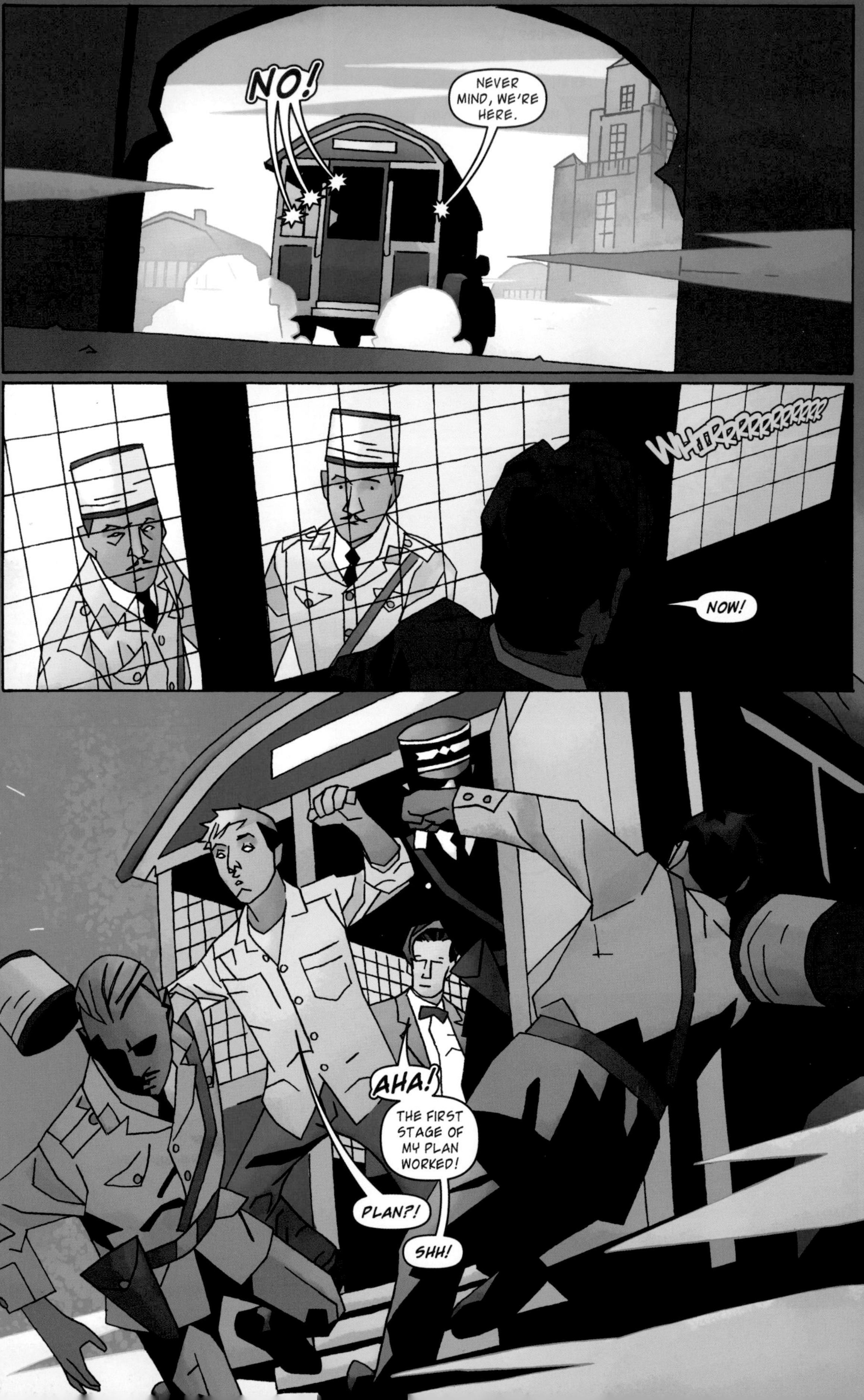
NO!
NEVER MIND, WE'RE HERE.
WHIIRRRRRRRRRR
NOW!
AHA!
THE FIRST STAGE OF MY PLAN WORKED!
PLAN?!
SHH!

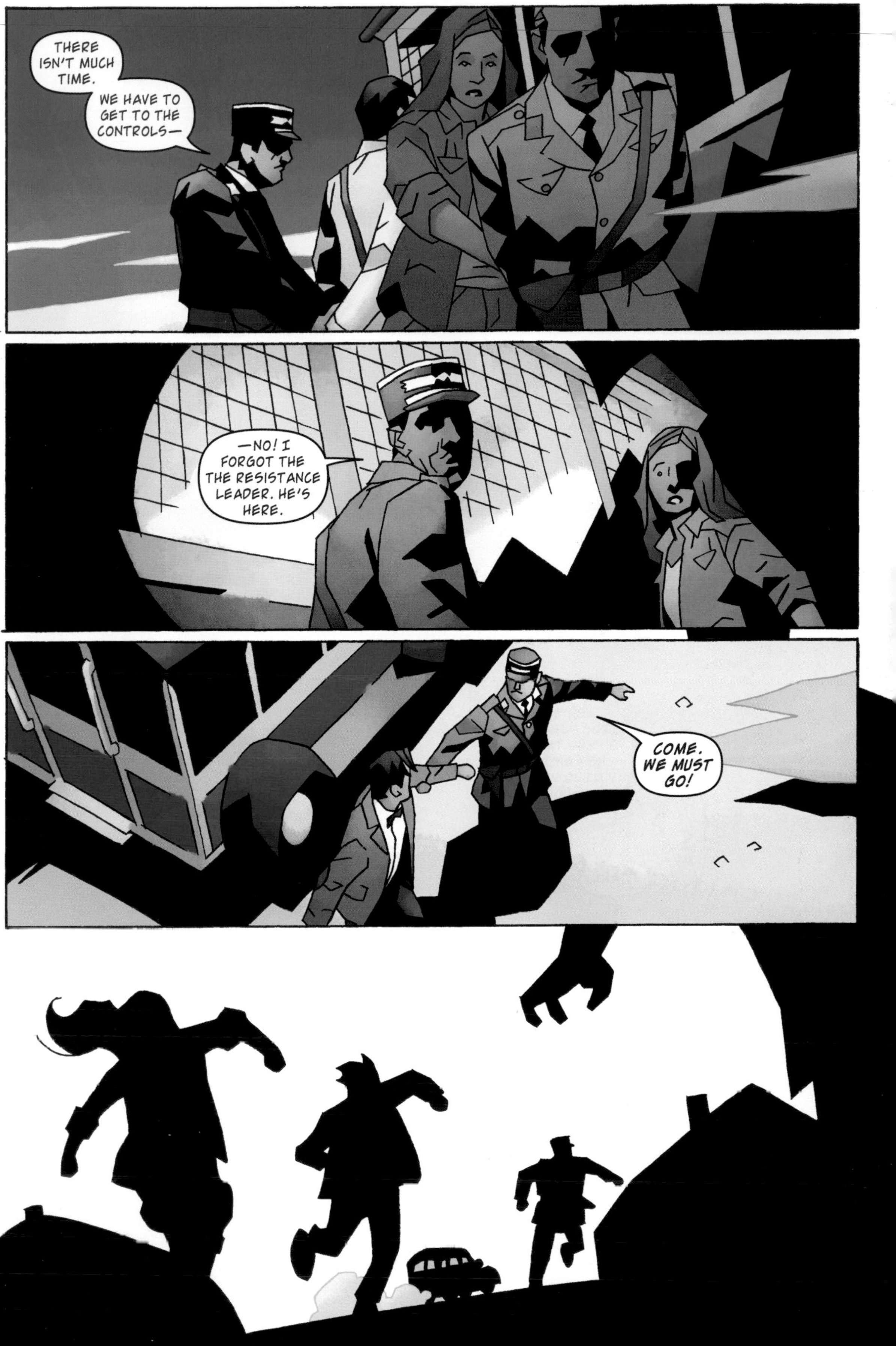
THERE ISN'T MUCH TIME.
WE HAVE TO GET TO THE CONTROLS—
—NO! I FORGOT THE THE RESISTANCE LEADER. HE'S HERE.
COME. WE MUST GO!

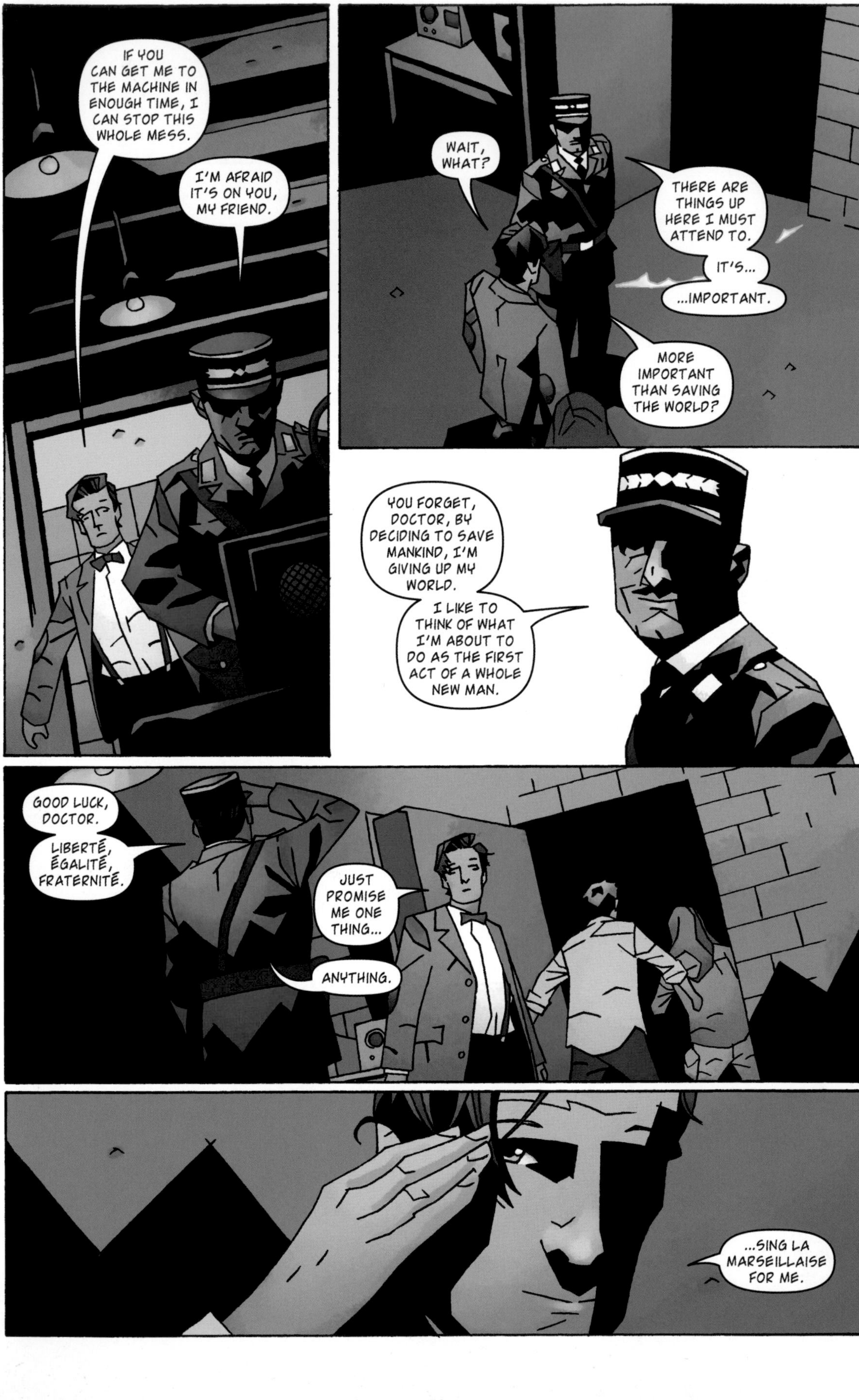
IF YOU CAN GET ME TO THE MACHINE IN ENOUGH TIME, I CAN STOP THIS WHOLE MESS.
I'M AFRAID IT'S ON YOU, MY FRIEND.
WAIT, WHAT?
THERE ARE THINGS UP HERE I MUST ATTEND TO.
IT'S...
...IMPORTANT.
MORE IMPORTANT THAN SAVING THE WORLD?
YOU FORGET, DOCTOR, BY DECIDING TO SAVE MANKIND, I'M GIVING UP MY WORLD.
I LIKE TO THINK OF WHAT I'M ABOUT TO DO AS THE FIRST ACT OF A WHOLE NEW MAN.
GOOD LUCK, DOCTOR.
LIBERTÉ, ÉGALITÉ, FRATERNITÉ.
JUST PROMISE ME ONE THING...
ANYTHING.
...SING LA MARSEILLAISE FOR ME.

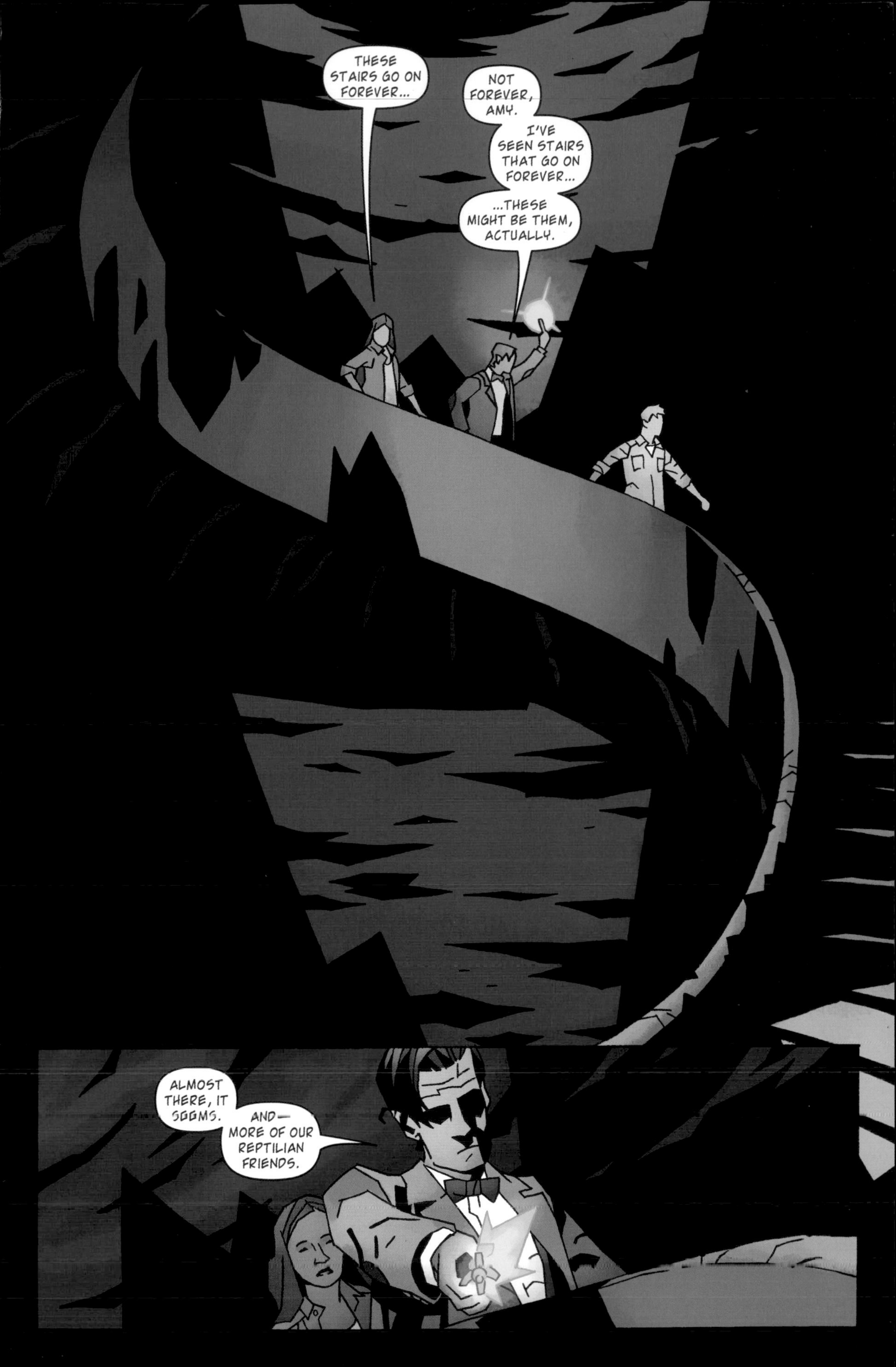
THESE STAIRS GO ON FOREVER...
NOT FOREVER, AMY.
I'VE SEEN STAIRS THAT GO ON FOREVER...
...THESE MIGHT BE THEM, ACTUALLY.
ALMOST THERE, IT SEEMS.
AND— MORE OF OUR REPTILIAN FRIENDS.

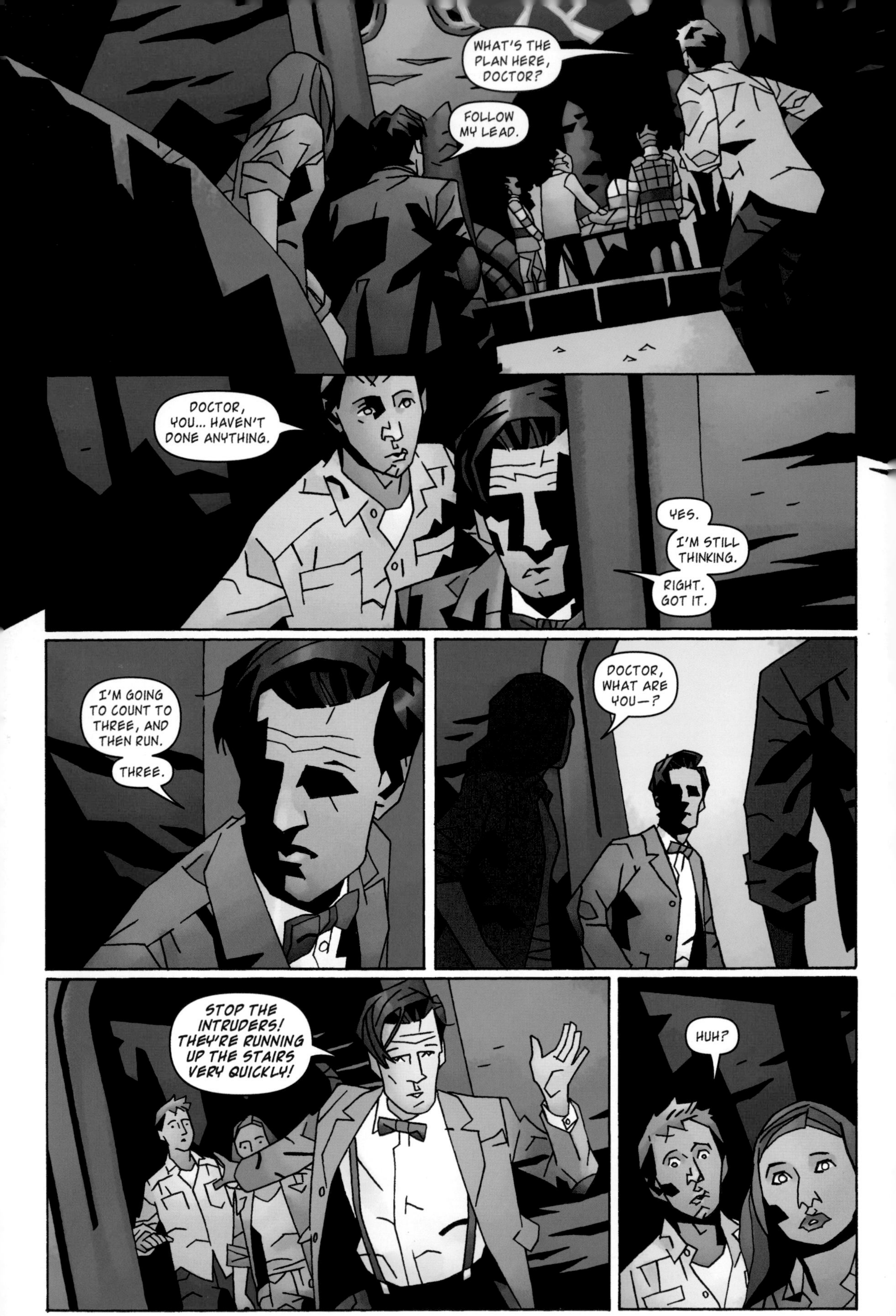
WHAT'S THE PLAN HERE, DOCTOR?
FOLLOW MY LEAD.
DOCTOR, YOU... HAVEN'T DONE ANYTHING.
YES.
I'M STILL THINKING.
RIGHT. GOT IT.
I'M GOING TO COUNT TO THREE, AND THEN RUN.
THREE.
DOCTOR, WHAT ARE YOU—?
STOP THE INTRUDERS! THEY'RE RUNNING UP THE STAIRS VERY QUICKLY!
HUH?

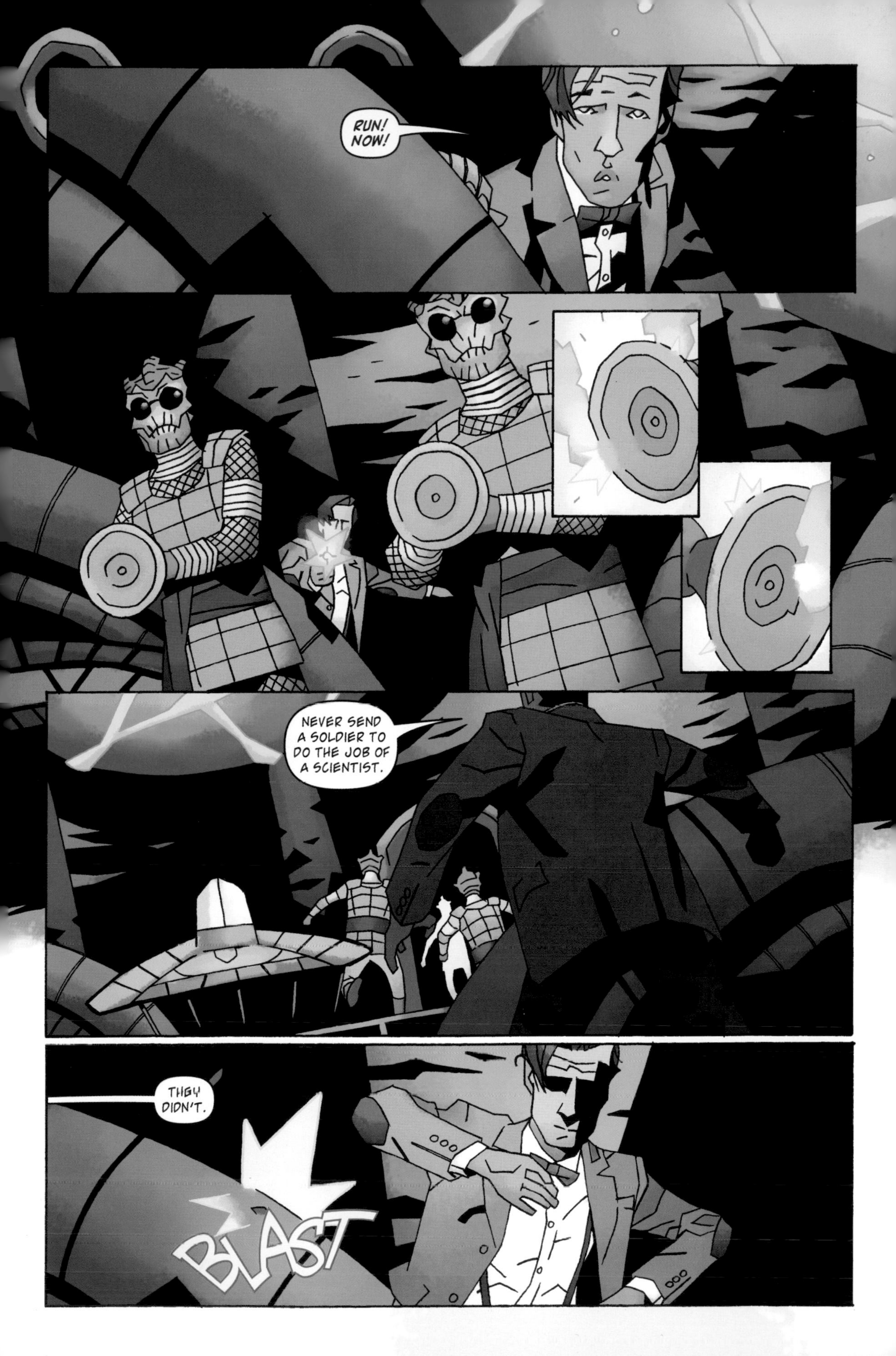
RUN! NOW!
NEVER SEND A SOLDIER TO DO THE JOB OF A SCIENTIST.
THEY DIDN'T.
BLAST

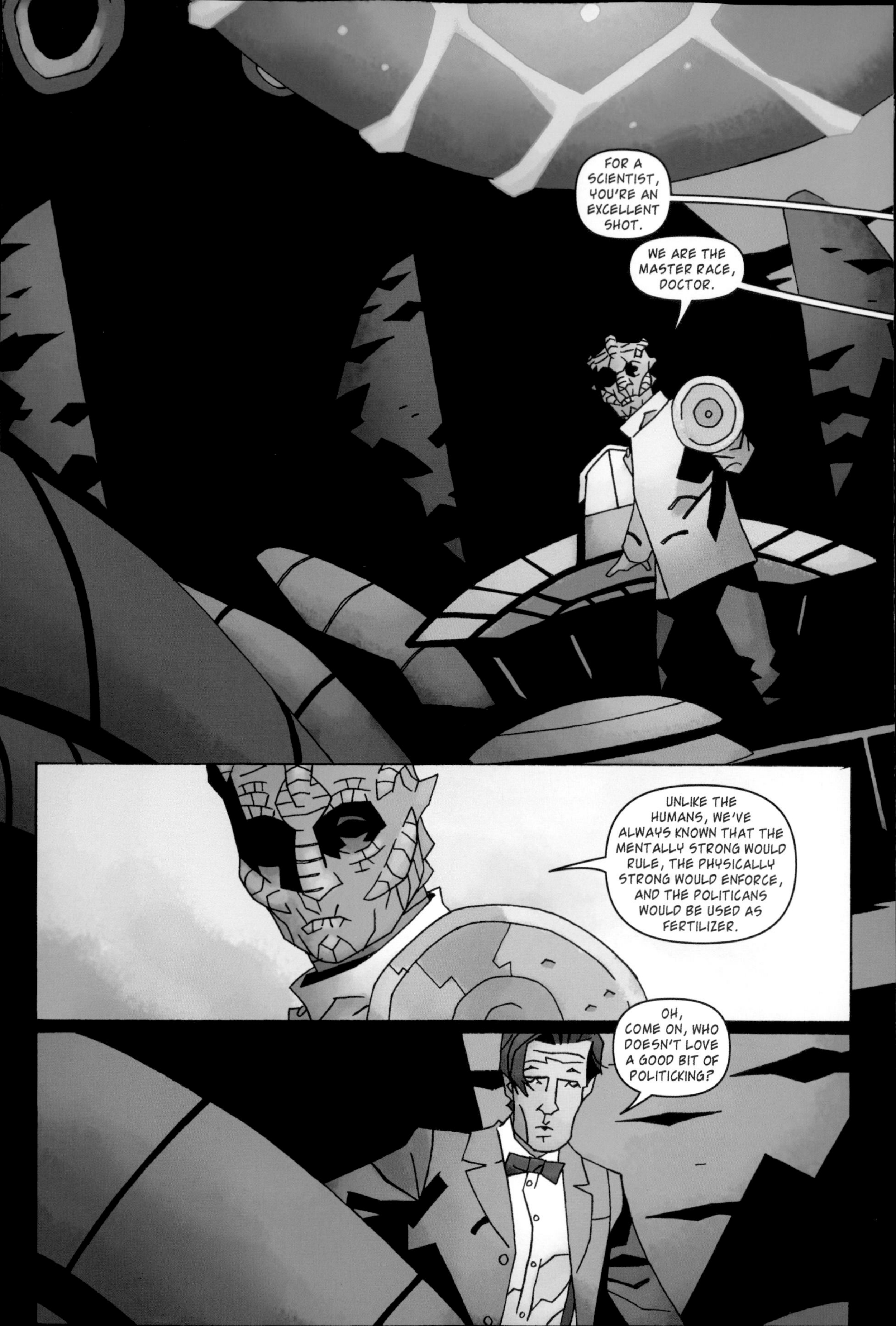
FOR A SCIENTIST, YOU'RE AN EXCELLENT SHOT.
WE ARE THE MASTER RACE, DOCTOR.
UNLIKE THE HUMANS, WE'VE ALWAYS KNOWN THAT THE MENTALLY STRONG WOULD RULE, THE PHYSICALLY STRONG WOULD ENFORCE, AND THE POLITICANS WOULD BE USED AS FERTILIZER.
OH, COME ON, WHO DOESN'T LOVE A GOOD BIT OF POLITICKING?

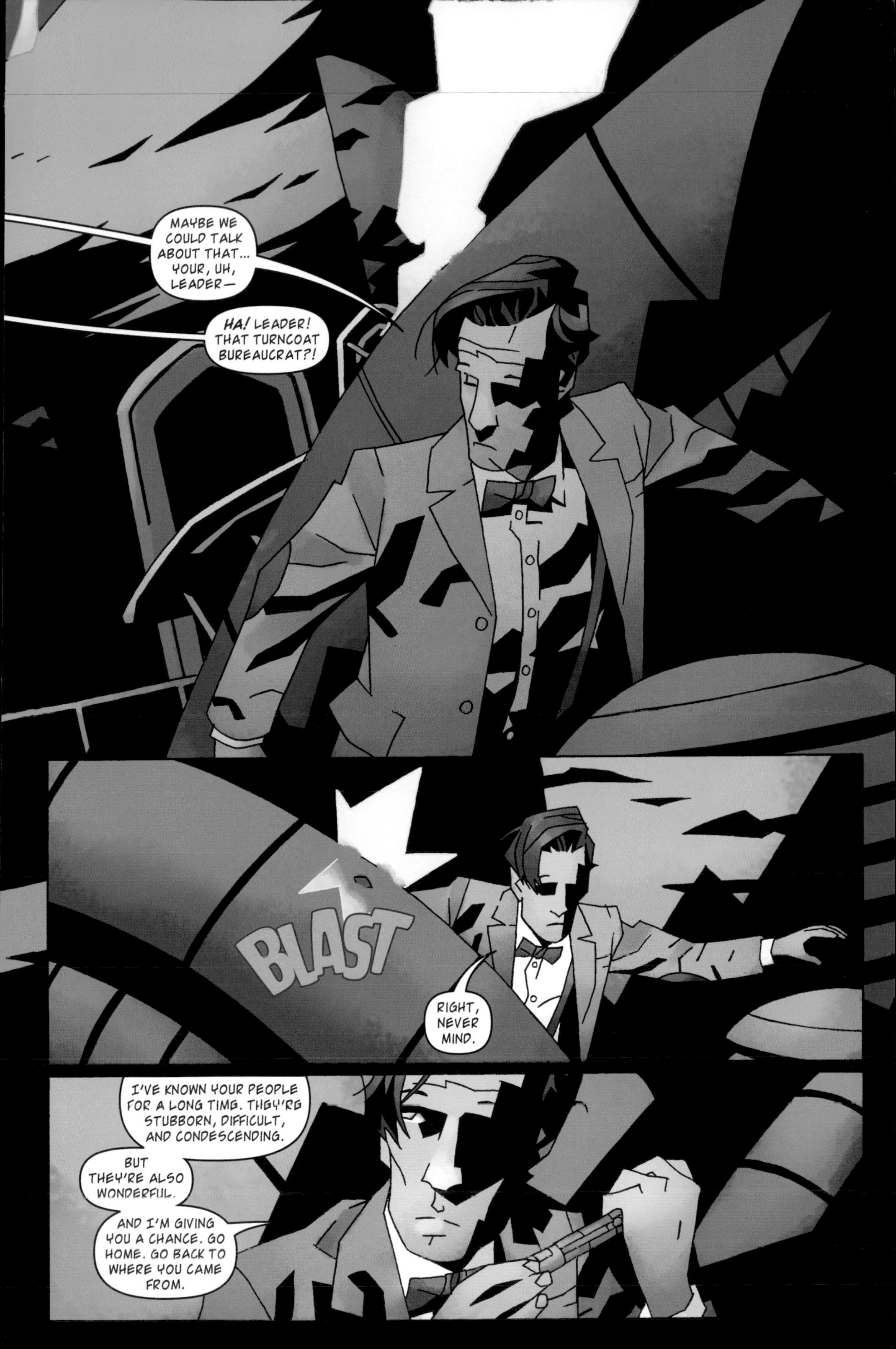
MAYBE WE COULD TALK ABOUT THAT... YOUR, UH, LEADER—
HA! LEADER! THAT TURNCOAT BUREAUCRAT?!
BLAST
RIGHT, NEVER MIND.
I'VE KNOWN YOUR PEOPLE FOR A LONG TIME. THEY'RE STUBBORN, DIFFICULT, AND CONDESCENDING.
BUT THEY'RE ALSO WONDERFUL.
AND I'M GIVING YOU A CHANCE. GO HOME. GO BACK TO WHERE YOU CAME FROM.

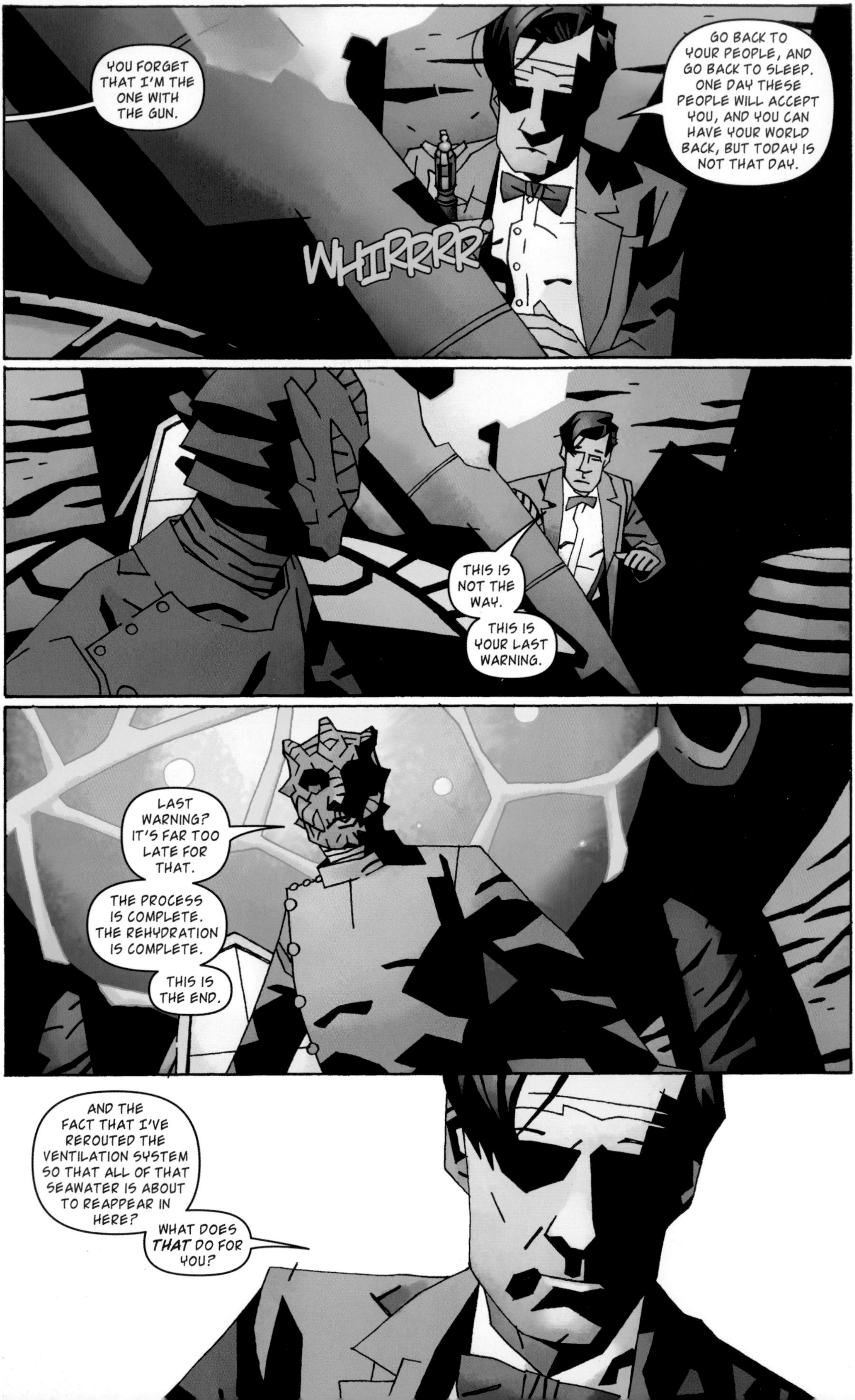
YOU FORGET THAT I'M THE ONE WITH THE GUN.
GO BACK TO YOUR PEOPLE, AND GO BACK TO SLEEP. ONE DAY THESE PEOPLE WILL ACCEPT YOU, AND YOU CAN HAVE YOUR WORLD BACK, BUT TODAY IS NOT THAT DAY.
WHIRRRR
THIS IS NOT THE WAY.
THIS IS YOUR LAST WARNING.
LAST WARNING? IT'S FAR TOO LATE FOR THAT.
THE PROCESS IS COMPLETE. THE REHYDRATION IS COMPLETE.
THIS IS THE END.
AND THE FACT THAT I'VE REROUTED THE VENTILATION SYSTEM SO THAT ALL OF THAT SEAWATER IS ABOUT TO REAPPEAR IN HERE?
WHAT DOES *THAT* DO FOR YOU?

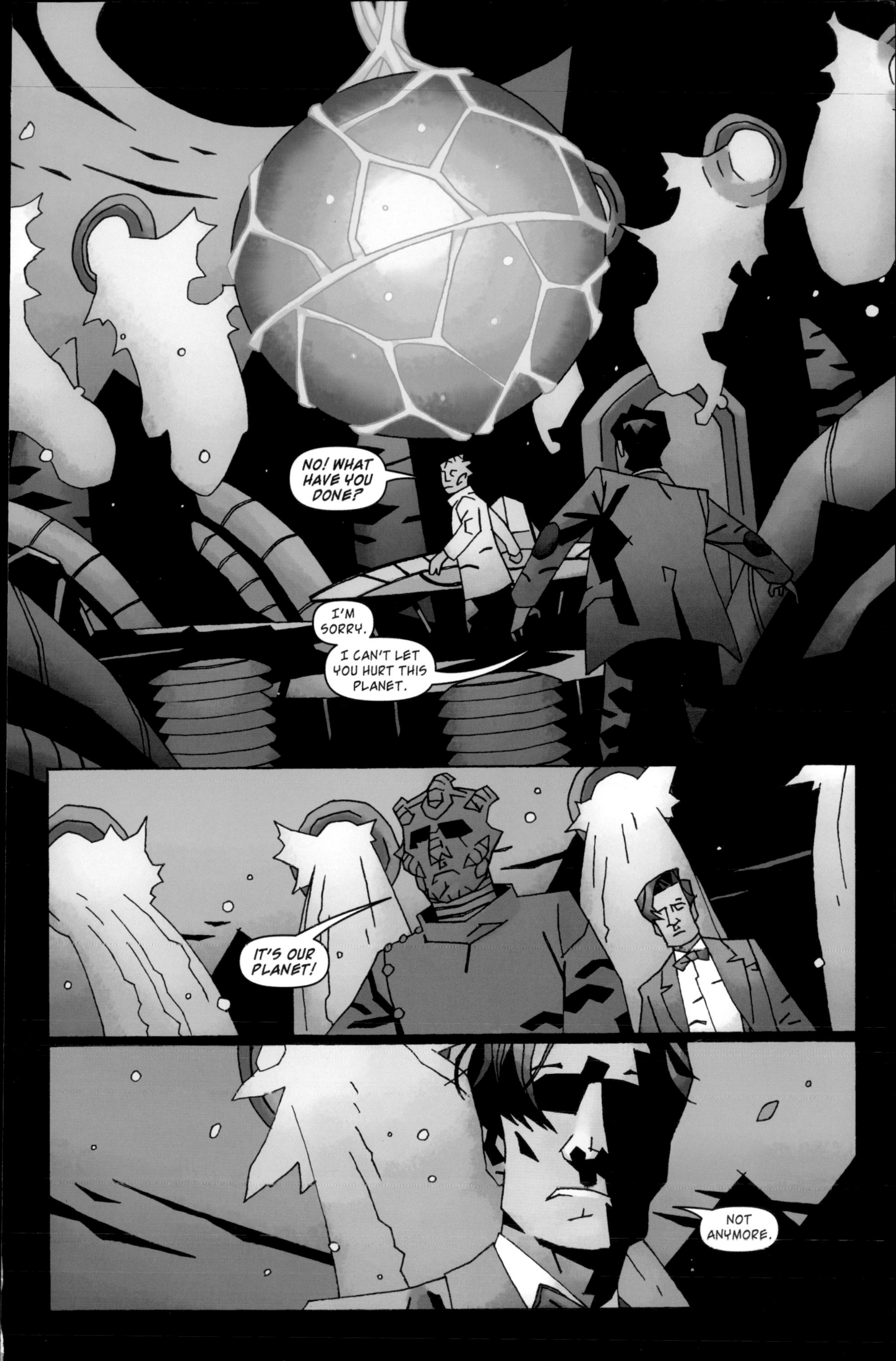
NO! WHAT HAVE YOU DONE?
I'M SORRY.
I CAN'T LET YOU HURT THIS PLANET.
IT'S OUR PLANET!
NOT ANYMORE.

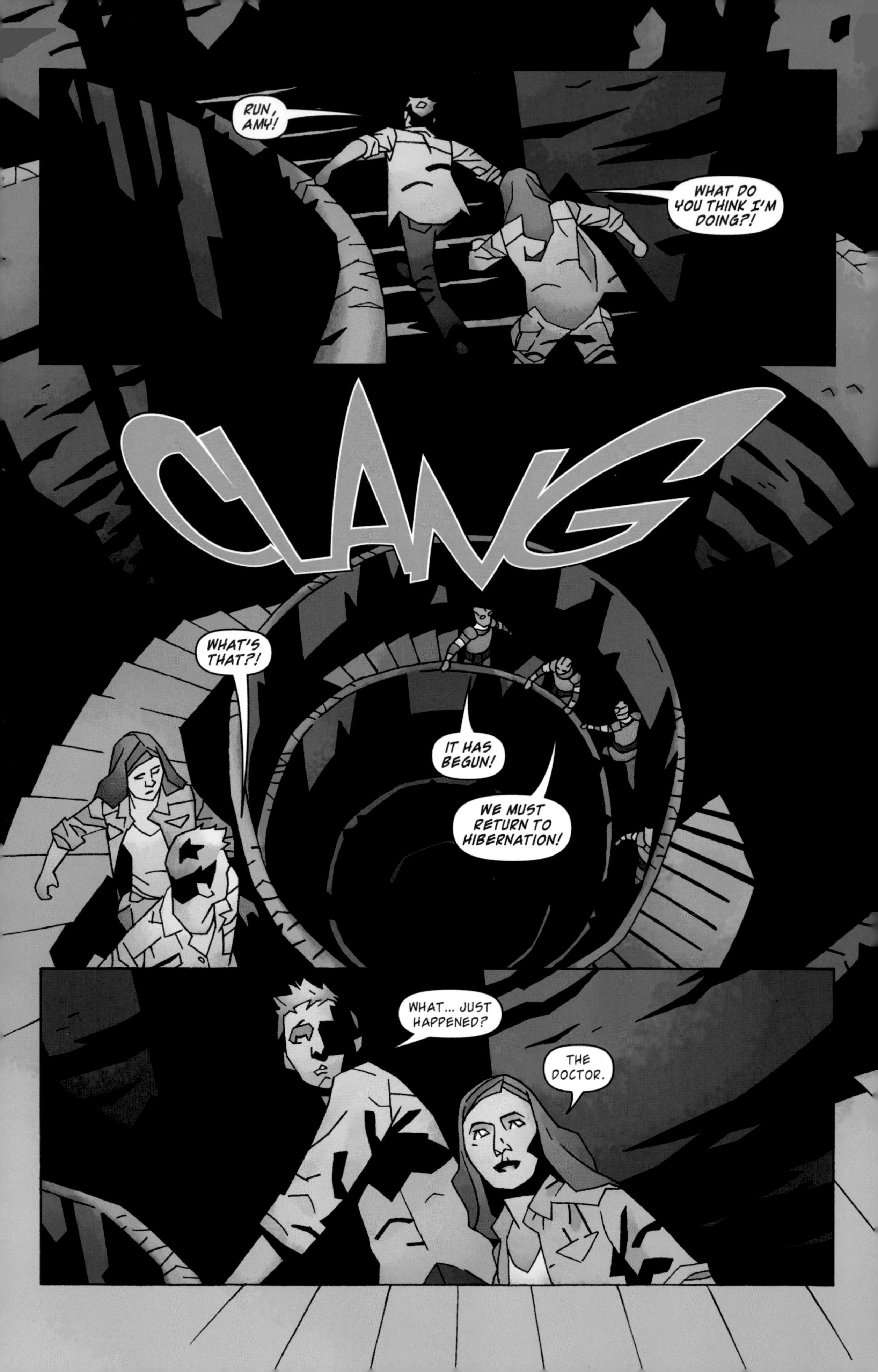
RUN, AMY!
WHAT DO YOU THINK I'M DOING?!
CLANG
WHAT'S THAT?!
IT HAS BEGUN!
WE MUST RETURN TO HIBERNATION!
WHAT... JUST HAPPENED?
THE DOCTOR.

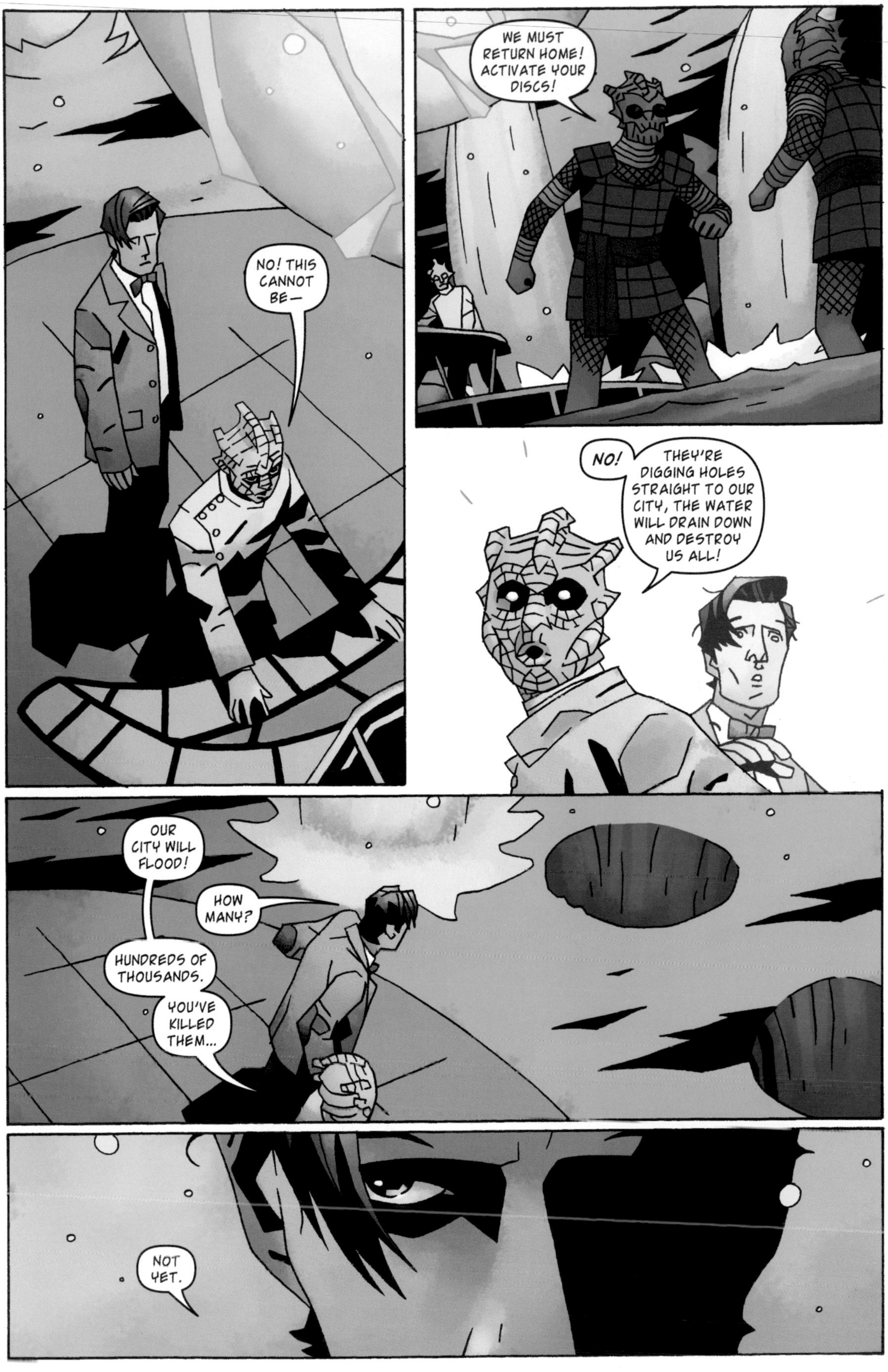
NO! THIS CANNOT BE—
WE MUST RETURN HOME! ACTIVATE YOUR DISCS!
NO!
THEY'RE DIGGING HOLES STRAIGHT TO OUR CITY, THE WATER WILL DRAIN DOWN AND DESTROY US ALL!
OUR CITY WILL FLOOD!
HOW MANY?
HUNDREDS OF THOUSANDS.
YOU'VE KILLED THEM...
NOT YET.

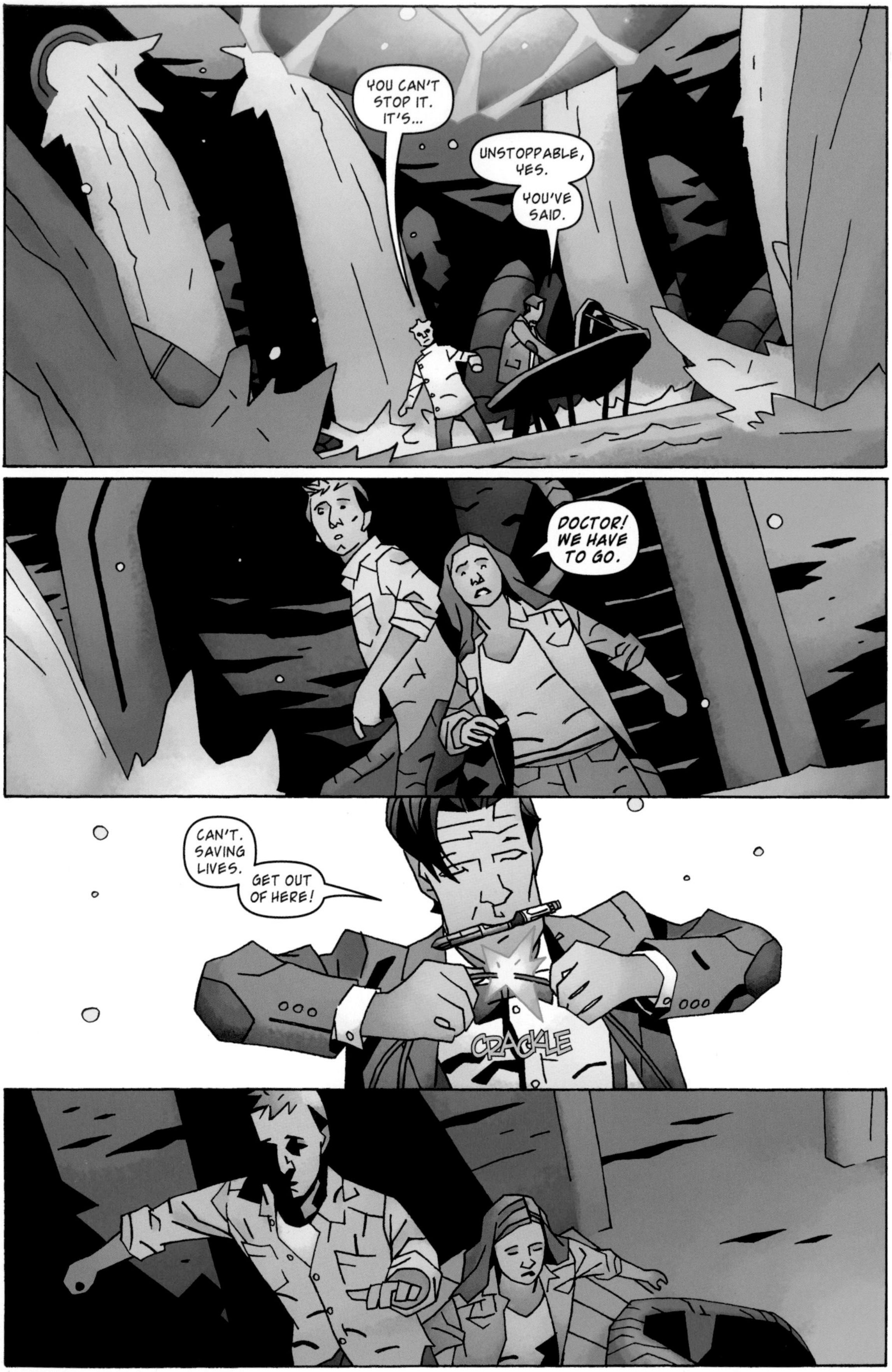
YOU CAN'T STOP IT. IT'S...
UNSTOPPABLE, YES.
YOU'VE SAID.
DOCTOR! WE HAVE TO GO.
CAN'T. SAVING LIVES.
GET OUT OF HERE!
CRACKLE

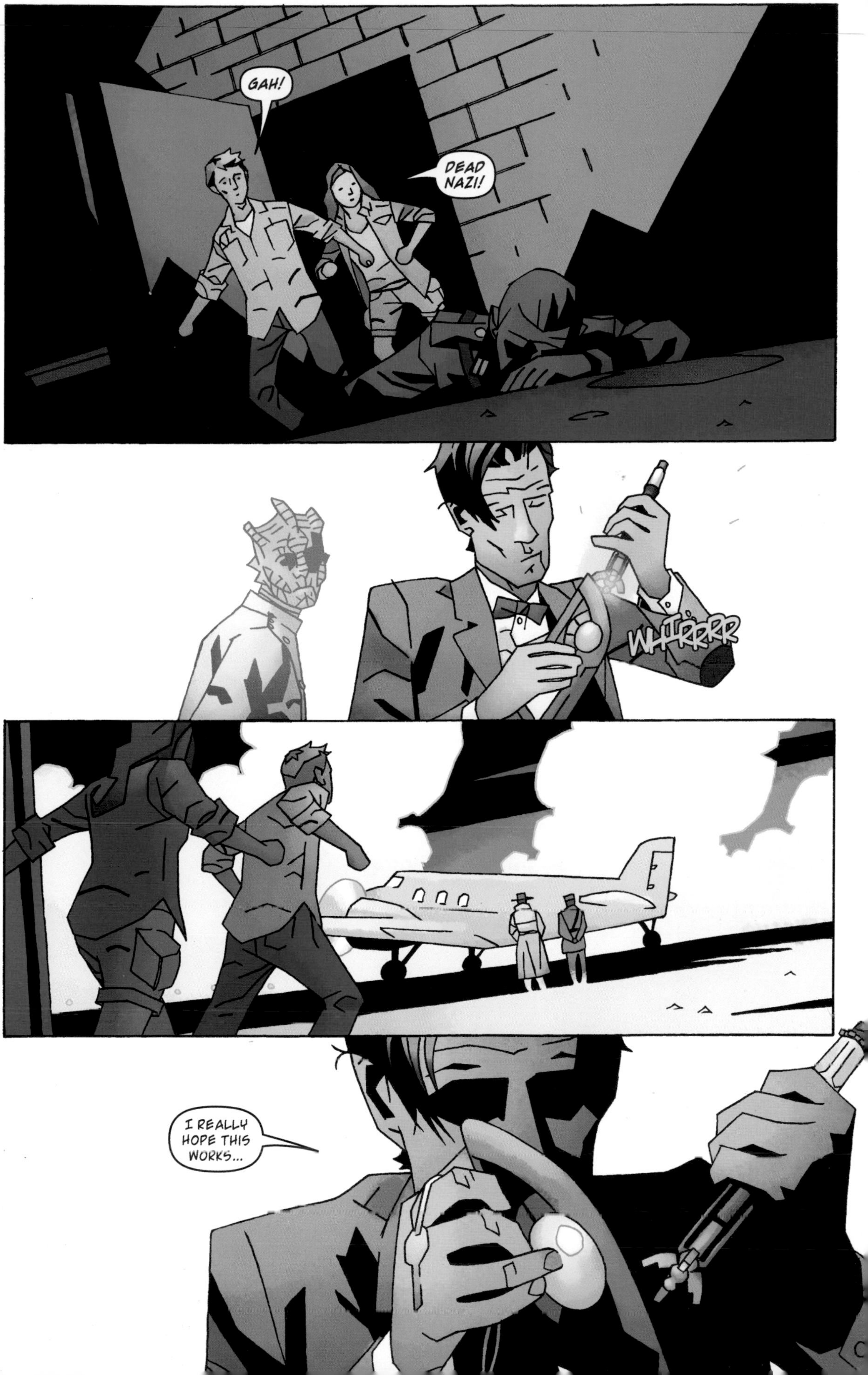
GAH!
DEAD NAZI!
WHIRRRR
I REALLY HOPE THIS WORKS...

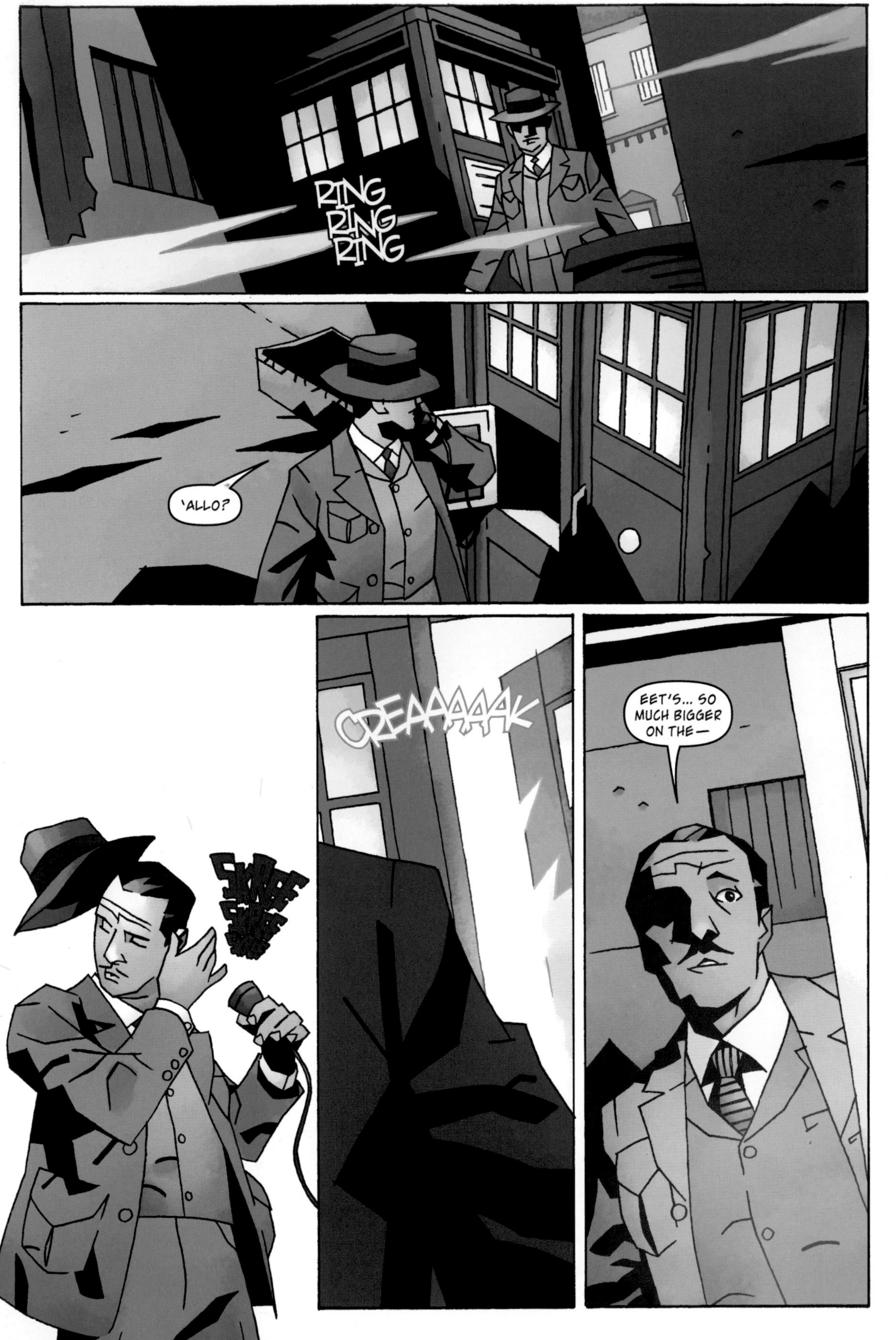
RING
RING
RING
'ALLO?
CREAAAAAK
EET'S... SO MUCH BIGGER ON THE—

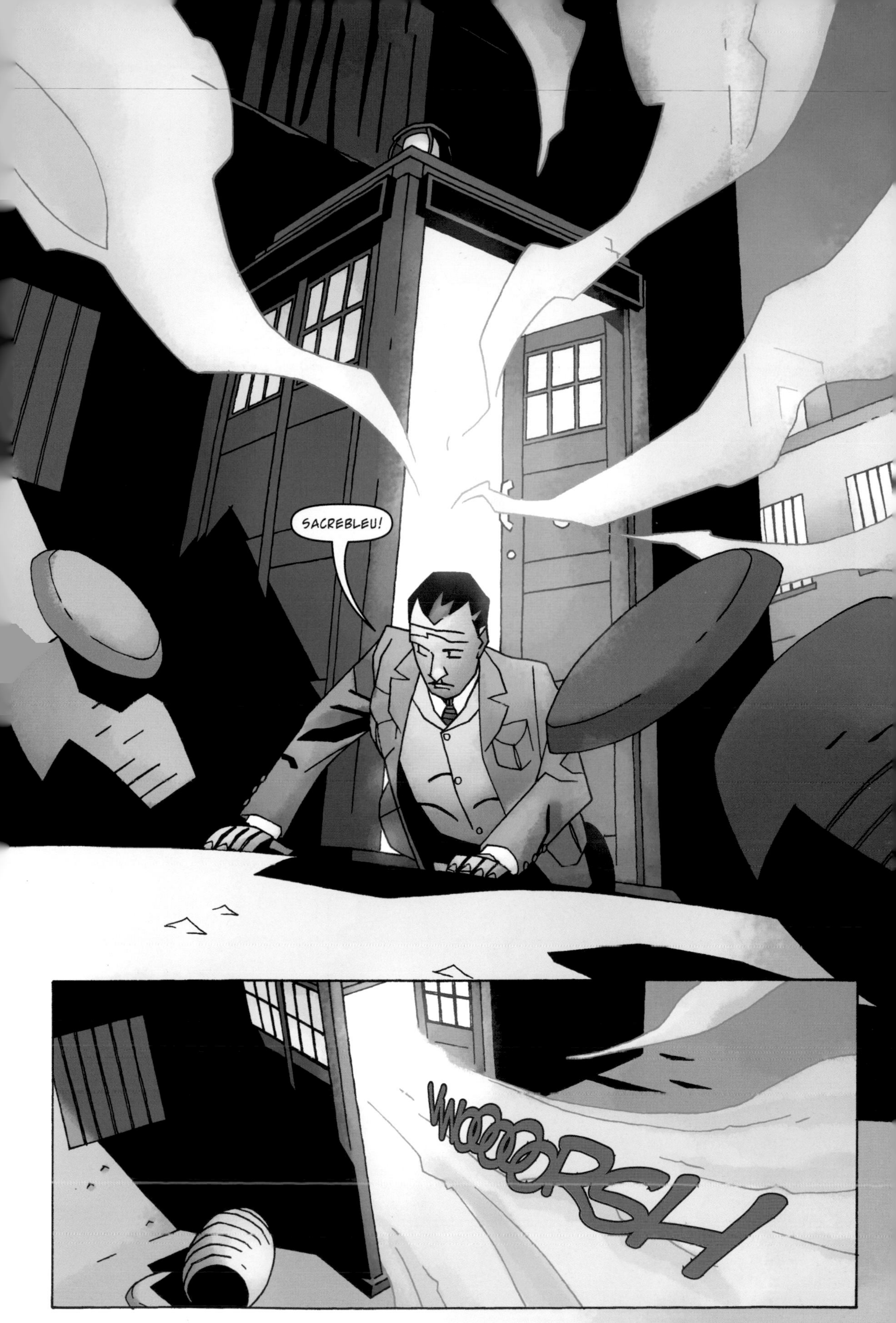
SACREBLEU!
VWOOORSH

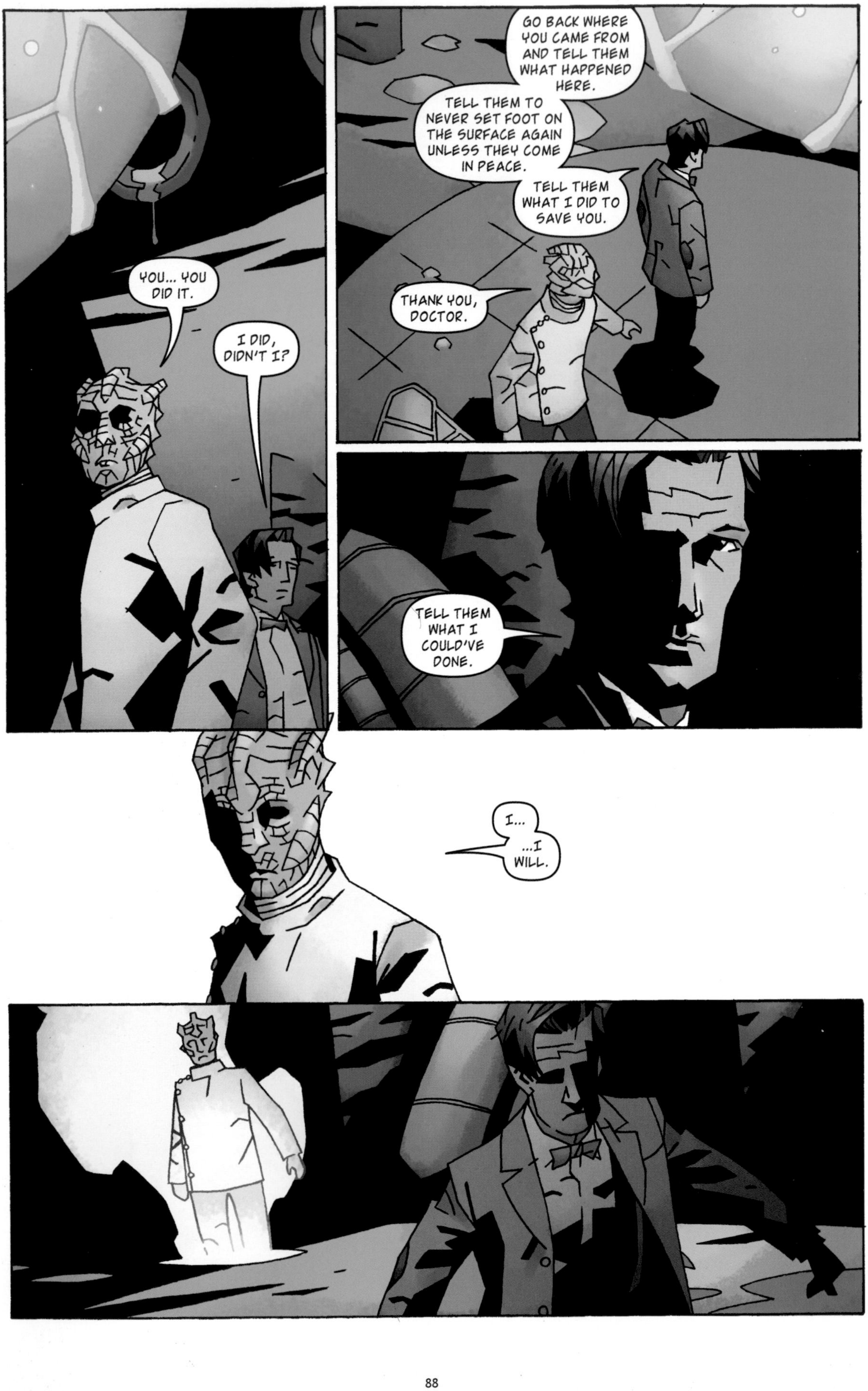

YOU... YOU DID IT.
I DID, DIDN'T I?
GO BACK WHERE YOU CAME FROM AND TELL THEM WHAT HAPPENED HERE.
TELL THEM TO NEVER SET FOOT ON THE SURFACE AGAIN UNLESS THEY COME IN PEACE.
TELL THEM WHAT I DID TO SAVE YOU.
THANK YOU, DOCTOR.
TELL THEM WHAT I COULD'VE DONE.
I...
...I WILL.

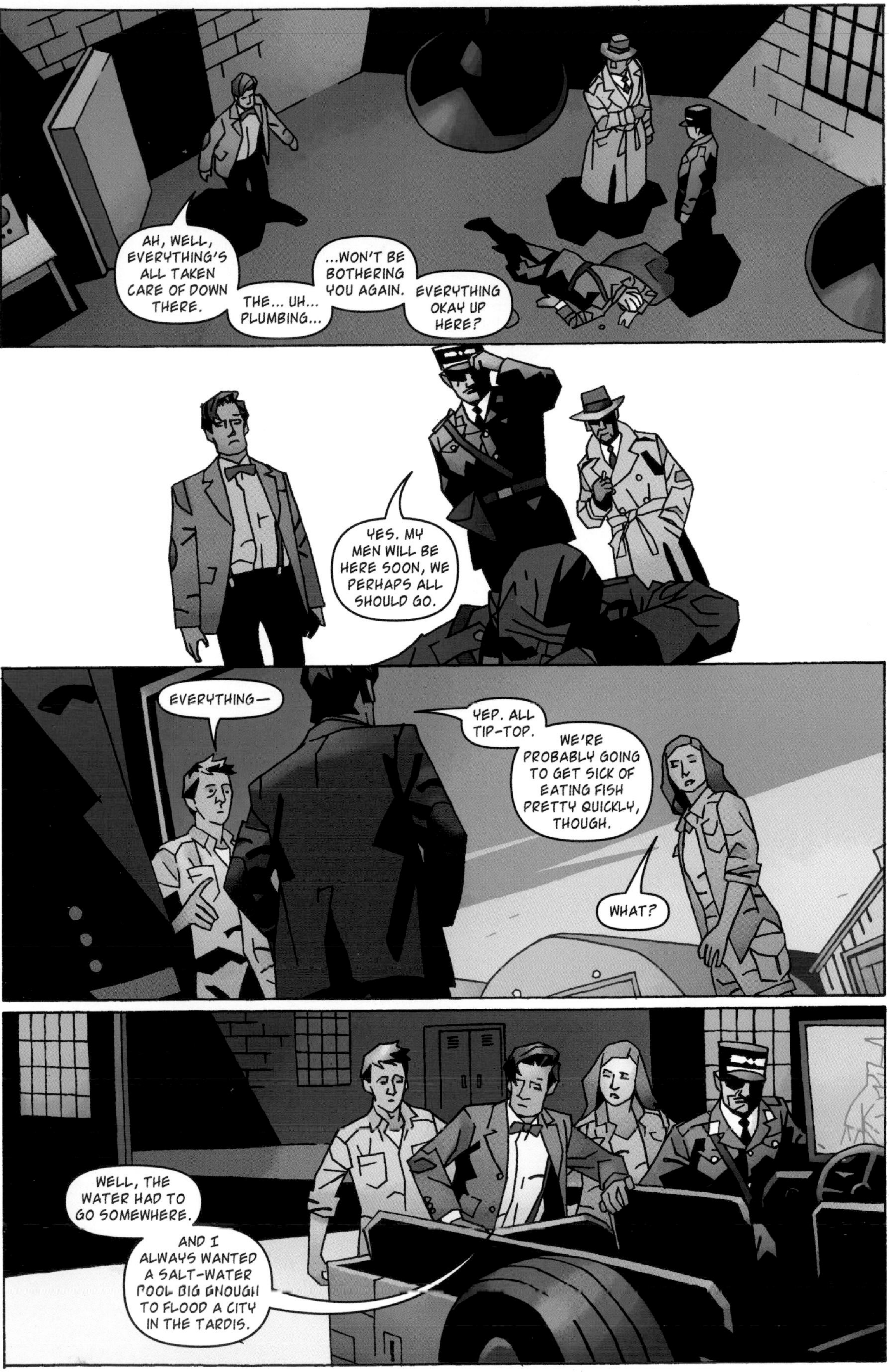
AH, WELL, EVERYTHING'S ALL TAKEN CARE OF DOWN THERE.
THE... UH... PLUMBING...
...WON'T BE BOTHERING YOU AGAIN.
EVERYTHING OKAY UP HERE?
YES. MY MEN WILL BE HERE SOON, WE PERHAPS ALL SHOULD GO.
EVERYTHING—
YEP. ALL TIP-TOP.
WE'RE PROBABLY GOING TO GET SICK OF EATING FISH PRETTY QUICKLY, THOUGH.
WHAT?
WELL, THE WATER HAD TO GO SOMEWHERE.
AND I ALWAYS WANTED A SALT-WATER POOL BIG ENOUGH TO FLOOD A CITY IN THE TARDIS.

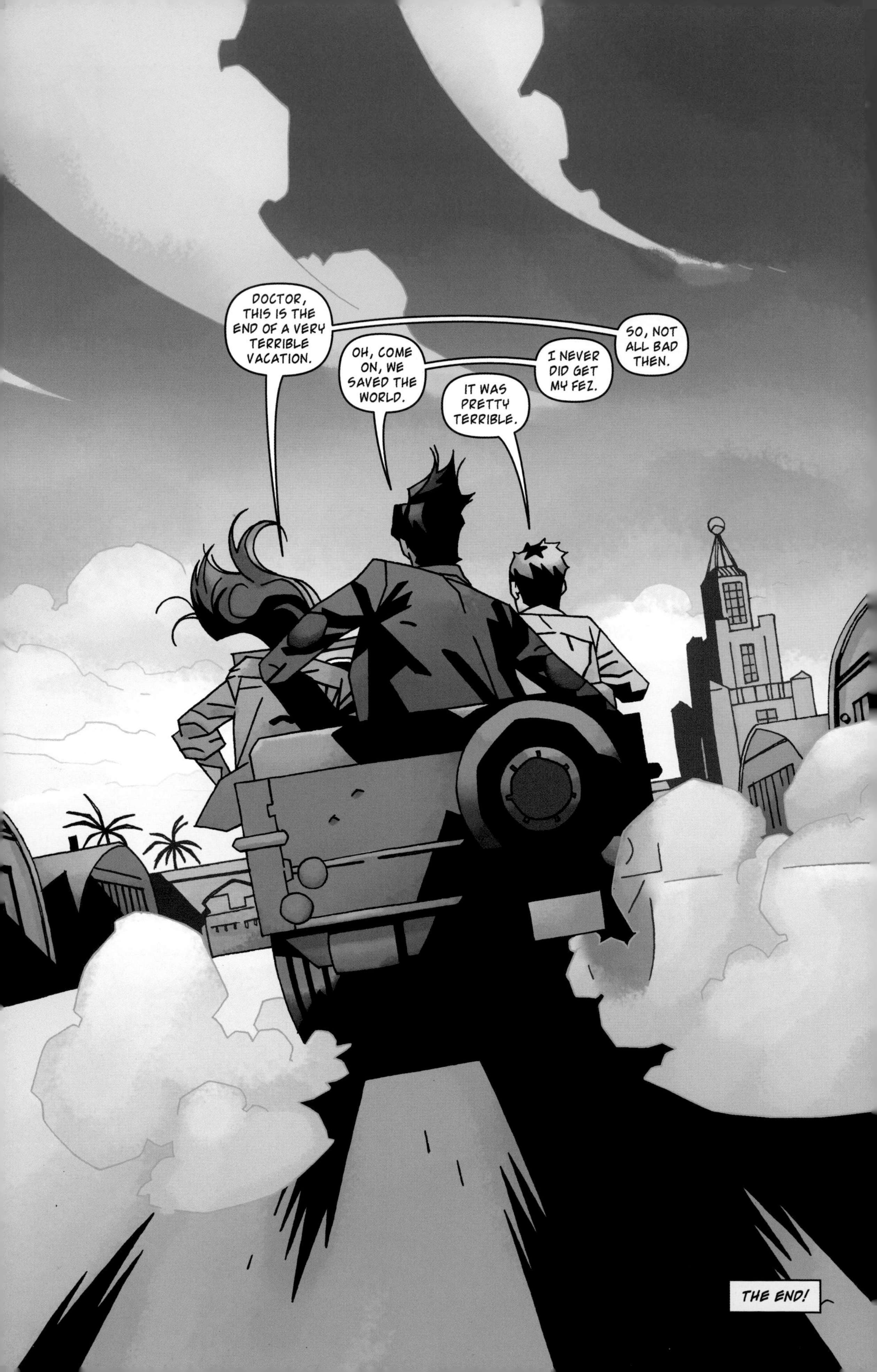
DOCTOR, THIS IS THE END OF A VERY TERRIBLE VACATION.
OH, COME ON, WE SAVED THE WORLD.
IT WAS PRETTY TERRIBLE.
I NEVER DID GET MY FEZ.
SO, NOT ALL BAD THEN.
THE END!

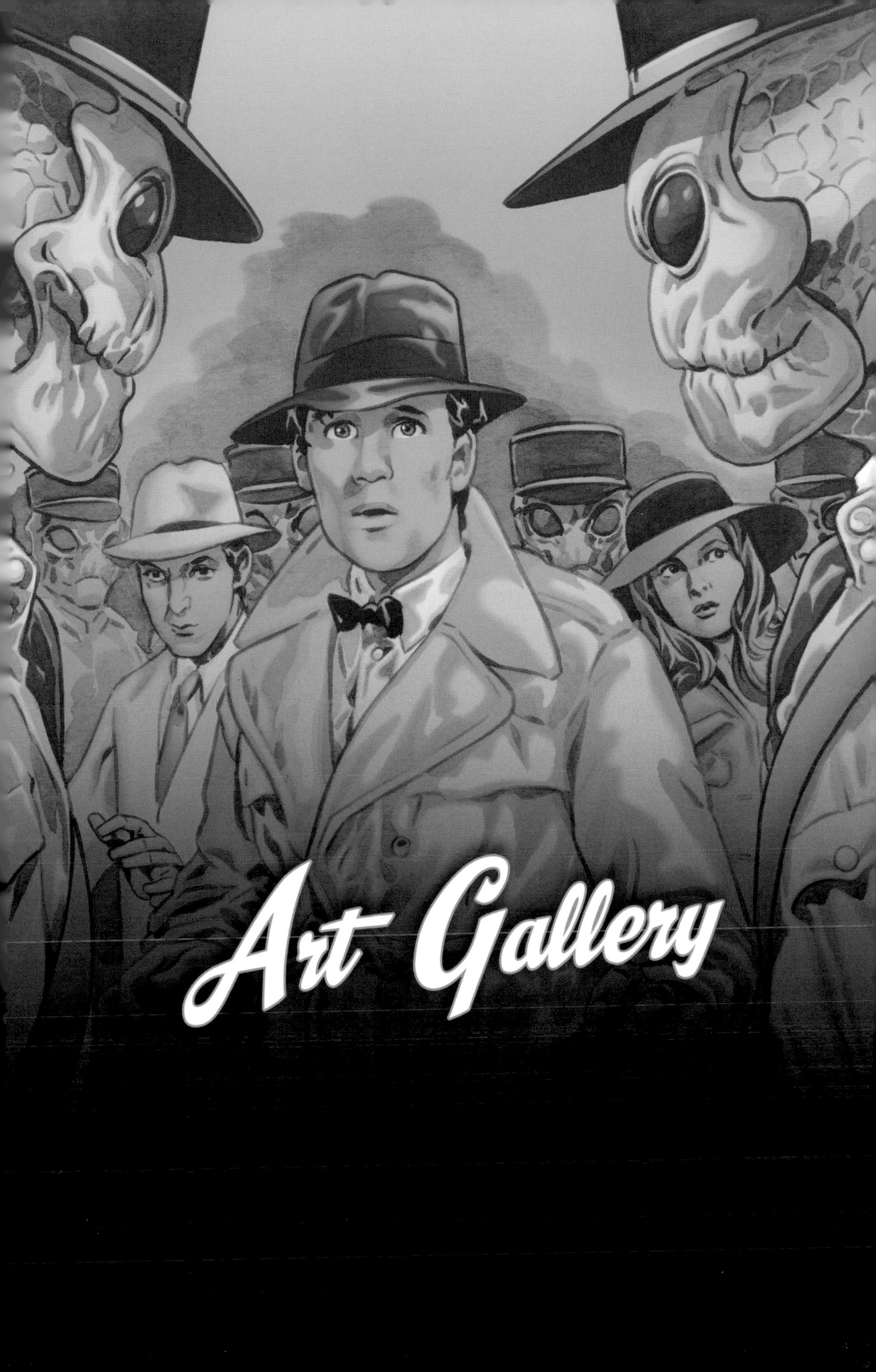
Art Gallery

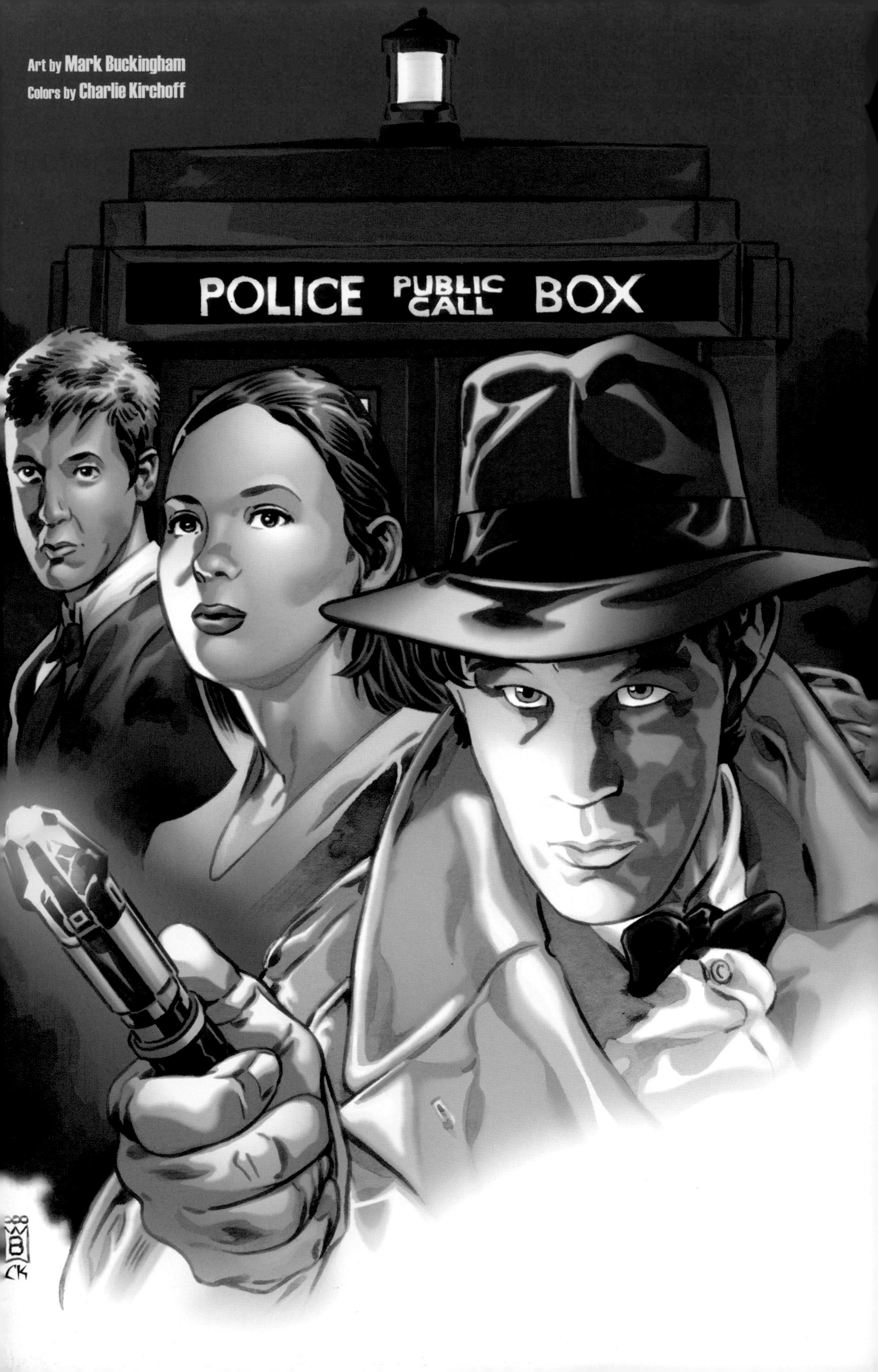

Art by Mark Buckingham
Colors by Charlie Kirchoff

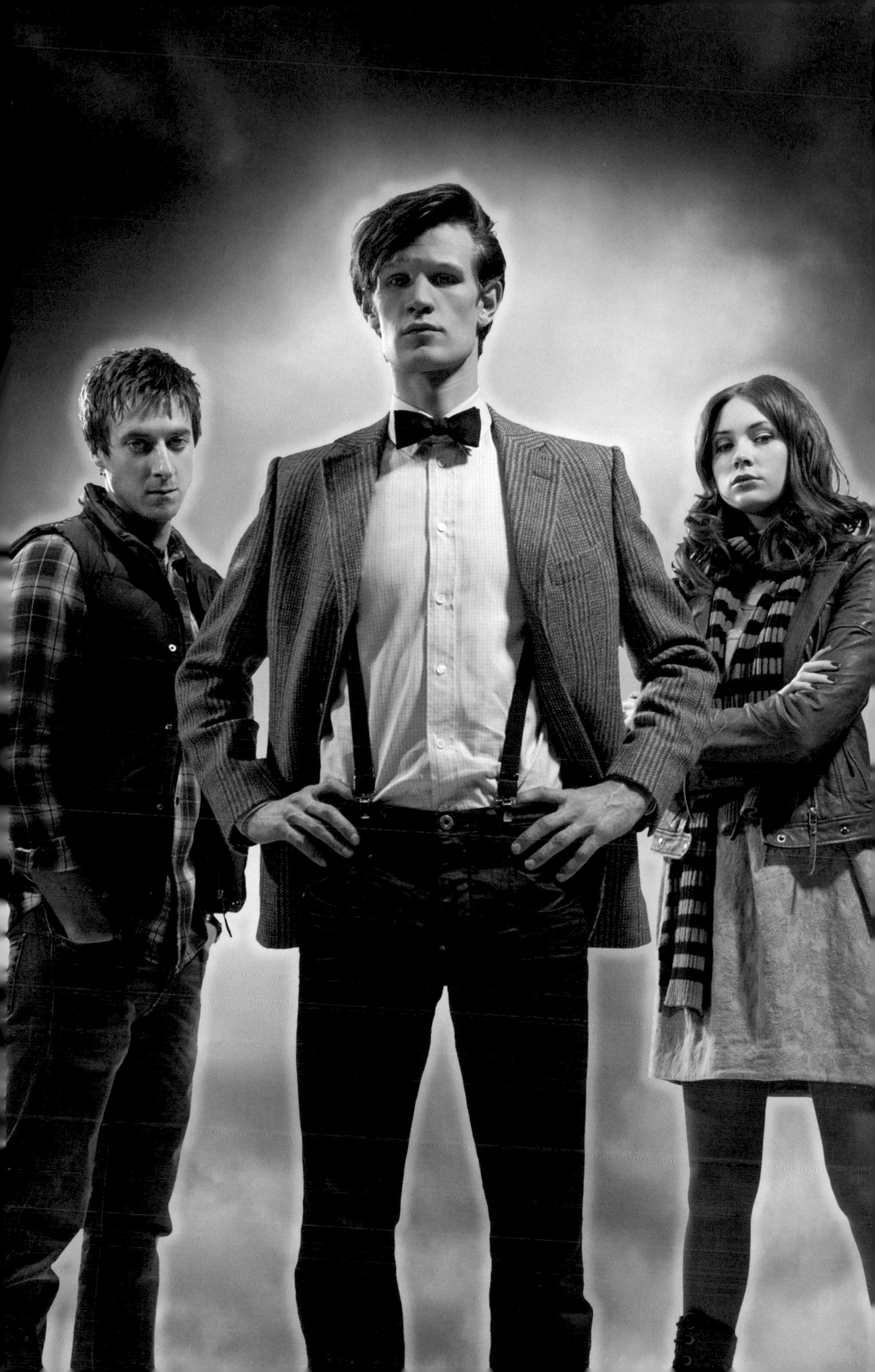

Art by Matthew Dow Smith

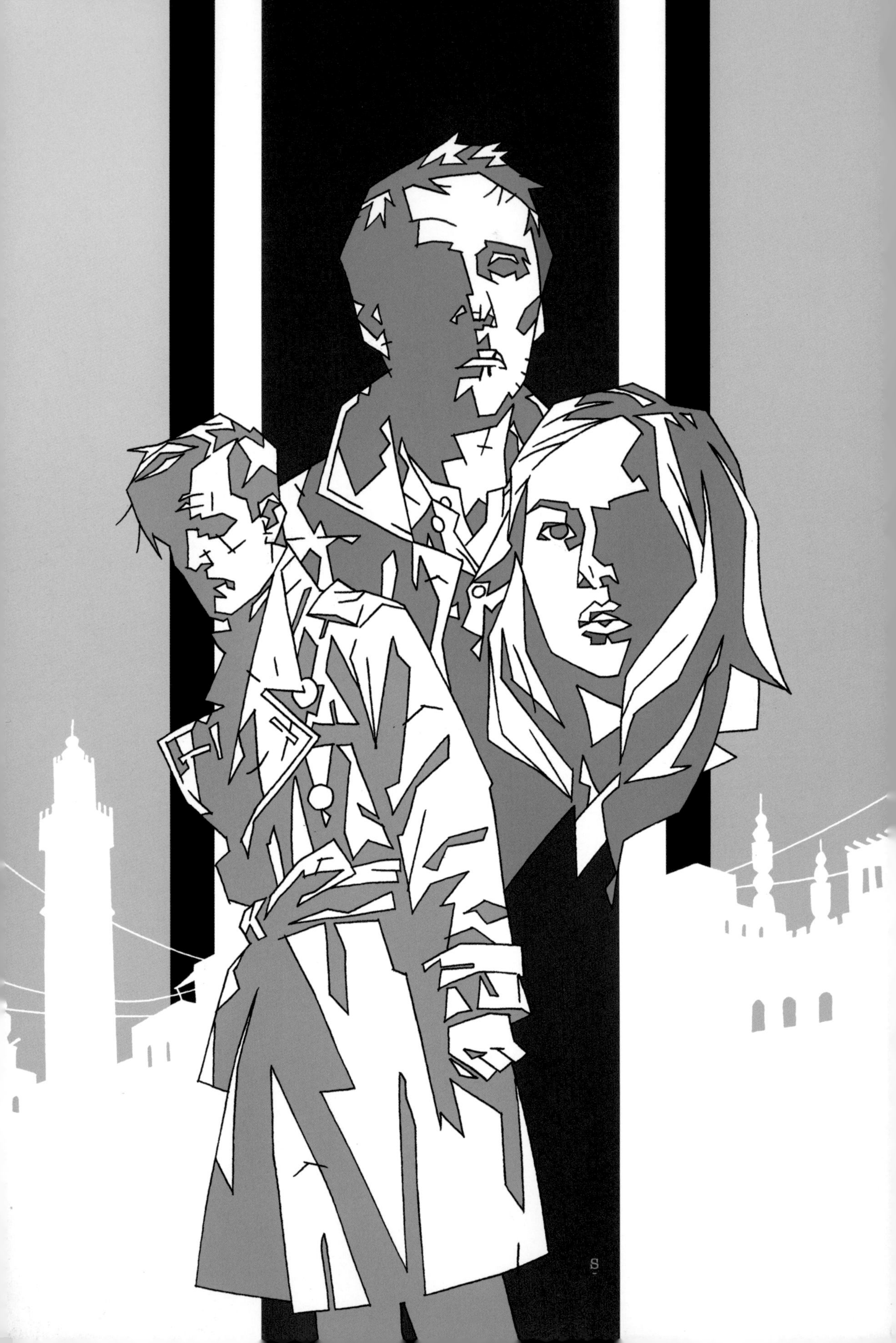

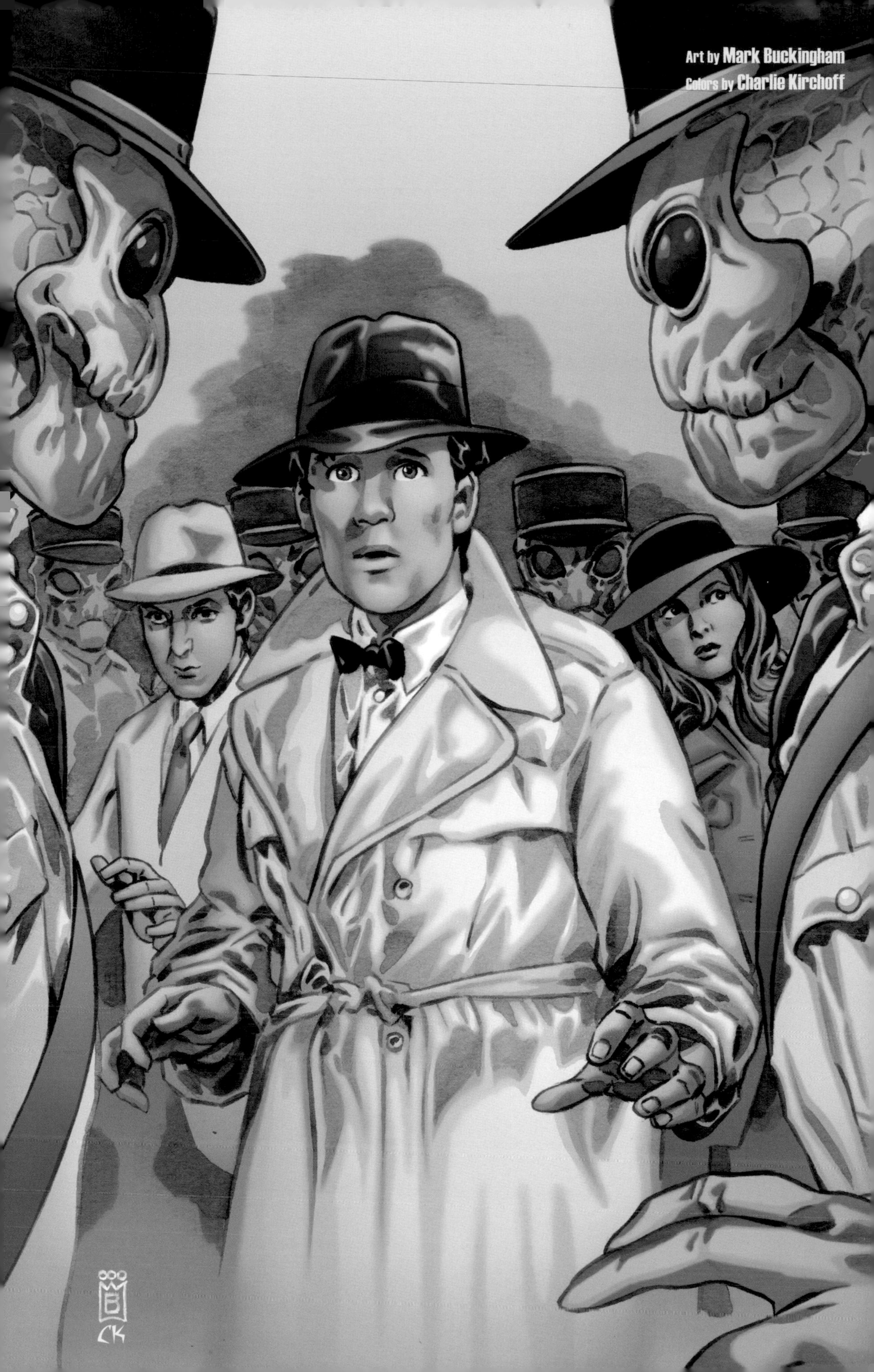
Art by Mark Buckingham
Colors by Charlie Kirchoff

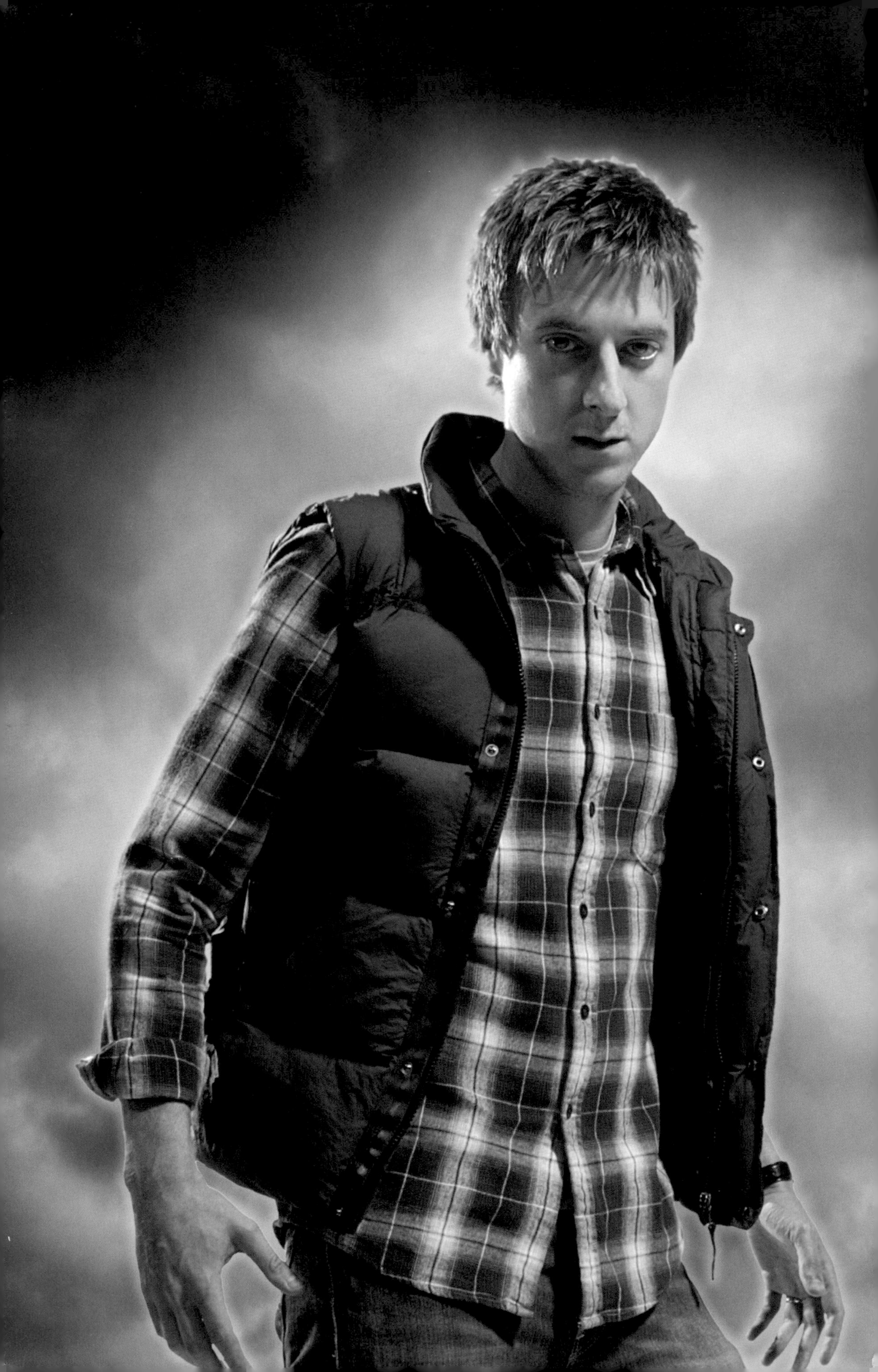

Art by **Matthew Dow Smith**

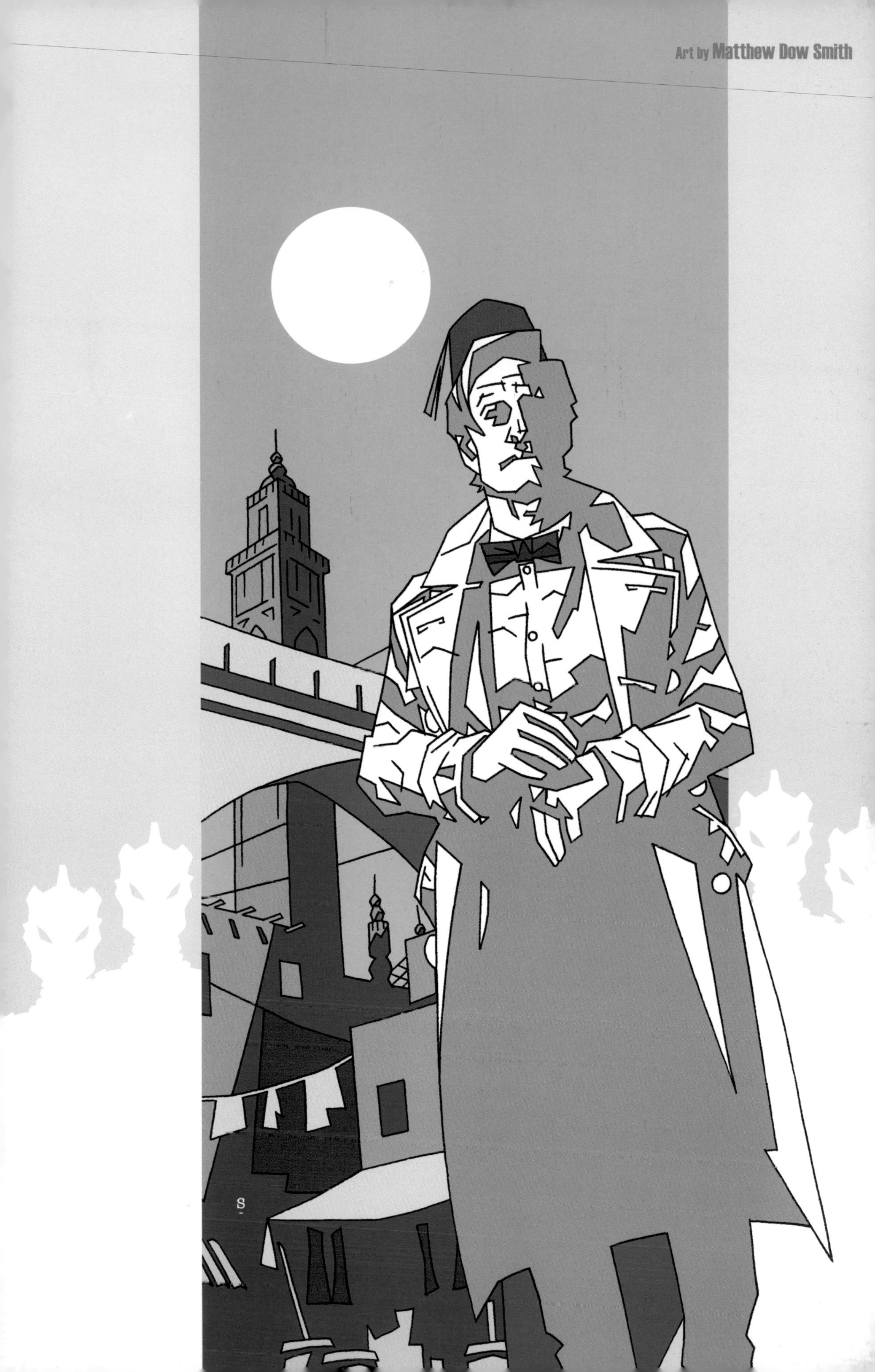

Art by **Mark Buckingham**

Colors by **Charlie Kirchoff**

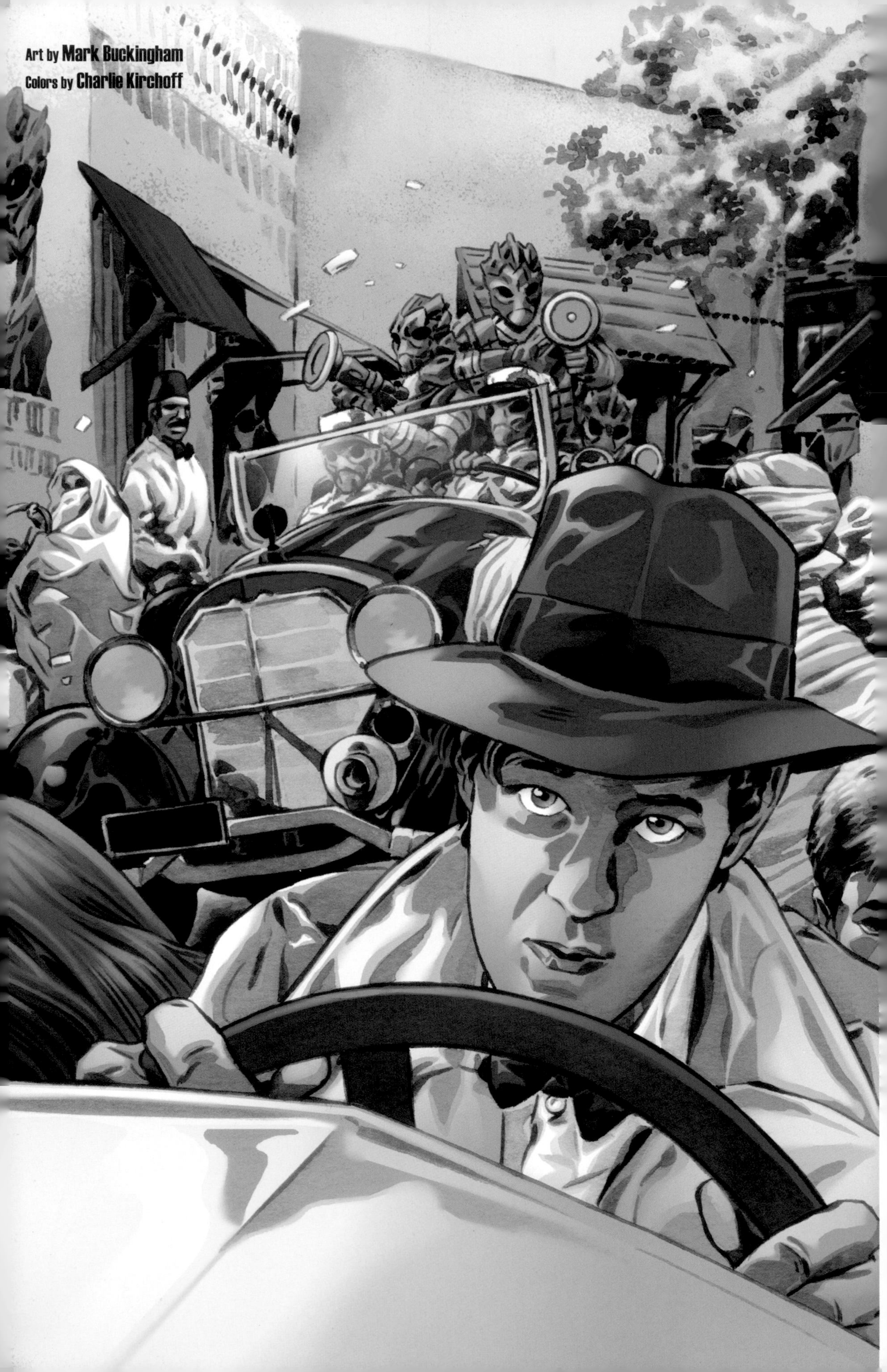

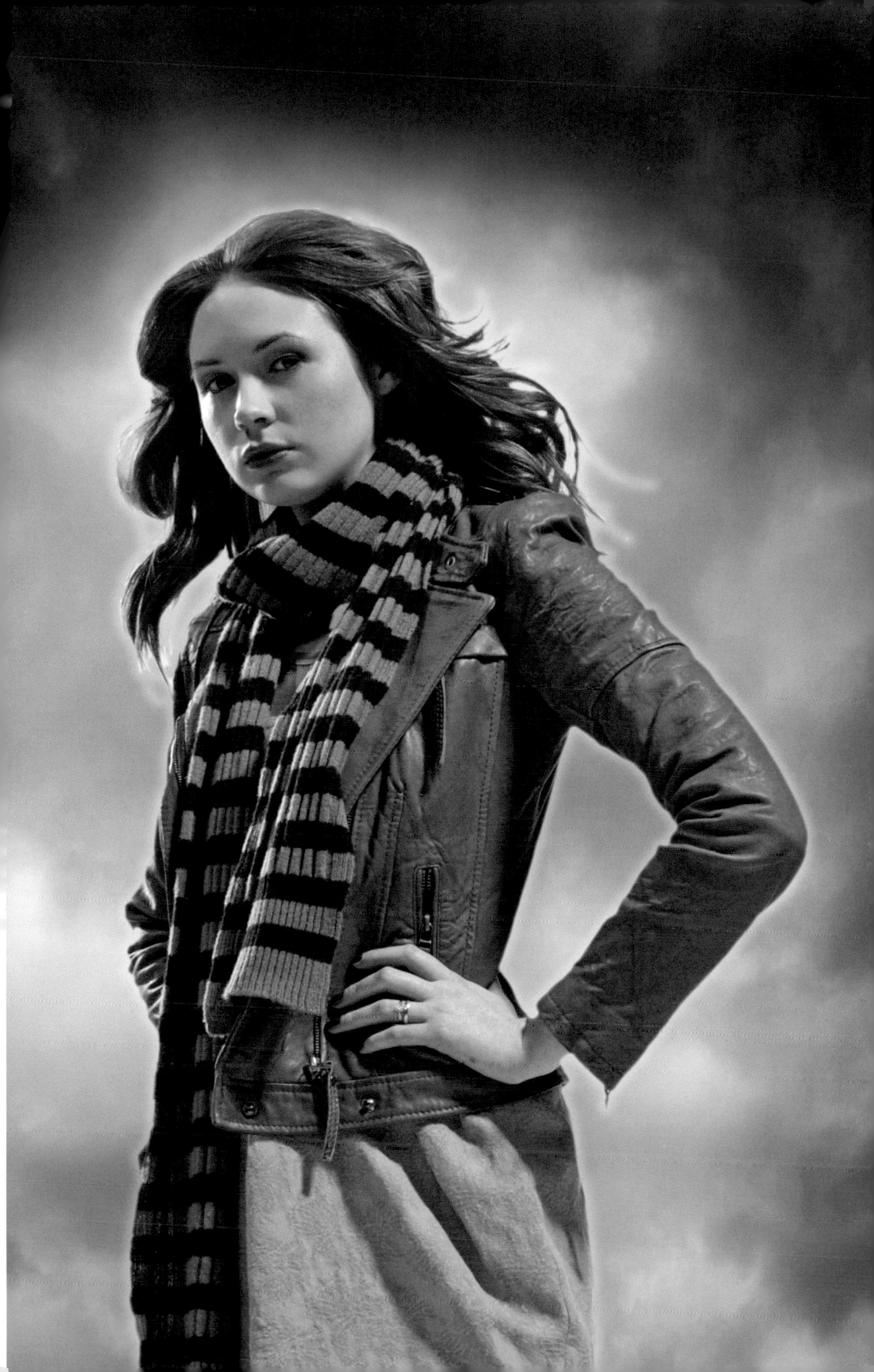

Art by Matthew Dow Smith

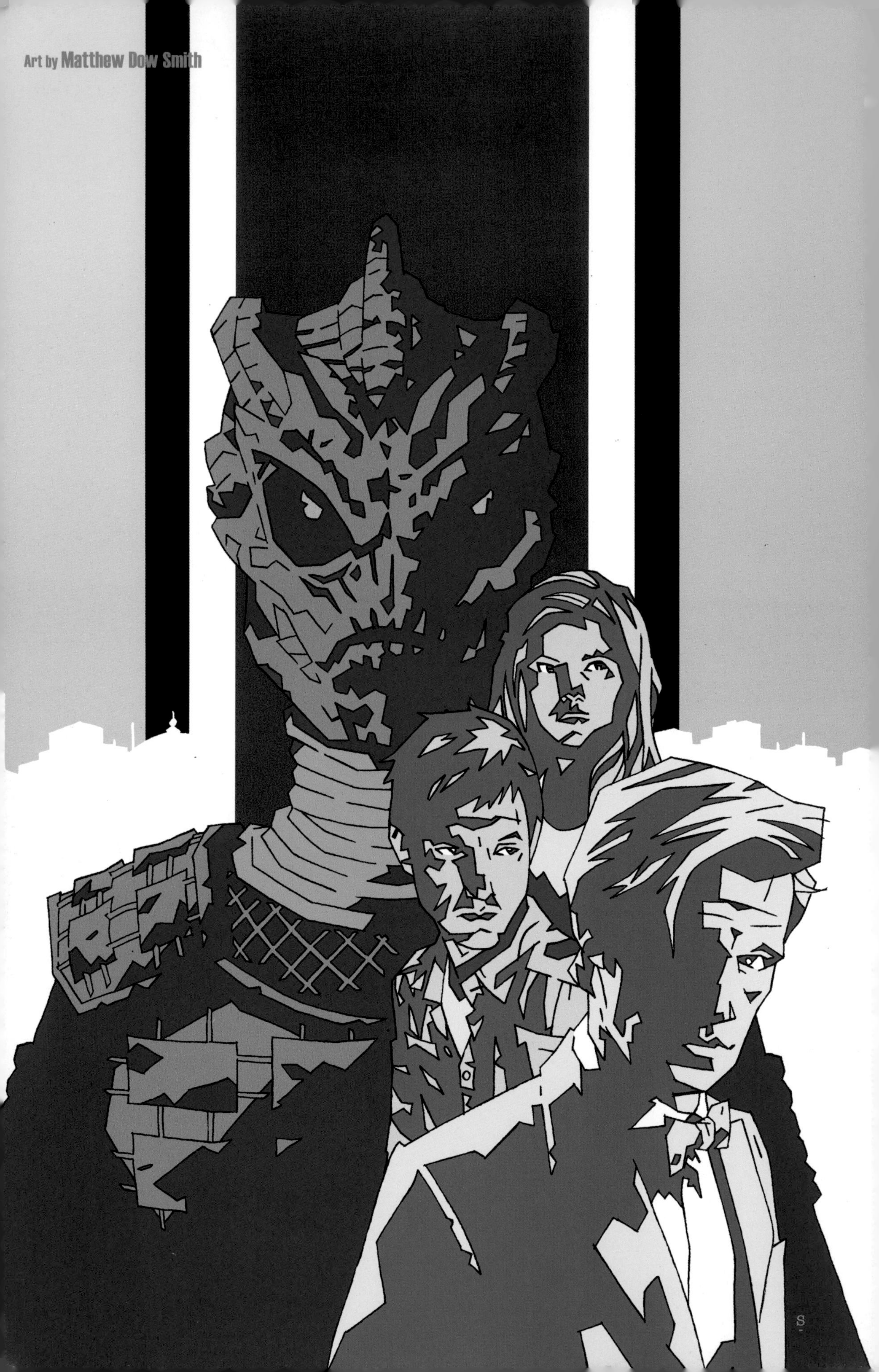
S

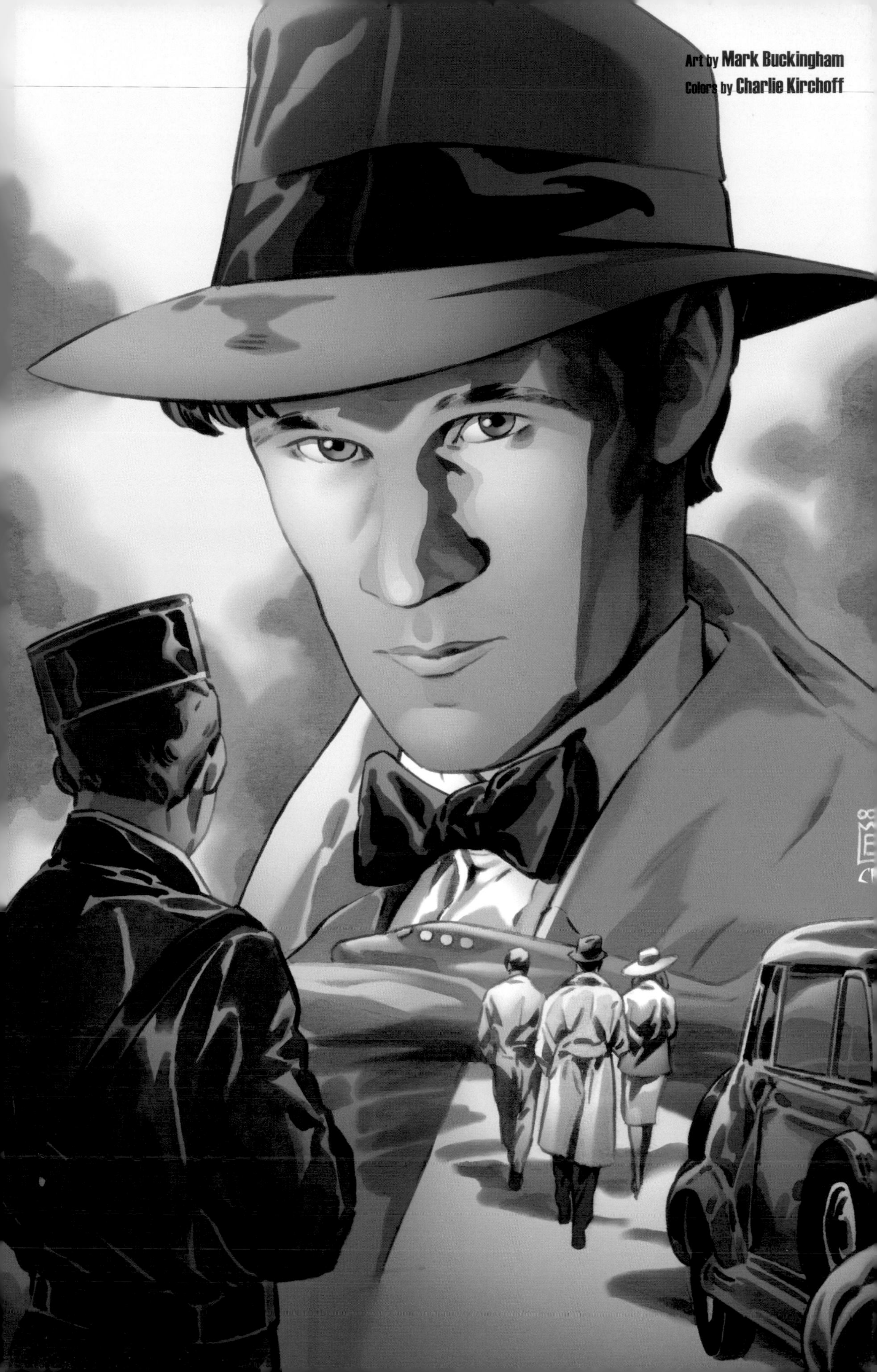
Art by Mark Buckingham
Colors by Charlie Kirchoff

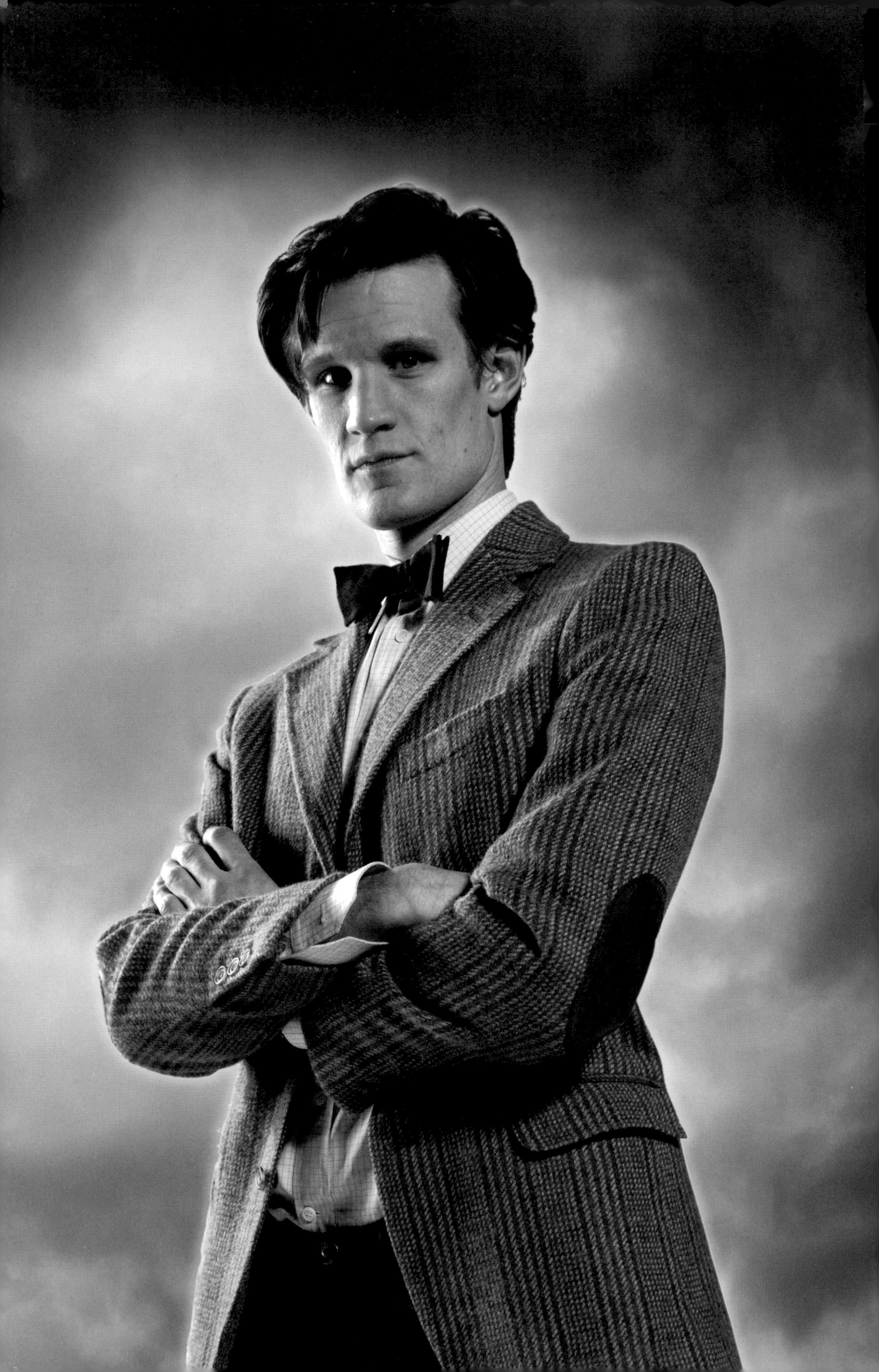

Art by **Matthew Dow Smith**

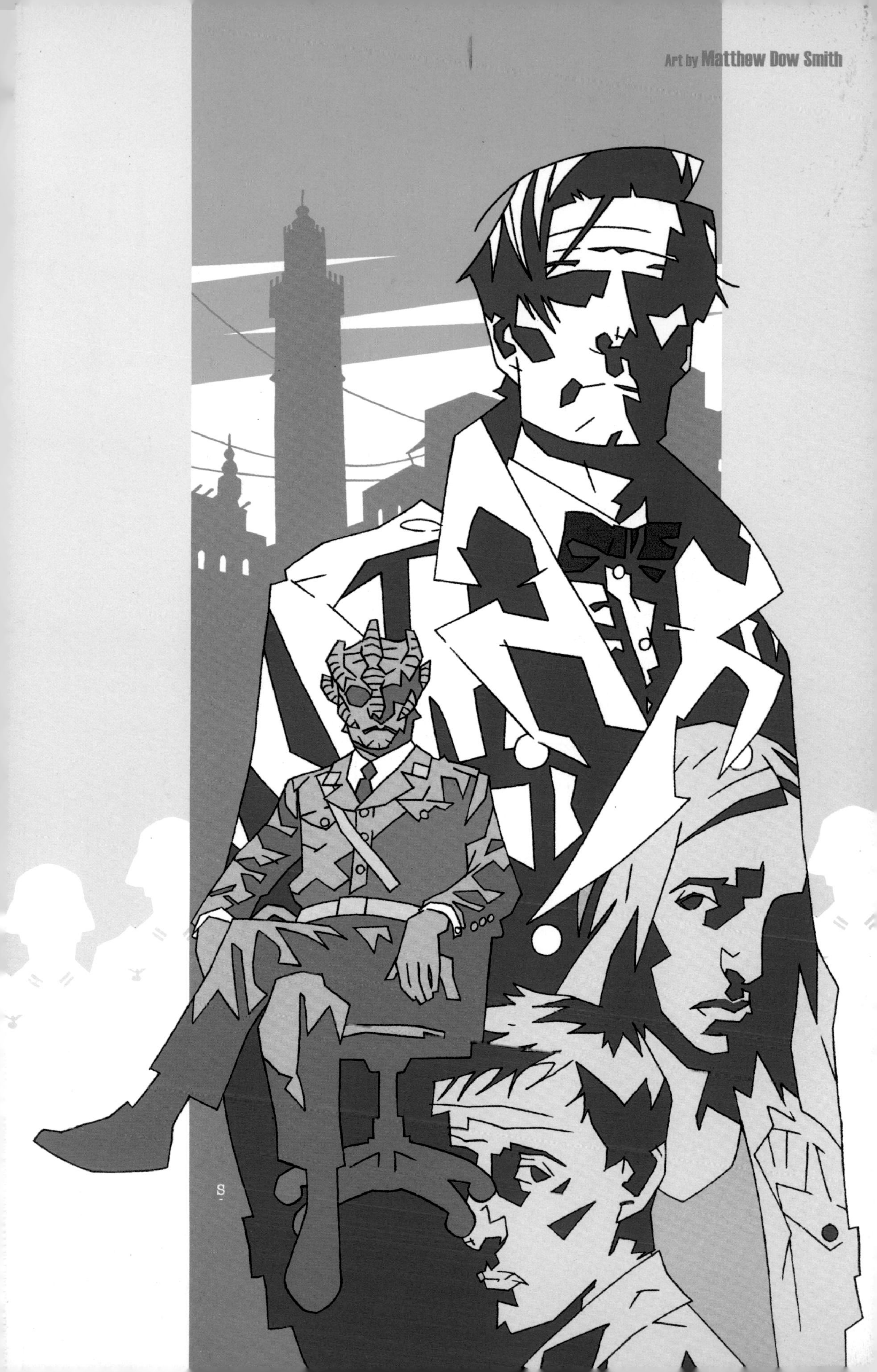

Keep up with

DOCTOR WHO

**Doctor Who:
Agent Provocateur**

ISBN: 978-1-60010-196-0

**Doctor Who:
A Fairytale Life**

ISBN: 978-1-61377-022-1

**Doctor Who:
The Forgotten**

ISBN: 978-1-60010-396-4

**Doctor Who:
Through Time And Space**

ISBN: 978-1-60010-575-3

**Doctor Who Series 1,
Vol. 1: The Fugitive**

ISBN: 978-1-60010-607-1

**Doctor Who Series 1,
Vol. 2: Tesseract**

ISBN: 978-1-60010-756-6

**Doctor Who Series 1,
Vol. 3: Final Sacrifice**

ISBN: 978-1-60010-846-4

**Doctor Who Series 2,
Vol. 1: The Ripper**

ISBN: 978-1-60010-974-4

IDW

www.IDWPUBLISHING.com